Convicting the Yorkshire Ripper

Convicting the Yorkshire Ripper

The Trial of Peter Sutcliffe

Richard Charles Cobb

PEN & SWORD
TRUE CRIME

First published in Great Britain in 2023 by
Pen & Sword True Crime
An imprint of
Pen & Sword Books Ltd
Yorkshire – Philadelphia

ISBN 978 1 39901 187 7

A CIP catalogue record for this book is
available from the British Library.

Typeset by Mac Style
Printed in the UK by CPI Group (UK) Ltd, Croydon, CR0 4YY.

Pen & Sword Books Limited incorporates the imprints of Atlas,
Archaeology, Aviation, Discovery, Family History, Fiction, History,
Maritime, Military, Military Classics, Politics, Select, Transport, True
Crime, Air World, Frontline Publishing, Leo Cooper, Remember
When, Seaforth Publishing, The Praetorian Press, Wharncliffe Local
History, Wharncliffe Transport, Wharncliffe True Crime, White Owl
and After the Battle.

For a complete list of Pen & Sword titles please contact

PEN & SWORD BOOKS LIMITED
47 Church Street, Barnsley, South Yorkshire, S70 2AS, England
E-mail: enquiries@pen-and-sword.co.uk
Website: www.pen-and-sword.co.uk

Or

PEN AND SWORD BOOKS
1950 Lawrence Rd, Havertown, PA 19083, USA
E-mail: Uspen-and-sword@casematepublishers.com
Website: www.penandswordbooks.com

Contents

Acknowledgements vi

Introduction vii

Chapter 1 The Yorkshire Ripper Murders 1

Chapter 2 Arrest and Confession 21

Chapter 3 The Road to the Old Bailey 35

Chapter 4 The Trial Begins 49

Chapter 5 'This Is Ripper Country' 100

Chapter 6 'I'm as normal as anyone' 121

Chapter 7 The Mission 134

Chapter 8 Psychiatry on Trial 174

Chapter 9 Summing Up and Verdict 194

Epilogue 211

Acknowledgments

Although my name appears on the front cover this book is the result of a fantastic team of individuals who have all come together to offer me their unique knowledge and skill to create what I feel is the most comprehensive study ever done on the trial of Peter Sutcliffe, aka, the Yorkshire Ripper.

Author and world famous photographer, Mark Davis for always being there for book research, crime scene investigations and the ability to capture the most amazing images. Your work will continue to fascinate many generations to come.

Author Chris Clark, without whom this book and previous work on the Yorkshire Ripper simply would not have happened. Many thanks for all your knowledge, ideas, and resources to keep me on the right track.

Chris Routh for his amazing knowledge and crime scene diagrams which bring the case to life for the modern reader. The work and dedication you put in goes above and beyond. Thank You

I also would like to thank the following individuals for their support and their friendship during the creation of this book, plus all those who have personally influenced my life at the time of writing.

My parents, brothers and my Son Brandon, who continue to offer all the support in every adventure and project I undertake. Kirsty, Ellise and Ella Giles for always being there for me. Liva Andruce, Rob Clack, Caroline Rhodes, Tom Davis, Ashlin Orrell, Neil Storey, Fiona Kay, Scott Nichol, Mel Simpson, Edward Stow, John Chambers, Martin Trueman, John Holloway, Annie Gilmour, Steve Blomer, Teresa Appleton, Darren Field, Daisy O'quigley, Mary Bear Taylor, Trish Routh, Mick Priestley, Anjum Fi, Jamie Biddle, Alan Clark, Sinnead O'Leary, Andre Price, Lindsay Siviter, Breen Lynch, Bernie Conroy, James Dawes, Niamh Newman, DC Henry Rogers and the Cumbria police force.

Introduction

This is a story you were never supposed to read today. It had all been decided behind the scenes that there was to be no trial, no jury. Just a quick court appearance then off to the mental asylum. You would never have known what actually happened. The files would be closed for over 100 years.

So this book is dedicated to Mr Justice Leslie Boreham, the judge who presided over the Yorkshire Ripper Murders trial, without whom this book and everything we know about the Ripper murders would not have come to light in our lifetime; and without whom, Peter Sutcliffe could have been released back into society.

No detective could have predicted that a single murder in the 1970s would herald one of the most notorious and long-lasting series of sadistic killings Britain has ever endured. Nor could anyone have envisaged the fear it would engender in Northern women and their families by the man dubbed by the newspapers as the 'Leeds Jack the Ripper Killer', or that he would remain free for so long.

The crimes committed by Peter Sutcliffe shocked the world, and even today his grim legacy continues to linger over his killing ground of Yorkshire.

When I first began researching the Yorkshire Ripper murders I amassed a large archive of documents, press reports and information not previously available to the public, and this ended up being my first book on the subject: *On the trail of the Yorkshire Ripper*, published by Pen and Sword Books in October 2019.

For the first time, all the crime scenes had been photographed, mapped out, and the murders described in detail.

However, I was left with a large amount of unused archive material surrounding the trial that followed Sutcliffe's arrest. I had witness statements, doctors' reports, and testimony from friends and family. It was a book that desperately needed to be written and provides a perfect sequel to *On the trail of the Yorkshire Ripper*.

Sutcliffe's trial in 1981 attracted vast crowds. The gallery was packed, the seats in court were packed and the press benches were packed; even seats that were normally allocated to relatives of victims went to reporters. Outside the doors of the Old Bailey in London, people slept in the street to be able to get a chance to get in to see the most infamous monster since Jack the Ripper face justice for his appalling crimes. It was a media circus. Most national newspapers had sent two or three staff each; including international reporters, there were thirty or forty journalists in court at any one time, yet the full circumstances of the trial and the arguments put forward by both prosecution and defence have remained largely unknown for the last forty years.

To my knowledge, this is the first book ever written which focuses primarily on Yorkshire Ripper trial, and presents the fascinating truth about what actually happened forty years ago, during the three weeks of what the press dubbed 'the trial of the century'.

I hope you find it equally fascinating and educational.

Richard C Cobb

Chapter 1

The Yorkshire Ripper Murders

It's quite appropriate that a real life monster like Peter Sutcliffe, aka The Yorkshire Ripper, should have died on Friday 13th, the end of a real life bogey man. The most notorious killer of his time was claimed in November 2020 by the most notorious killer of modern times, Covid-19. But although he may be gone, the Ripper murders have left their mark on society no less than on the battered bodies of his victims.

For nearly four decades, the murderous onslaught and afterlife of Peter William Sutcliffe has filled miles of newsprint, numerous books and days of television, securing his place as one of the most notorious serial killers in criminal history. But the vital statistics are human – the thirteen women he is known to have brutally murdered and the seven he failed to kill. Their lives and those of thousands of others, including dozens of children and hundreds of relatives and friends, are marred forever by his legacy.

For five years Sutcliffe led a double life – pretending to be an ordinary working man while going out at night and killing women. He fooled his wife, his employers, his co-workers, his neighbours and – when he was finally caught – he almost fooled the police.

When Wilma McCann's body was first discovered on a playing field in Leeds in October 1975, the investigation officers said they were looking for a 'vicious and sadistic killer'. Just how vicious and sadistic the whole country was later to discover as twelve more murders over the next five years provided a catalogue of atrocities which shocked even the most hardened of detectives.

Wilma McCann's death was savage and brutal – she'd been hit over the head with a hammer, which smashed her skull; as she lay dead or dying on the ground, her killer removed her clothes to reveal her breasts and abdomen before stabbing her repeatedly. These were to be the classic signs of a Yorkshire Ripper attack. And police would learn to fear them.

Over the next five years twenty women would be attacked in the grim backstreets of Leeds, Bradford, Huddersfield, Halifax and Manchester; thirteen of them were murdered. Their deaths were violent, their bodies were mutilated and defiled. And while the killer was free, no woman was safe. In recent years it's become clear that there could have been even more victims, some of whom will never see justice done.

There are three other figures who feature prominently in the Yorkshire Ripper story, all in their own way are victims.

George Oldfield was the Assistant Chief Constable of West Yorkshire Police, and at one time the most famous detective in the United Kingdom. He had the job of tracking down the Ripper and he failed; it was failure he felt personally and one from which he never recovered. Eventually, after suffering a heart attack, he had to be taken off the case. Then there was the terrible toll on the officers under his command. Hundreds of officers had worked night and day for months turning into years sifting through the mountain of information supplied by the public. Strains on family and social life among some members of the police were inevitable and in some cases the sheer physical pressure of work became unbearable.

Ronald Gregory, Chief Constable at West Yorkshire Police, once backed George Oldfield all the way, but in the end was forced to put someone else in charge of the case. Some of the severest criticisms would be reserved for him. As Chief Constable he refused to release a hard-hitting report detailing his force's failure; on his retirement he was to publish his memories and was paid handsomely by a newspaper for his story.

Then there is Peter Sutcliffe's wife, Sonia. The pair first met in 1966, he was 20 and she was 16; Sonia's family had left Czechoslovakia and moved to the UK. They married in 1974, at Clayton Baptist Church on School Street, Clayton, in Bradford. She now has to live the rest of her days as the 'wife of the Yorkshire Ripper'; she said she had known nothing of her husband's other life, but fingers were pointed at her just the same. Every aspect of her life was laid bare for all to read about during the trial and, like her husband, Sonia has rarely found peace from the media even today.

But the real victims are the thirteen women who died; some of whom lived on the fringes of society, earning their livings from prostitution in the red-light districts of northern cities. There was also a building society clerk, a civil servant and two students, and another was just 16 – fresh out of school and with a life full of promise ahead of her. There are a further seven women who survived an attack by the Yorkshire Ripper; physically and emotionally scarred, they will remember for ever the night he destroyed their lives.

On 20 January 1976, Emily Jackson, 42, became the official second victim of the Ripper; she was a part-time sex worker, whose description as such after her murder was a source of astonishment to her friends and neighbours in Churwell, where she lived. Her husband, Sydney, was a local roofing contractor; Emily helped with the paperwork and, because he did not drive, she drove the old Commer van for him from job to job. He would wait in the local pub while Emily conducted her business out on the streets of Chapeltown. She too was attacked with a hammer, she too died in the red-light area of Leeds. Her death was similar to Wilma McCann's, but in addition to the same terrible injuries there was also a boot print on her thigh, as if her killer had stamped on her body.

An incident room was opened at nearby Millgarth Police Station as the biggest manhunt the country had ever seen was about to begin. Posters of Emily appeared in shop windows, on buildings and on the sides of police cars touring the streets. Appeals were made over Tannoy systems, at cinemas, bingo halls, plus football and rugby matches. Over the course of a year, police checked thousands of vehicles, made almost 4,000 door-to-door enquiries and took over 800 statements. Officers leading the inquiry at the time even spoke to doctors about any suspect patients who could have done such a thing. No stone was left unturned, but the killer still eluded them.

But from the very start the investigation was flawed. The killer had already attacked other women prior to the McCann murder.

These early attacks took place on several women all of whom survived. Anna Rogulskyj, aged 36, was attacked with a hammer at around 1.30 am on Saturday, 5 July 1975, in Keighley and Olive Smelt, a 46-year-old office cleaner, was attacked by the Yorkshire Ripper on Friday, 15 August 1975, in Halifax.

Tracy Browne was 14 when, on Wednesday, August 27 1975, she was attacked with a hammer by Peter Sutcliffe on a lonely farm road at around 10.30 pm. Tracy and her twin sister, Mandy, had been in Silsden, near Keighley (where Anna Rogulskyj had been attacked). They were supposed to be home at 10.30 pm and Mandy had left for their home, about a mile outside of Silsden, earlier than Tracy did. Fortunately, Tracy survived the attack.

Detailed and accurate photofits were drawn up, but their cases were never linked. Had they been, then the Ripper's reign of terror might not have been as long and infamous.

Marcella Claxton, aged 23, was attacked in Leeds in the early hours of Sunday, 9 May 1976. She was lucky to be one of the few women who survived, but unfortunately the police did not link the attack to the Yorkshire Ripper series, though they did re-examine the file later down the line. The police of the mid-1970s had little if any experience of serial killers, but any doubts the police had about the man they were up against were dispelled in 1977, when 28-year-old Irene Richardson was murdered on the Soldiers Field area of Roundhay Park in Leeds, in almost exactly the same spot that Marcella Claxton had been attacked nine months earlier. Soldiers Field is located at the southern end of Roundhay Park; it is a recreation area for organised sport and so called because the Army used to train there in the 1890s.

Irene Richardson was discovered on the morning of 6 February 1977. By 9 am the crime scene in Soldiers Field had been sealed off. Wooden duckboards had been placed on the ground leading up to where the body lay and a 35ft plastic screen concealed the body from public eyes. Suspecting this could be the same person who killed Wilma McCann and Emily Jackson, Professor David Gee was once again brought in to examine the murder scene. He arrived shortly after 10 am and was followed fifteen minutes later by Edward Mitchell, one of the forensic scientists from the Harrogate laboratory. Investigating the case from the police side was DCS Jim Hobson. A Leeds man born and bred, Hobson joined the force in 1951 and was promoted to sergeant by 1958. He became DCS in 1975. Irene Richardson lay face down in the shaded grass area at the rear of the sports pavilion, just hidden from view of the road

With the murders of Wilma McCann and Emily Jackson there had been very little evidence left at the crime scene to help investigators, but with the murder of Irene Richardson, the police discovered an important clue. Fresh tyre marks discovered close to the body revealed that the killer had driven his car onto the soft ground of Soldiers Field. The police were able to determine the tyre marks as being two India Autoway tyres and a Pneumant on the rear offside, all cross-ply. DCS Jim Hobson decided to concentrate the bulk of the investigation onto finding the car that made the prints. Provided the killer didn't change the tyres, he felt confident that a thorough search of vehicles using the same tyres would bring results.

Although police were careful not to disclose exact details of the horrific injuries, it didn't take long for the press to learn about their severity. It was a news editor's dream – sex workers were being stalked on the dark, foggy streets of Yorkshire by an unknown killer who cut their throats and ripped open their stomachs.

The legend of a new 'Jack the Ripper' took root, as bigger and bolder headlines graced newspaper stands up and down the country. And this was just the beginning. The comparisons between the Yorkshire Ripper and Jack the Ripper, who terrorised the streets of London in 1888 and butchered five East End prostitutes, were inevitable. The Victorian Ripper knew his territory, lured his victims into quiet traps and killed them quickly. His signature was to slit his victims' throats and most were mutilated, with intestines pulled out and body parts cut off.

What's more, that Ripper had never been caught. As the attacks in West Yorkshire and Lancashire continued, many doubted his modern namesake would be either.

Meanwhile, the women working on the streets fifteen miles away in Bradford's red-light district had been unaffected by the fear that plagued the 'sisterhood' in neighbouring Leeds, where the murders meant sex workers walked the streets in teams, conspicuously noting punters' number plates. In Bradford, they still felt safe enough to come out on their own from 4.30 pm, looking for trade among workers leaving factories. This was soon about to change.

Patricia Atkinson was murdered in Bradford on 23 April 1977. Only ten days before her murder she had moved into Flat 3 of 9 Oak Avenue, a 1960s purpose-built block of flats, two storeys high at the front and three at the back and comprised of many cheap, self-contained bedsits. Atkinson occupied a small flat to the right-hand side of the property, in the middle of the ground floor. Her battered body would be discovered lying on the bed.

Her murder was unusual in the Yorkshire Ripper case for it was the first and only time the killer would strike indoors. All murders before and after would be committed outside, either on the streets, in back alleys or on waste ground. It was also the first of the murders to have occurred in Bradford, which threw more strain on the fledgling police investigation which, until then, had only been concerned with Leeds.

At this crime scene boot prints were found, this time on her bed sheet where she had been killed. It was clear that the Ripper had expanded his territory to include Bradford and now the police were well aware that they were facing a brutal assassin who would not respect geographic bounds.

The Leeds Ripper was now the Yorkshire Ripper.

The police also struggled with getting public support in the early days of the manhunt as the attitude of many Yorkshire citizens had been clouded by the idea of prostitution. People had convinced themselves that as long as decent, respectful women were not conducting the seedy hazardous occupation and only sex workers were being murdered, there was nothing to fear. The fact that sex workers were always at risk from unbalanced men who could assault, or even kill them, when faced with their sexual inadequacies didn't seem to matter to most people reading the news, and they judged that the women were working the streets out of choice. Sympathy and understanding was sadly lacking in many households across the district.

This attitude quickly changed with the murder of Jayne MacDonald, a 16-year-old shop assistant and much-loved daughter, whose only mistake was to take a short cut home through Chapeltown; her body was found on the morning of 26 June 1977 in a children's playground. Like others before her, she'd been hit over the head with a hammer, once dead the Ripper had set to work on her body, tearing at her flesh with sharpened screwdrivers.

Confronted by the seeming powerlessness of the police to catch the perpetrator, women were frightened, indignant and in some cases inclined to take direct protective measures of their own.

Jayne MacDonald was laid to rest in Harehills Cemetery in Leeds and just over two years later she was joined by her father Wilfred, who died in October 1979. Those who knew him said he never recovered from the sight of his murdered daughter and developed breathing complications soon after her death. It's probably more accurate to say the poor man died of a broken heart.

The world's focus and immense pressure was now on West Yorkshire Police to deliver decisive action. They would have to double their efforts. The Ripper must be caught. West Yorkshire's Chief Constable Ronald Gregory decided to put his senior, most experienced, detective in charge of the Ripper investigation. Assistant Chief Constable (ACC) George Oldfield would become the most famous and most visible police officer in the Ripper inquiry. He had succeeded Donald Craig as head of West Yorkshire CID in 1973. Donald Craig had solved all of the seventy-three murder inquiries he had led in the three years he was head of the department. Now the focus was firmly on George Oldfield to live up to the reputation of his predecessor. He was an old fashioned policeman with a lifetime experience of being a detective, he would devote every waking moment to catching the Ripper and expected every officer under his command to do the same. He was thorough and methodical, liked and respected. In one of his first television appearances he tried to appeal to the Ripper directly:

> I would like to say to you, we are getting nearer and nearer to you and it's only a matter of time before you are caught. In your own interests, in the interests of the relatives and friends of past victims and in the interests of your own relatives and friends, it is now time for you to come forward and give yourself up.

Part of the difficulty in the manhunt was that the Ripper not only appeared to possess psychopathic ingenuity in planning and executing his crimes, but also an ice-cold patience in deciding where and when to strike. Those that did brave the gloomy streets had to be on their guard, they went home in twos and threes. For the unwary, death was constantly lurking

There was an essential mystery which press, police and public alike could not answer. How could a murderer who left so many apparent clues and be so determined to kill again and again, evade capture in Britain's biggest ever manhunt?

They would later learn that the answer to this mystery lay in a cavalcade of cruel hoaxes, false assumptions and over-looked clues, in an enquiry which was a huge and unyielding operation, with all the facts but without the common thread to bind them all together.

In the late 1970s police computer systems like HOLMES (Home Office Linked Major Enquiry System) as used today, simply did not exist. So,

George Oldfield introduced the idea of index cards for all officers gathering statements and information. Anything which an officer felt was relevant to the case, including details of a person of interest, would be written down on one of these cards and placed in the files alphabetically. However, the sheer volume of information that had to be written down swamped the investigation. Forensic reports, witness statements, intelligence-gathering etc – it was too much for the clerks and detectives assigned to administer the running of the investigation. The result of the log-jam of information was that many detectives found themselves checking out leads that had already been covered, sometimes months before, by their own colleagues. And reports compiled by some officers that could have proved vital were not seen for months by senior men tasked with coordinating the enquiry.

The killer was there, staring them in the face. All the facts they needed to catch him were in the system, but they simply couldn't see him.

The tyre tracks left behind at the Irene Richardson murder were the subject of intense investigation. Their rear track width applied to twenty-six different vehicles, which seemed to narrow it down to the quite positive delight of DCS Jim Hobson who was leading the tyre investigation. But when the statistics came back, it highlighted the monumental task that lay ahead. A staggering 100,000 vehicles in West Yorkshire would have to be checked, and hopefully before the killer changed any of his tyres. Today that process could be done at the touch of a button, but in the 1970s, before modern computer data, the investigators had to arrange with all the local taxation offices to compile a list of the cars that belonged in the relevant category. Once this was done, teams of officers would physically go out at night and check the tyres of all the cars. This included a check on cars parked in side streets and pub car parks in the red-light district. Measurements would have to be precise as a simple quarter of an inch more or less would add a dozen more cars to the list. If the owner changed just one tyre, it would render the exercise pointless.

The check on all the possible car owners with the right tyres was three quarters complete when George Oldfield made a disastrous decision and decided to abandon that particular line of inquiry. This outraged Jim Hobson, who had spent so much time and energy on it. He argued that most of the vehicle owners had already been questioned and there was only a small number left. Despite his protests, he was overruled and it was made clear that there simply wasn't the manpower to run several murder investigations, plus the tyre inquiry, which had yet to yield any results. The workload would have to be shifted elsewhere. This would prove to be a fateful decision. The Ripper's car was on the uncompleted list.

On the night of Saturday, 9 July 1977, the Yorkshire Ripper struck again. This time he chose Bradford and his victim was Maureen Long, a 42-year-old mother. He had picked her up in his car after she had left a nightclub on Manningham Lane. Heavily intoxicated she had accepted his offer of a lift. He attacked her with a hammer on waste ground just off Bowling Back Lane. After she had slumped to the ground, he pulled down her tights and panties and stabbed her in the chest, stomach and back. One wound stretched from her breasts to below the navel. During the attack, the Ripper was disturbed by a barking dog, so he left Maureen for dead. Incredibly the woman survived, and hours later her cries brought residents of a nearby caravan park to her rescue.

The police fingertip search of the scene uncovered the partial bloody palm print on a piece of discarded ceramic sink and although convinced the print belonged to the attacker, it wasn't good enough to be used for any detection. But the investigators, led by George Oldfield, must have felt an immense sense of relief to know that a woman had survived a guaranteed Ripper attack. They could now gain an accurate description of their nemesis. To the dismay of the police however, Maureen Long was suffering from amnesia.

She remembered being in the night club and retrieving her coat from the cloak attendant. She vaguely remembered walking along the road in the direction of the city centre and being picked up in a white car with a black roof. She noted the car was probably a Ford model.

Unfortunately, her description of the man who had attacked her was not very accurate. She described him as: a white male, mid-30s and well built. She said he had puffy cheeks, thick eyebrows and blond hair which was collar length.

In October 1977, the Ripper expanded his killing ground to Manchester, where he murdered sex worker Jean Jordan, also known as Jean Royle. She was one of the many poverty-stricken residents at Lingbeck Crescent in the city during the 1970s. There, she scraped a living alongside her common-law husband, Alan Royle, and their two children. Jean's body was found in the allotment grounds next to a cemetery, her injuries were horrendous and an attempt had been made to cut off her head. The events of the murder resulted in the Yorkshire Ripper leaving a clue that could be (and was) directly traced to him.

Jean Royle was murdered on 1 October and her body hidden in the allotment; the killer returned nine days later to drag the body out into the open where it would be found on Monday morning – 10 October. It would seem the act of returning the body was an attempt to recover the incriminating evidence; when he failed, he carried out the worst attack and mutilation of any of his victims.

In a small compartment at the front of Jean Jordan's handbag police found a brand new £5 note and quickly assumed the killer had given her this as advanced payment for sexual favours. This was the evidence the killer was so desperate to obtain.

Jack Ridgeway was head of the Manchester CID during the Ripper inquiry and would deal with two of the Yorkshire Ripper murders, Jean Jordan and the later killing of Vera Millward. He knew right away that the best clue to the identity of the killer was this £5 note. The note was passed to the Bank of England, which was asked to trace where it was issued. Detectives learnt it had been sent from its printing works to the Leeds branch of the Bank of England, just a few days before the murder. The trail then led to a parcel of notes, which had been dispatched to Midland Bank and then dispersed to several branches in Leeds and Bradford. The suspicion was that the fiver had been distributed as part of a firm's payroll. The serial number of the note, AW51 121565, was released to the press and people were asked to check notes they had received in their pay as it was one of sixty-nine consecutively numbered notes. Delays with trying to trace other notes from the same batch – by starting the inquiry too late and not immediately informing the public about it – resulted in a lost opportunity to restrict the number of people who could have received the note. Manchester Police were drafted into West Yorkshire, and the Shipley branch of Midland Bank became the focus of their attention. Staff at the branch were asked to help identify which batch of notes the fiver had come from. Thirty-four firms in West Yorkshire, which could have issued the fiver in a pay packet, were scrutinised by police. They included T. & W.H. Clark (Holdings) Limited of Canal Street, an engineering company in Bradford, which had received money for the payroll at the relevant time. A list was obtained of every single employee so they could be seen individually by police.

As they sat there questioning potential suspects, they didn't realise that the man they sought was literally staring down at them as they conducted their inquiries. Among those employees was a long-distance driver Peter William Sutcliffe. A conscientious and meticulous driver according to his employers, and his log books reflected the care he took of his lorry. In their eyes, the quiet and shy young man was a model employee and so when it came to marketing, they had picked Sutcliffe to feature in Clark's annual calendar. One of images shows him sitting in his truck in the driveway of Clarks. This image had now been enlarged, framed and hung in the main reception room behind the detectives. Sutcliffe was interviewed twice in the £5 note enquiry and managed to slip through the net.

While all this was going on, Leeds police decided to clamp down on sex workers in the Chapeltown area. Over the next few weeks, 152 women were arrested and reported for prostitution and a further sixty-eight were cautioned. Knowing very well that this tactic could only work for so long, they advised the street workers to let a friend know if they decided to go off with a stranger, or at the very least take the registration of the vehicle. Policewomen volunteers, posing as sex workers, were deployed to the street corners of the red-light district in an attempt to lure the killer. It was a dangerous and risky tactic but they were monitored at all times by other police officers close by and instructed to never get into a car. They were equipped with shortwave radios so officers were able to take down descriptions of kerb-crawling punters, as well as the make and model of their cars. A system of flagging was also introduced. Police would go undercover and make notes of car registration numbers of anyone seen cruising the area. If a car appeared more than once, the owner became a suspect; three times and they would be brought in for questioning. For West Yorkshire Police, the day-to-day costs were stacking up. So far, over 175,000 people had been interviewed with a further 12,500 statements taken down – not to mention the 100,000 vehicles that needed checking. At one point, 250 officers were working full time on the case and a total of 343,000 hours in wages had been paid out.

Marilyn Moore was a 25-year-old sex worker when she too was attacked and left for dead by the Ripper on waste ground in Leeds on 14 December 1977. Once again he was disturbed in the act and had to flee the scene. Marilyn provided one of the best photofits of the suspect from a known Ripper victim (unknowingly, the police already had an even better description of the Ripper from survivor Tracy Browne, but her case was never linked). This was just one of the many little mistakes that occurred during the five-year manhunt.

Yvonne Pearson, a 21-year-old sex worker, became the seventh woman to be murdered by the Ripper murdered on January 21, 1978. She was beaten to death on waste ground off Arthington Street Bradford and her killer concealed the body under a discarded sofa that lay nearby. Because of this her body was not found until two months later, in which time he had already gone on to commit his eighth murder. Helen Rytka, an 18-year-old sex worker, was murdered by Peter Sutcliffe on 31 January 1978, only ten days after the murder of Yvonne Pearson. Her body was discovered in the rear yard of a timber factory. She had been beaten with a hammer and repeatedly stabbed around the chest and torso. The Yorkshire Ripper had, once again, expanded his territory to now include the red-light district of Huddersfield.

The passage of time has allowed us to examine the whole Ripper investigation and pinpoint key mistakes made by the police during the manhunt. These mistakes changed policing procedures forever and no doubt has aided investigative techniques over the last forty years.

By far the biggest mistake concerned a tape recording which arrived one morning in the post addressed to George Oldfield. Oldfield called a press conference and, at 2 pm on Tuesday, 26 June 1979, he walked into crowded a lecture theatre at the West Yorkshire Police training academy in Bishopgarth. Dozens of news reporters and journalists had amassed for what would prove to be one of the most sensational moments in British criminal history. On the table in front of Oldfield was a portable tape recorder and, as silence fell upon the room, DSI Dick Holland leaned over Oldfield's shoulder and pressed the play button. There was a hiss as the first few inches of blank tape rolled through the machine, and then an unmistakable Geordie voice filled the room:

> I'm Jack. I see you are still having no luck catching me. I have the greatest respect for you, George, but Lord, you are no nearer catching me now than four years ago when I started. I reckon your boys are letting you down, George. Yer can't be much good, can yer? The only time they came near catching me was a few months back in Chapeltown when I was disturbed. Even then it was a uniform copper, not a detective. I warned you in March that I'd strike again. Sorry it wasn't Bradford. I did promise you that but I couldn't get there. I'm not sure when I will strike again but it will be definitely some time this year, maybe September or October, even sooner if I get the chance. I'm not sure where. Maybe Manchester; I like it there, there's plenty of them knocking about.
>
> They never learn, do they, George? I bet you've warned them, but they never listen. At the rate I'm going I should be in the book of records, I think it's eleven up to now, isn't it? Well, I'll keep on going for quite a while yet. I can't see myself being nicked just yet. Even if you do get near, I'll probably top myself first. Well, it's been nice chatting to you, George. Yours, Jack the Ripper. No good looking for fingerprints. You should know by now it's clean as a whistle. See you soon. Bye. Hope you like the catchy tune at the end. Ha ha!

The recording was followed by twenty-two seconds of the song *Thank You for Being a Friend* by Andrew Gold.

No murder enquiry had ever been handed a clue like it, its effect was sensational; the Yorkshire Ripper was now taunting Oldfield and promising to kill again. The tape changed the whole course of the inquiry with tragic and fatal consequences.

> Well we already know quite a lot about him, the big thing about the tape and the interest as far as we are concerned is that it narrows down our field of inquiry, we know now that we are definitely looking for a man who originated in the North East.

Oldfield had no doubt; he was convinced the voice was the Ripper's. This was the man he'd been hunting for so long, this was the man who carried out such terrible murders, and this was the man who had taken over George Oldfield's life. Perhaps he believed it because he wanted to believe it, because he desperately needed a clue such as this, as he listened to the tape under the glare of the television lights, George Oldfield appeared tired and ill, and he was.

But the tape wasn't the only clue linking the Ripper with the North East, there were two letters signed Jack the Ripper, postmarked Sunderland. Forensic tests concluded whoever had sent the letters, sent the tape as well.

The letters referred to the murder of a sex worker in Preston, Joan Harrison, she had not been linked to the Yorkshire murders. The police had established that whoever had killed her had blood group B, and a gap in his front teeth. Saliva on the envelopes also revealed the sender had blood group B as well. The clues would have matched the real Yorkshire Ripper, he did have group B, and he had a gap in his front teeth – but he didn't kill Joan Harrison. It was cruel irony, but those clues could still have been used to track him.

There was one niggling doubt about the letter, whoever wrote it didn't seem to know anything about the murder of Yvonne Pearson, who certainly was a Ripper victim, dead at the time the second letter was posted, but her body hadn't yet been discovered.

Vera Millward, a 40-year-old sex worker, living in a run-down council flat in Hulme, Manchester, was murdered by the Yorkshire Ripper on 16 May 1978, three-and-a-half months after the killing of Helen Rytka. Her body was discovered in the grounds of Manchester's Royal infirmary and bore all the hallmarks of a Ripper murder. She would be the last sex worker to be murdered, but certainly not the last woman. There was now a lull in the murders; one psychiatrist suggested the Ripper may have settled down, got married and given up his senseless killing, but he was wrong.

On 4 April 1979, Josephine Whitaker, a 19 year old building society clerk in Halifax was bludgeoned to death on her way home from her grandparents' house. Again, her murder had all the hallmarks of the notorious killer and the police now knew the Ripper was no longer interested in just sex workers. The pervasive police presence in the known red-light areas of the Yorkshire Ripper's 'territory', had caused the killer to widen his search area for suitable victims. This would cause near-panic throughout West Yorkshire as it soon became clear that any woman, not just sex workers, were at considerable risk every time they ventured out at night.

Two further clues were discovered at the scene which helped police build up a picture of the man they were looking for; there were traces of an oil found only in engineering factories and there were more boot prints – one was worn away on the right sole, suggesting the Ripper might be a driver of some kind, perhaps for an engineering firm.

Armed with these new clues, detectives visited hundreds of firms and questioned the workers. Clarks was one such firm, again Peter Sutcliffe was questioned and again he slipped through their net. He later said the policeman who questioned him was holding a print of the very boots he was wearing at the time.

The hoped-for breakthrough with the tape recording hadn't materialised, voice experts decided whoever made it came from Castletown near Sunderland; police interviewed every man who lived there, nobody stood out as a suspect but police persisted with the idea that the Ripper was a Geordie

Barbara Leach, a 20-year-old university student about to start her third and final year in social psychology, was brutally murdered in the early hours on Sunday, September 2 1979, just west of Bradford city centre. She had been drinking with college roommates in the Mannville Arms pub and when they left around 12.45 am, Barbara had decided to get some fresh night air and go for a walk. She was later found battered and stabbed near Bradford University her body, covered with an old carpet, had been wedged into a bin recess area at the rear of a house.

By now there was great anxiety about the way the hunt was being handled; the police had interviewed thousands and thousands of people but were no nearer catching the Ripper. Why not call in Scotland Yard, was a common question posed by the press. Oldfield always used to point out dryly that 'Scotland Yard hadn't caught their own Ripper yet'.

Commander Jim Neville, a senior ranking officer from Scotland Yard was eventually brought in, but left within a month saying politely that everything was being done correctly, although he did voice doubts about the tape inquiry. His appointment was seen as merely a box-ticking exercise to please any police critics.

Another major initiative was being taken up at the time; police set up surveillance points in red-light areas and logged down the licence plate numbers of any car entering the area. The numbers were then fed into the Police National Computer and analysed for patterns. The Ripper's car was logged more than fifty times; his reasons for driving through red-light areas were always convincing, at least to everyone except detective constable Andrew Laptew, who recommended to superiors that they should take a closer look at him. His report was marked 'no further action'. It was another missed opportunity in an investigation that was losing its way

The Ripper hunt was now so big and so complex it had got completely out of hand. The thousands of calls received after the tape recordings were released, and the follow ups generated by the surveillance operations made matters worse. At one stage they were nine months behind interviewing people, there simply wasn't the manpower to conduct the inquiry and any follow up inquires

A police roadshow toured the North of England playing the tape and showing the letters – none of it helpful. West Yorkshire police also circulated a checklist to other forces with which they could base their suspect elimination:

1. Not born between 1924 and 1959
2. If he is an obvious coloured person
3. If his shoe size is size 9 or above
4. If his blood group is other than B
5. If his accent is dissimilar to a North Eastern (Geordie) accent.

Peter Sutcliffe's unmistakeable Yorkshire accent was his strongest alibi

Marguerite Walls was a 47-year-old civil servant who worked at the Department of Education and Science office in Pudsey, Leeds. On Wednesday, August 20 1980, she became the twelfth victim of the Ripper as she made her way home from work around 10.30 pm. She was attacked in New Street, only half a mile from her house, then dragged into the grounds of a large mansion estate. There, while kneeling on her chest, the Ripper strangled her, stripped her of all her clothing except her tights, and when he made his escape, he partially covered the body with grass cuttings and leaves.

That year would see three more women attacked by the Ripper, two of whom were lucky to survive.

Upadhya Bandara was a 34-year-old doctor from Singapore who had arrived in England in August 1979. She had won a scholarship from the World Health Organization and was studying a postgraduate course in Health Service Studies at the Nuffield Centre for International Health and Development at Leeds University. On the night of Wednesday, 24 September 1980, she had been visiting friends and started to walk home in Headingley, Leeds, an area popular with students. Her route took her down Chapel Lane, a narrow, dark and deserted cobblestoned alleyway, which ran down the back of the large terraced houses of St Michael's Crescent.

It was here that she suddenly heard footsteps approaching from behind. Thinking it must be someone in a hurry home, she moved to the side to allow them to pass. But they didn't pass her by. Instead, Sutcliffe struck her on the back of the head with a hammer, stunning her. As she turned to fall into the wall she lunged again, this time striking her on the front of the head. She collapsed onto the cobbles and, although dazed, she remembered the feeling of rope being looped around her neck and suddenly restricting her air supply and constricting her windpipe. It was the same rope the Ripper had used on Marguerite Walls just over a month before in Leeds. He used it to drag Upadhya to a secluded bin area that serviced the adjacent properties. Her shoes were scraping along the floor as he dragged her but he felt they were making too much noise, so he stopped and tried to pick her up, holding her under the armpits and moving her towards the bins. But with two arms now carrying the her, he couldn't hold the rope properly and this allowed Upadhya enough time to push her fingers between the rope and her neck and give her a small but precious amount of air.

Having heard the commotion, Valerie Nicholas and her husband Hugh, at 5 St Michael's Crescent, decided to investigate. Their appearance startled the Ripper and he abandoned his attack and fled back up Chapel Lane to the safety of his car, which he had parked round the back of the Arndale Centre. Valerie and Hugh Nicholas had heard the sound of his footsteps as he ran off, and when they opened the back gate they found the battered and unconscious Dr Bandara lying among the bins. Valerie attended to her wounds while Hugh phoned for an ambulance and the police. Upadhya was still unconscious, but started to come round once the ambulance arrived on the scene. Later, in hospital, when she had regained her senses, she described her attacker as aged 25, around 5ft 4ins in height, with black hair and a full beard and moustache. Once again, the police were faced with another assault on a lone woman at night, with head injuries caused by a blunt instrument and another similar description of a young man with dark hair and a beard. This was an almost identical description given by Marcella Claxton, Marilyn Moore and Tracy Browne.

Just over a month later, 16-year-old Theresa Sykes was attacked in Huddersfield. It was during Bonfire Night, Wednesday, 5 November 1980. She had been making her way back from the shops when she became aware of a man following her. As she approached her house the man caught up with her and hit her over the head with a hammer. She collapsed but managed to grab a hold of the weapon and her screams alerted her boyfriend, Jim Furey, who came to her rescue and proceeded to chase after her attacker, losing him in the darkness. Theresa was able to give another good description of her attacker, claiming he had black hair, a beard, and a moustache.

Less than two weeks after this attack the Ripper ventured back to Leeds to commit his final murder. Jacqueline Hill, aged 20, a student in the third year of her English degree course, was returning home to her students' hall of residence in Headingley, Leeds, on a wet, rainy, Monday, 17 November 1980. Jackie had decided to take the Number 1 bus from Beeston to Holt Park. This dropped her off opposite the front of the Arndale Centre. From there it was only a two-minute walk to her student residence at Lupton Flats. The 5ft 6in student, with short dark brown hair, was wearing a two-tone checked grey duffle coat with a detachable hood and plastic toggles. She was wearing dark blue jeans, brown shoes and an off-white fluffy woollen scarf and Fair Isle patterned mittens. She carried a cream handbag. As she made her way up Alma Road she was struck from behind with a hammer and then dragged into an overgrown wasteland area at the rear of the Arndale centre.

Her lifeless body was discovered the next morning by Mr Donald Court, one of the managers from the Arndale Centre, as he was taking the previous day's takings to the bank. His journey took him along Alma Road and up the service ramp located at the back of the building. After walking half way up the ramp, he stopped to switch the heavy bag of change into his other hand. At this point, he looked directly onto the waste ground below and saw what he first took to be a tailor's dummy lying in the undergrowth. As he stared, he realised to his horror that it was a woman and he ran to fetch help from a nearby shopkeeper.

Jackie Hill's murder, more than any other, brought home to the police, the press and the public, the type of man they were up against. The murder of a young student, so close to the university campus where many other young girls were staying, eventually led to violent demonstrations and women's rights marches through Leeds

If no woman could go out alone in the north of England, what kind of society were we living in? Such was the extent of public frustration that Prime Minister Margaret Thatcher threatened to come up and take charge of the investigation personally.

Ronald Gregory was now forced to shake up the Ripper squad by replacing George Oldfield with Jim Hobson and bringing in four senior officers from forces other than West Yorkshire; it was now dubbed the 'super squad '.

Explaining his decision to reshape the investigation Gregory said:

I think the time had come, you could say the time had come a few murders ago, and it's certainly come for a rethink about the investigation. Public concern and considerably amount of pressure on what we are going to do next for we can't carry on in the same groove because we've had no success up to now.

So would Jim Hobson succeed where others had failed?

Hobson himself would comment on the chances:

Oh I'm certain it can be done, the morale of the force is very high and despite what people say about public confidence I'm sure we have the confidence of the public behind us … this case won't be solved by detectives but will be down to the officers on the ground, sooner or later, they will be in the right place at the right time.

His words were prophetic, by January 1981 the Yorkshire Ripper's reign of terror would finally come to an end.

But who would the Ripper turn out to be?

Would he be old or young; black or white; a loner or a family man? Would he have a criminal record or a history of mental problems? What fooled so many was that the most remarkable thing about him, was he was unremarkable; a Yorkshireman with ordinary parents, a wife and steady job.

Peter Sutcliffe

Peter Sutcliffe, by all accounts, was a nobody. If some men are said to be low profile in their introversion, then Sutcliffe was positively underground.

His father, John, was a dominant extrovert and his brothers shared many of their father's manly characteristics. John Sutcliffe was a self-proclaimed 'man's man', a local boy-about-town, as well as a famed footballer, cricketer and actor – a man for all seasons. Peter, by contrast, was small and weedy from the start. He weighed in at just 2.3 kilos (5 lbs) when he was born on 2 June 1946.

His parents were living in a row of terraced cottages: 2 Heaton Royd, Ferncliffe, Bingley, and John Sutcliffe was a journeyman baker in those days. Peter's mother, Kathleen Sutcliffe (née Coonan), was of Irish extraction; her family hailing originally from Connemara. She is still fondly remembered in Bingley and the local area as a woman who was kind, decent, honest and good-looking. As their family started to grow, the Sutcliffes moved out of their tiny stone cottage onto a sprawling council estate, to 70 Manor Road, Bingley. There, John and Kathleen went on to have more children – Anne, Michael, Maureen, Jayne and Carl – before moving one last time to a four-bedroomed, semi-detached property at 57 Cornwall Road, also in Bingley. All the Sutcliffe children went to the same local Roman Catholic schools, St Joseph's and Cottingley Manor School, but although bright and quick-witted, Peter did not excel academically. He didn't adjust well to school and was detached from other children of his age. He would spend playtimes on his own and was never involved in the normal rough and tumble of the playground.

At home, he was also quiet and loved reading and being at his mother's side. Unlike his brothers, Peter was socially awkward and never quite managed the art of surviving daily life comfortably in the council-estate world of Bingley, a somewhat dour town just 6 miles north of Bradford along the Aire Valley.

His weak build and shyness made him an easy target for school bullies and by the time he moved to Cottingley Manor Secondary School in 1957, the bullying became so bad that he played truant, sometimes for weeks on end, hiding all alone in the attic with just his thoughts for company. To the rest of his family he was seen as a puny and introverted boy who clung to his mother's skirts, following her everywhere. As he entered his teenage years, he didn't take any interest in girls and his thoughts were focused on motorbikes and cars; he was always fascinated by anything mechanical. When he turned 15 in 1961, he left school and began a £2.50-a-week job on 17 August, as an apprentice engineer at a local firm, Fairbank Brearley. He left less than a year later, never completing his apprenticeship and the reasons are unknown.

At 16, he bought his first motorcycle and began to assert himself a bit more confidently. He quickly gained a reputation as reckless on two wheels. According to his father, it was as if he had at last found something he was good at. He also started going out more with boys of his own age. Once, three or four of his male friends got together to try and form a pop group and he also became keen on shooting rats with an air gun. As his confidence grew, he took an interest in bodybuilding and would spend hours alone training with a bullworker, gaining upper arm and chest strength.

On 27 May 1962, he went to work in a fibre factory for about two years, but during this time he started to develop a habit of being late for work, which would eventually lose him the job. In fact, over the next couple of years it would cost him around eleven jobs. For a man who must later have used a near-phenomenal sense of split-second timing, his timeless approach to life in his youth seems odd. For the next couple of years, Peter drifted through a variety of undistinguished, dead-end jobs, going from one to another seemingly rudderless and without ambition, yet oddly never short of money.

In 1963, aged 17, he obtained a learner driver licence and was stopped and reported by Keighley Police for driving a car unaccompanied, and failing to display L-plates. There would be a similar case against him in May 1964. That same year, he took a job that marked an important milestone in the making of the Yorkshire Ripper. He went to work as a gravedigger at Bingley Cemetery. He actually worked two stints at the cemetery, because he left for a while to work for the water board at Gilstead filter beds – but was sacked for bad timekeeping. He returned to gravedigging in June 1965 and stayed there until November 1967 before he was sacked once more for bad timekeeping. His boss at that time, Douglas McTavish, recalled later: 'I had to sack him. He should have started work at 8 am but kept arriving at 8.30 am and 8.45 am. When the other men started arriving late as well, I gave him his last chance but he was late again.'

Rumours circulated after his arrest that Sutcliffe had in fact been sacked from his job for opening the coffins and stealing jewellery from the corpses.

Sutcliffe drifted around different jobs and began sporting a neatly trimmed beard; he was nicknamed 'Jesus' by his workmates. Friends and family noted that he became withdrawn from conversations and when he did talk, he would discuss death or his job digging graves. Curiously, he also spoke of his sisters' moral welfare. He preferred the solitude of his own bedroom, into which his family were not allowed, and would become agitated when his sisters' boyfriends came round for dinner. He would frequent several pubs with his work colleagues but would always bring the conversation back to his fascination with death.

In 1966, when Sutcliffe was 20, he met two people that were to play a major part in his later life. Trevor Birdsall, an 18-year-old Bingley lad, became his best friend and would be the person who came closest to witnessing first-hand the beginning of Sutcliffe's reign of terror. Unfortunately Birdsall did nothing about it until after the thirteenth and last victim, who died in November 1980. He then wrote an anonymous letter to the police suggesting they should look into Sutcliffe's activities. Nothing happened; the letter got swallowed up among the hundreds of others being processed. Eventually, Birdsall was persuaded by his girlfriend in December 1980 to go to the police and make a statement, but even that was still waiting in the queue of paperwork by the time Sutcliffe was arrested.

The other person was 16-year-old Sonia Szurma – the first girl he ever took home to meet his mother. Sonia seemed to understand him. He met her when he was frequenting the Royal Standard pub, one of his favourite haunts on Manningham Lane in Bradford. They were an odd couple; whereas Peter had left school at 15, Sonia had seven O Levels, plus piano qualifications. He was an ex-gravedigger, she had ambitions to become a teacher, but they seemed to hit it off and were often seen kissing and cuddling in the corner of a bar.

For the next few years, life seemed to be going well for the young Peter, with a steady job and a girlfriend he thought the world of. However, the events of 1969 brought his world crashing down. It soon became apparent that his mother, Kathleen, was having an affair with a neighbour, a local policeman. His father arranged for his children, and Sonia, to be present at a Bingley hotel for a grand and humiliating confrontation. Kathleen arrived at the bar believing she was meeting her boyfriend, only to find her entire family waiting. In an act of vengeance, her husband degraded her in front of them by forcing her to show the whole family the new nightdress she had bought for the secret occasion. It destroyed the innocent image Peter always held for his mother.

A further devastating blow was his discovery that in late July of the same year, Sonia had been secretly meeting with another boyfriend, a local Italian ice-cream salesman named Antonio. She had been spotted by Peter's brother Mick, who promptly told Peter what was going on. Peter decided to confront her, but she refused to answer any of his questions or tell him whether their relationship was over. That night a bitter and wounded Sutcliffe decided he would take revenge by going with a prostitute. This would be turn out to be a crucial event in the life of Peter Sutcliffe, the full details of which are laid out later in this book and provide a possible motive for the Yorkshire Ripper murders.

Despite these circumstances the couple did manage to stay together and on 10 August 1974, Sonia Szurma celebrated her 24th birthday by becoming became Mrs Sonia Sutcliffe at Clayton Baptist Church on School Street, Clayton in Bradford. The wedding was performed in front of fifty guests by Reverend William Nelson.

The marriage certificate got Sutcliffe's age wrong – it said he was 29 but he had celebrated his 28th birthday only two months earlier. For his best man Sutcliffe chose an old school friend from Cottingley Manor School, Ron Wilson, but only after two other friends had turned down the offer.

The decision to marry had followed long and serious talks with Sonia's father who was assured they planned to save every penny they could for a deposit on a house of their own. So, after a honeymoon in Paris, it was back to live with Sonia's parents at Tanton Crescent, Bradford. Their prospects of buying their own home were boosted when Peter eagerly accepted the offer of £400 redundancy at Anderton International and used £200 of that to pay for lorry driving lessons at Apex Driving School in Cullingworth. From here Sutcliffe found a job as a long-distance driver with the Bradford firm, T. & W.H. Clark (Holdings) Limited.

Here he would stay until his eventual arrest.

Chapter 2

Arrest and Confession

'I hope the officer in Sheffield isn't too ugly, I promised to kiss whoever caught the Yorkshire Ripper.'

Ronald Gregory, Chief Constable, West Yorkshire Police

Melbourne Avenue in Sheffield was an area where many of the street sex workers who worked the Hanover area of the city took their clients. The quiet tree-lined avenue was situated in the up-market residential area of Broomhill and contained large, stone Victorian and Georgian properties with long, shaded driveways. Most of these houses had been converted into business premises. At number 3 there sat a large three-storey Victorian property with a long sweeping driveway that curled round to the back of the building. Visiting the scene today it's easy to see why this particular spot was a popular choice for those sex workers seeking privacy with their clients. The drive way was set back from the tree-lined avenue, and with high walls and bushes either side it would have afforded cover to carry out their business discreetly. It was also close enough to the boundary of the red-light district so they could be back quickly for another client.

As for the building itself, it too was once a residential property but had been converted into commercial use. In 1981 it was home to the Federation of British Engineer's Tool Manufacturers, and was better known as Lights Trade House. Sheffield still teemed with hundreds of tiny businesses producing goods from locally made special steels, small workshops, manufactured cutlery, silverware and pewter ware as well as hand-made tools like drills, slit saws, scythes and sickles. Lights Trade House represented these businesses. In its heyday more than thirty different associations were based there.

Its decline came as global companies tended not to be interested in maintaining an involvement in national trade associations and by the time it closed its doors in 2002, most of the main groups had already gone their separate ways, linking up with larger umbrella organisations from their sector. Only a handful of organisations were still based there, some with only overlapping memberships and secretariats.

The current occupiers of Lights Trade House do not want to be associated with the building's history.

At around 10.50 pm on 2 January 1981, a routine police patrol car was making its journey from the nearby Hammerton Road police station to the red-light district of Hanover Square. The driver was 31-year-old Probationary Constable Robert Hydes and his supervisor, 47-year-old Sergeant Robert Ring, a man with many years' experience in policing the city. Both officers were working the 10 pm to 6 am shift. PC Hydes had been assigned to Hammerton Road station after completing his seven-month South Yorkshire Police training. As part of his mentoring of the young constable, Sergeant Ring would accompany him on a routine patrol of the red-light district to show the new officer how to handle the issue of curb crawlers operating in the area. They cruised around the usual sites of Broomhall Street and Hanover Square before deciding to journey up to Melbourne Avenue, a well-known hangout for sex workers.

Cruising slowly down the narrow tree-lined Avenue, Sergeant Ring glanced to his left and saw a brown Rover car parked up in the driveway of number 3. Sensing this could be a curb crawler with a sex worker, he instructed PC Hyde to go and investigate. The patrol car swung into the drive and parked directly in front of the Rover. The headlights now lit up the Rover car and it was clear there were indeed two occupants inside, a man and a woman.

Upon instruction from Sergeant Ring, PC Hyde approached the car. The male driver wound his window down and, following a routine questioning, gave his name as Peter Williams. While this was going on, Sergeant Ring had made his way to the back of the car and noted down the licence plate number as HVY 679N. He then went to join his colleague at the driver's window and asked the driver to identify the woman sitting next to him. 'She's my girlfriend' was the answer, and when asked what her name was, he said, 'I don't know, I have not known her that long.'

Sergeant Ring sharply replied, 'who are you trying to kid, I haven't fallen off the Christmas tree.' To which the driver said: 'I'm not suggesting you have.'

Sergeant Ring returned to the police car and radio-checked the Rover's registration number via his pocket radio through to Sheffield Police Headquarters Control Room, who checked on their Police National Computer terminal linked to the national system. The system was still in its infancy but was still able to come back with a result. The licence plates were registered to a Mr Aslam Khan, not Peter Williams, and – more importantly – they actually belonged to a Skoda, not a Rover. Returning to the car, Sergeant Ring informed the driver that the plates were wrong and reached through the car window and took the car keys out of the ignition. PC Hyde then took the car's tax disc from the window for further examination. A closer look at the licence plates revealed that the Skoda plates had been crudely taped over the original Rover plates with black electrical tape.

A decision was made to bring the driver and his female companion to the nearby Hammerton Road police station for further questioning. The woman was escorted to the police car by PC Hyde, while Sergeant Ring went to radio the station to inform them of the arrest; after doing so he turned to go back towards the Rover and he heard a scuffling sound coming from the side of the building. He then noticed the driver was no longer in the vehicle but was emerging from shadows near a stone porch that abutted onto the building behind his car.

'What are you doing there?' Ring said: 'I've fallen off that fucking wall,' said the driver. 'I wanted to piss.' Ring told him to go to the toilet at the front of the building where he could see him, but the man said he wouldn't bother.

The driver was then officially arrested by Sergeant Ring on suspicion of stealing licence plates. Before leaving in the police car he grabbed his coat, which lay on the back seat of the Rover, and put it on. When he climbed into the back of the police car, it had already been established by PC Hyde that his female companion was Miss Olivia Reivers, a well-known local sex worker who worked the Hanover Square area of Sheffield.

Arriving at Hammerton Road police station, the arrested man requested to use the bathroom. This was allowed and upon his return he was questioned further regarding the accusation of theft. Here for the first time he revealed himself to be Peter William Sutcliffe from Bradford, claiming he had stolen the licence plates because he had been caught drink driving the previous year and would no doubt be banned from driving once he had gone to court. He felt there was no point in renewing his car insurance which was up shortly and so he stole the plates. It was a fairly plausible story and under normal circumstances he would have been booked and released on bail to appear at a Petty Sessions court in the future. The whole process could have lasted ninety minutes and he would have been free to leave.

But the desk sergeant wasn't happy and his gut instinct told him that this Bradford man seemed a bit too far from home for his liking. He also remembered that West Yorkshire Police were keen to question any man caught in the company of a sex worker. The desk sergeant decided to make a call to the Millgarth police station in Leeds to check if they had any information on Peter Sutcliffe.

It soon transpired that the Ripper squad had already interviewed Sutcliffe several times in the past. He worked in the mechanical trade, a profession the Ripper was likely to work in following the discovery of oil stains on the body of Halifax victim Josephine Whitaker, and his alibis seemed to have come only from family. More importantly, in past interviews he had repeatedly denied ever being with sex workers.

It was now approaching 2.30 am on Saturday morning and following his instinct, the desk sergeant decided to lock Sutcliffe in the cells for the night and contact Dewsbury police station to inform them of the arrest; he asked if they could send someone in a car to pick him up and question him further. Around 5.00 am Dewsbury station contacted Sheffield police to say that once the new shift came on duty at 6.00 am they would send somebody to collect Peter Sutcliffe for further questioning. They also offered to collect Sutcliffe's Brown Rover that was still parked up in Melbourne Avenue.

At 8.55 am Sutcliffe arrived at Dewsbury police station in the back of a West Yorkshire Police car, he was accompanied by three officers, two were in the lead car with Sutcliffe and the third was driving Peter's brown Rover. His jacket pockets were searched, a standard police procedure which, unbelievably, was not carried out in Sheffield. In his pockets detectives found money, a pair of his underpants and a piece of blue and red plaited nylon rope about 3ft long. Asked what the rope was for, he said it was lifting things such as car engine parts. This rope was knotted with two knots at each end and two additional knots a few inches apart near the middle. When asked about this he replied it was to make it easier to grip the rope.

Peter was then asked to remove his clothing so they could be examined thoroughly. When he stripped off his trousers the officers found that he was wearing a rather odd garment underneath. They appeared to be special leggings next to his skin which he explained as being leg-warmers. They consisted of two sleeves of a jumper made of a silky material and crudely sewn together upside down and pulled up to the waist with a leg to go in each arm; there was a large gap in the leggings which exposed his private parts. More revealing was the fact he had sown in extra padding around where his knees would go. No significance was placed on these bizarre leggings at the time, but I will return to these later in the book.

The officers also learnt that Peter Sutcliffe had a wife waiting for him at home. Sonia Sutcliffe would later recall the events that night:

I had a phone call from Pete [on Friday night] to say he had trouble with his car. That was around 9 pm. That's all I heard. Having waited in a state of uncertainty, all night, the next I knew was that on Saturday morning at around 10 am there was a knock on my door at our house on Garden Lane, Heaton. I had locked up but the bolt wasn't on because I had been expecting Pete's return at any time. So I thought, why should I answer the knocking when I knew he had his key?

About five minutes later and the phone rang, and it was the local police and that police officers were at my door and that Pete had been held overnight at Sheffield police station. And that was the first inkling I had of Pete's whereabouts. About four o'clock that afternoon I asked the police on the phone about getting there to see Pete. I hadn't seen him since Friday and I had no idea what was going on. The officer told me he would phone back. He did so but it was three hours later about 7 pm. The officer said words to the effect of, there's no point in coming because you won't be able to see him. I was just left wondering. At around 10 pm the police called back to say I would be taken to see Peter tomorrow, that would be Sunday.

As Sonia waited most of the day to hear more news about her husband's arrest, further police interviews were continuing over in Dewsbury station. Sutcliffe did not appear surprised at such attention for such a minor offence, told police officers he was a lorry driver from Bradford and had made regular deliveries to Sunderland in his 32-ton 'artic', he talked about his interest in cars and said that he had been interviewed as part of the £5-note enquiry and the Jean Jordan murder. He also said detectives had questioned him about his car being flagged up in the red-light areas of Bradford, Leeds and Manchester.

By now the interviewing officers were beginning to become more and more suspicious of Sutcliffe, especially since he also had a size eight shoe and a gap in his teeth. One of his cars had also been a white Ford with a black roof. Hadn't the one driven by Maureen Long's attacker been similar?

Blood and hair samples were taken and the interviews continued. He was asked about his car being seen in Manchester; he denied ever being there. He gave the excuse that his job took him home through the red-light districts and that he had already been interviewed and given the police samples of his handwriting. He discussed his alibis and the fact that he had been at home with his wife on Bonfire Night when Theresa Sykes was attacked.

By 5.30 pm on Saturday evening, Detective Sergeant O'Boyle felt it probably was a false alarm, and that Peter Sutcliffe was unlikely to be the Ripper. He didn't have the Geordie accent and his handwriting didn't match the 'Wearside Jack' letters. He was prepared to recommend that Sutcliffe be released.

Chief Superintendent John Clark, in charge at Dewsbury, was not so convinced, and still considered Sutcliffe to be a major suspect in the Ripper case. Clark expressed his 'displeasure' at the lack of importance attached to the man they held in custody to the duty officer at the Leeds Incident Room. He insisted another officer be brought in to question Sutcliffe. Probably not wanting to get a hard time by his superiors, O'Boyle decided to stay on when his shift finished at 6.00 pm to help out his replacement, a Detective Inspector John Boyle who had been sent down to take over. The interviewing continued into the night, pretty much repeating all the things which had been asked previously. At one point in the interview it was decided to send out for fish and chips. Sutcliffe joked that he would go get them, but they would be cold by the time he got back.

At this point the interviewing officers didn't really have much, other than circumstantial evidence; besides, in the five years they had spent in the hunt for the Yorkshire Ripper, they had seen similar circumstances before in dozens of potential suspects. In all likelihood, Peter Sutcliffe would be free to leave within a short period of time; they couldn't legally hold him for much longer anyway.

It was now 10.00 pm on Saturday night and over in Hammerton Road police station in Sheffield, Sergeant Ring had once again clocked on for another 10 pm to 6 am shift. It's no exaggeration to say this work shift was one of the most important timings in the history of crime. As he arrived into work, he was amazed to discover that the man he had arrested in Melbourne Avenue was still being held for questioning by the Ripper Squad. He had thought, like everyone else, it was just a routine case of licence plate theft, but now he realised there could be something far bigger going on. It was then he made the most important decision of his career. In the back of his mind he vaguely recalled seeing Sutcliffe go to the side of the house on the night he was arrested. The officers had been too busy dealing with Olivia Reivers to initially notice how Sutcliffe had disappeared from the driving seat of his car only to reappear from the side of the building moments later, giving the excuse he needed to urinate. He and PC Hyde decided to return immediately to the Lights Trades House and explore the area where Sutcliffe had gone. They arrived shortly after 11.00 pm.

The area was pitch dark and the two officers made their way up the driveway armed with torches; they weren't sure what they were looking for but made a thorough search along the drive up towards the stone porch area where Sutcliffe had gone.

Around to the back of the porch the officers were greeted by the oil-storage tank. A quick shine of the torch along the side of the tank and there, to their disbelief, they found a ball-pein hammer lying among the leaves. At first they thought it might have been left by a workman, but then Sergeant Ring said, 'Yeah but who owns the knife?' His torch had caught the shiny reflection of large kitchen knife lying close to the hammer. One can only imagine what a moment that must have been for the officers when it suddenly dawned on them that they had possibly captured the Yorkshire Ripper.

He radioed back to the station where he was given a rather frantic answer of, 'Don't touch anything, a photographer is on the way.' West Yorkshire Police were also informed of the crucial find and now, at 00.10 am on Sunday morning, Inspector Boyle decided to telephone his Ripper Squad superior, Detective Superintendent Dick Holland at his home in Elland, Leeds. This was it, the moment he had waited five years for. Sutcliffe had been arrested sixteen hours earlier and only now, for the first time, there seemed like a real breakthrough. On the orders of Dick Holland, an officer was immediately assigned to sit with Sutcliffe in the cell with him.

At 9.00 am Dick Holland was briefed at Bradford Police Station and Inspector Boyle and Sergeant O'Boyle had been immediately sent back to Sheffield to re-interview Olivia Reivers. Holland would now personally go to number 6 Garden Lane and confront Sonia Sutcliffe.

Sonia remembered the visit clearly:

At 11 am in morning while I was watching a German language television programme, four police officers arrived. They came in and insisted, almost from the start, that I switch the programme off. I turned down the sound to comply. But that wasn't enough, they wanted it off and immediately subjected me to detailed questioning.

Thinking the officers were there only to give her a lift to the station to see her husband, she said:

Aren't we going to get moving? But they wanted to keep questioning me and they also kept grumbling about how cold they were. Later on in the papers I saw a quote by one of them likening my house to a morgue. Really? That would have been pathetic if it wasn't so absurd, anyway it was hardly surprising as I purposefully hadn't put the heating on thinking we would be leaving for Dewsbury police station immediately.

The four officers were in fact Detective Chief Inspector George Smith, Detective Superintendent Dick Holland, Detective Sergeant Desmond O'Boyle, and the young policewoman, Detective Constable Jenny Crawford Brown.

Sonia continues: 'We got to Bradford police station around noon. There they began the run down off my life, with Mr Smith asking for all sorts of facts and figures and very personal questions. This continued until around 8 pm that night.'

Sonia was questioned about her husband's whereabouts on the key nights of the murders and attacks, she couldn't remember those particular details and dates, but it transpired that out of all the nights in question Sonia remembered Bonfire Night the most, because she and her husband were supposed to have gone out to watch the fireworks but he phoned to say he couldn't make it, arriving home around 10.00 pm that night. This revelation had now blown apart Peter Sutcliffe's claim of being at home at 8.00 pm when Theresa Sykes was attacked. Sonia would also identify the kitchen knife found in Sheffield as one she had bought in a set years ago.

Over in the Sutcliffe's home in Garden Lane, Dick Holland had moved to the garage and ordered his officers to start bagging up various tools, including screwdrivers, chisels, hammers and a hacksaw. The hacksaw was a key piece of evidence which he knew about and the fact that the Ripper had tried to cut Jean Jordan's head off with a hacksaw was purposefully withheld from the press, public and most of the ground detectives. This may or may not have been a great move considering several past interviews had resulted in Sutcliffe's house and garage being searched by officers. The hacksaw that hung in his garage was the one used on Jordan, yet no detective knew about it during those searches.

Now they had the weapons and they had a lot of circumstantial evidence to go with it, but in 1981 DNA profiling was yet to be discovered, so there was no way of proving whether they were the same weapons that had been used in previous murders. Could they really prove Sutcliffe had committed all the Yorkshire Ripper murders? The question now was, could they get him to crack under questioning?

Inspector Boyle had all the info he needed and this time he was joined by Sergeant Peter Smith, specially requested by Dick Holland because of his long service on the Ripper Squad and intense knowledge of the case.

At 12.00 pm the interviews continued at a slow pace and gradually built up speed and pressure. They went through all the details previously provided by Sutcliffe, only this time they were tying him up. He was pressed heavily about the amount of times his car had been logged in red-light areas in Leeds, Bradford and Manchester. How could he explain his car being seen in Manchester if he'd never been there? He replied that it must be some mistake. Here the detectives called his bluff and told him they had double checked all the records and it was definitely his car. Sutcliffe began to get rattled and started mumbling that his car had broken down in Bradford city centre, he had left it in the car park at Bradford Central Library, and that: 'someone must have used it to go to Manchester and put it back on that spot'. It was quickly pointed out to him that that the person would have to have fixed his car first, then taken it to Manchester only to bring it back again and park it in the same spot. Sutcliffe knew his excuses were unravelling fast.

By 2.00 pm Boyle and Smith were now pressing Sutcliffe hard, particularly about the night of Theresa Sykes's attack on 5 November 1980. His alibi had been shot down by Sonia admitting he hadn't been at home at 8.00 pm, but that he had come in around 10.00 pm. They now felt the time was right to press him on why he had gone to Sheffield that night.

Boyle: 'Why did you go to Sheffield that night?'

Sutcliffe: 'I gave three people a lift to Rotherham and Sheffield from Bradford. They stopped me on the M606 and offered me £10 to take them home, so I did.'

Boyle: 'I don't believe that. I believe you went to Sheffield on Friday night with the sole purpose of picking up a prostitute.'

Sutcliffe: 'That's not true. It was only after I got to Sheffield and had declined an offer to go with a prostitute that I decided to use the money I got from the hitch-hikers and go with one.'

Boyle: 'When you were arrested in Sheffield you had a prostitute in your car which had false plates on it. I believe you put them on to conceal the identity of your vehicle in the event of it being seen in a prostitute area.'

Sutcliffe: 'No, that's not true. To be honest with you, I've been so depressed that I put them on because I was thinking of committing a crime with the car.'

Boyle: 'I believe the crime you were going to commit was to harm a prostitute.'

Sutcliffe: [Clearly rattled] 'No, that's not true.'

Boyle: 'Do you recall that before you were put in a police car at Sheffield you left your car and went to the side of a house?'

Sutcliffe: 'Yes, I went to urinate against the wall.'

Boyle: 'I think you went for another purpose.' [No response from Sutcliffe. He sat looking at the floor. Boyle allowed a moment to let it all sink in before continuing.] Do you understand what I am saying? I think you are in trouble, serious trouble.'

Sutcliffe: [Long pause before speaking] 'I think you have been leading up to it.'

Boyle: 'Leading up to what?'

Sutcliffe: 'The Yorkshire Ripper.'

Boyle: 'What about the Yorkshire Ripper?'

Sutcliffe: 'Well, it's me.'

Both officers leaned back in their chairs, glancing slightly towards one another as the gravity of what they just heard sank in. Five years had seemed a lifetime and here it was, finally over. The most notorious serial killer since Jack the Ripper was sitting right in front of them.

Outside the interview room Dick Holland had decided it was time to make a phone call to the man he regarded as his superior officer and it wasn't going to be Detective Chief Superintendent Jim Hobson, the man officially put in overall charge of the Ripper Squad. The phone call went to his old boss, George Oldfield, who was having his Sunday dinner at the time. Oldfield dropped everything to hurry across to face his nemesis. When he got there he was told Sutcliffe was ready to confess to all the murders but had only one request. That he get to tell his wife before anyone else did. The request was granted.

Sonia recalled the moment she first learnt her husband was the Yorkshire Ripper:

> In the middle of my interview Superintendent Holland and Sergeant O'Boyle went off to Dewsbury, where I heard later a jubilant press conference was going to take place. I remained at Bradford police station from 8 pm to 10 pm during which time I was given a hamburger to eat. I was waiting for the OK from the police to be allowed to go to Dewsbury and to see Pete, still not knowing what was going on. I said, has Pete had anything to eat, an officer replied, we're not inhuman you know.
>
> Perhaps it was 10.30 pm when we finally got to Dewsbury, I'm not sure. But I'm sure about what happened next. At about 10.30 pm the police brought Pete into a room in the police station where I was waiting. There were various other police officers in there. They were all watching me, scrutinising me. Pete just looked at me and then he said those awful words 'it's me'.

All the questions relating the Yorkshire Ripper now made sense to Sonia and she just stared at her husband in disbelief.

> I said, is it? Is it really? And he said yes it's me … Just like that.
>
> I saw him twice that night for about five minutes on each occasion. I suppose I was given about an hour and a half for the news to sink in. Jenny the policewoman stayed with me. At that point Mr Smith offered me a glass of Scotch whisky which released my tension.

Over in Dewsbury at 9.00 pm, Chief Constable Ronald Gregory appeared before the press and cameras, he was accompanied by a jubilant George Oldfield and Jim Hobson. Among a sea of flashing camera lights, Gregory read out the following statement:

> A man was detained in Sheffield by the Sheffield police in connection with a matter which was identified as theft of number plates of a motor car and the number plates had been stolen from the West Yorkshire area.

He was brought to West Yorkshire as a result of discussions between the South Yorkshire police and the West Yorkshire police; further inquiries were made and this man is now detained here in West Yorkshire and he is being questioned in relation to the Yorkshire Ripper murders.

It is anticipated that he will appear before the court in Dewsbury tomorrow. I cannot say where he is at the moment because a lot of enquiries have to be made. Mr Oldfield and Mr Hobson and other senior investigating officers have to make a number of inquiries tonight but I can tell you that we are absolutely delighted with developments at this stage, absolutely delighted.

He then opened the conference up to questions from the press.

Q. Can you give us any details at all about the murders?

A. No, not at this stage because a man is being interviewed at this very moment in time. But indications are that there will be a charge later tomorrow.

Q. Can you tell us whether he has a Geordie accent?

A. I cannot tell you that because I've not heard him speak.

Q. Can you give us any details of the arrest, circumstances of, if not actual details?

A. All I can say is that he was detained in Sheffield. He was with a lady ... he was detained in relation to an incident in Sheffield, and he was detained, let me tell you, by a sergeant, two outstanding police officers, a Sergeant Ring of the South Yorkshire police, Robert Ring, and a Constable Robert John Hyde of the South Yorkshire police. They're uniformed officers who have my heartfelt thanks, who made this original detection and as a result of questioning later on by West Yorkshire police we have reached the present stage but it is just the initial stages and I thought you should know now before we go any further.

Q. Are you scaling down the operation with the general hunt for the Yorkshire Ripper from this moment on?

A. Right.

Ronald Gregory would later come under harsh criticism by legal representatives in the way he had conducted this press conference. In the eyes of the law Peter Sutcliffe was still an innocent man but here was the Chief Constable and his senior officers being paraded in front of the world laughing and rejoicing, signalling to everyone they had got their man. It would later be pointed out that the entire sorry spectacle could have given legal grounds for a mistrial.

Meanwhile, in another section of Dewsbury station, Sonia was in hysterics and being comforted by Constable Jenny Crawford Brown.

> Suddenly during a two-minute sob on jenny's shoulder I saw out of the corner of my eye some of the top brass come in. They went out again, they obviously thought it was an inappropriate moment for their intrusion. A quarter of an hour or so later at 1 am they came back. CID chief George Oldfield sat down next to me and tried to present a concerned image.
>
> He began by saying 'you know who I am, don't you? 'Taking it for granted that I would. I just stared ahead as he rattled on. My priority was to let my parents know.
>
> Oldfield said to me, oh no I wouldn't advise you do that; the press will get you.
>
> What on earth are you on about, what do you mean?
>
> He said 'we've had a press conference, you know, and they are all waiting outside'

By now it was 1.15 am and Sonia felt it was too late to phone her and that she would rather tell them face to face. But unknown to her, the press had already descended upon her parents' house at Tanton Crescent, Bradford. They had begun banging on the door and a rather frightened Maria Szurma, mother of Sonia, phoned the police.

At 2.30 am Sonia was given fresh bed linen and offered a room to sleep in a police accommodation building next to Dewsbury police station. Unknown to her she was, understandably in the circumstances, being placed on suicide watch.

> I asked for a bath or a shower. Jenny the policewoman – we were now on first name terms – asked 'do you want to come back to my place'. It was a kind gesture; I said to her, how can I stay at yours, I can't even visit my parents. Jenny then went to bed in another room and I had another policewoman with me all night. She said it was instructions. She also insisted I keep the door open when I had a shower, I said I wanted it shut but she said, no its orders. The policewoman who stayed in my room sat up reading and smoking. The light had to remain on but I couldn't sleep at all that dreadful night.
>
> At 6 am there was a change of shift, a policewoman called Linda came in. I got up and dressed and the woman gave me a newspaper. It was a daily paper. I started reading but when she realised what I was reading

she grabbed it back. I said come on you've just passed me your paper; you've just handed it to me. Everyone else in the street is allowed to read the paper I don't see why I shouldn't be allowed to do so. She said it was orders. I demanded to speak to someone in more authority but was told they were all still asleep. The whole episode was devoid of human consideration. For here I was, at the bleakest moment of my life.

Over the next twenty-four hours – apart from a break when Sutcliffe was returned to his cell to rest from 3.30 am to 8.30 am on the Monday morning – O'Boyle and Smith took perhaps the most incredible statement ever given by a killer. Sergeant Smith sat at the desk and wrote down the words while Sutcliffe sat in front of the desk but sideways, resting one arm on it. Sergeant O'Boyle paced about the office while asking the questions. Sutcliffe's detailed accounts left no doubt in the minds of the detectives that this was indeed the Yorkshire Ripper. As he would chillingly state, all the details were locked in his head, 'reminding me of the beast that I am'.

After five years the Yorkshire Ripper investigation had resulted in 2¼ million police man-hours being spent, 250,000 people interviewed, 157,000 cars checked, 28,000 official statements taken and 27,000 houses visited.

It was the largest murder inquiry in the history of the British police and the ultimate irony was that it was solved almost by accident.

In the subsequent search of Sutcliffe's truck, detectives found road maps such as an, A-Z of Leeds, Bradford, Manchester and Liverpool. There was also an atlas of the grid of Britain's motorways. They were stacked together and squeezed into a navy blue plastic-come-leather shopping bag along with a weekend magazine and copies of the lorry driver's monthly magazine 'Headlight'. Still in the lorry cab was a blue cotton jacket, a sleeping bag and two oil-stained boiler suits.

A further search of the leather shopping bag revealed a rather bizarre note tucked inside a plastic pouch, an obscure message painstakingly written and worked over again in Biro. It read:

In this truck is a man whose latent genius, if unleashed, would rock the nation, whose dynamic energy would overpower those around him. Better let him sleep.

This message has never really been explained but it gives a small insight into the warped mind of Peter Sutcliffe.

Later his employer went on TV to say:

He was a very quiet chap, he was very sensitive. If you told him off tears would come to his eyes and he would think the whole world was against him. I was surprised he was arrested because he had already been interviewed twice within the last twelve months by police. All the staff here have been interviewed, some of us had our clothes taken away. In our opinion Peter had been cleared of suspicion, he was a good, clean and honest worker. He delivered machine parts such as axles and engineering equipment to firms throughout the country. He always kept himself to himself and his main interest seemed to be repairing cars, he was very reserved and did not associate with the other drivers.

As the world woke to the news that the Yorkshire Ripper had possibly been captured; newspapers across the country, and especially the Yorkshire area, reported at the sense of joy being felt in and around the streets and pubs of all their major towns and cities.

The *Yorkshire Post* reported:

Last night there was a near carnival atmosphere in the red-light district with Sheffield and other northern cities almost like the old days. Publicans on both sides of the Pennines have not seen so many girls about in ages. In Manchester's Moss Side, Bradford's Lumb Lane and the Chapeltown area of Leeds, smiling street walkers plied their trade in greater numbers than for the past three or four years. 'It almost reminds you of the January sales' said one officer from the West Yorkshire Police. 'You could say business is booming.'

Since 1975 the world's oldest profession has always been one of the riskiest in the vice district of North industrial cities. Fear of attacks had driven many northern street girls to work in the Midlands or London. Girls who stayed on operated in pairs for protection. Potential clients had also been scared away from the red-light districts because of the increased police patrols in Manchester's Moss Side. Late last night a prostitute called Sarah said 'it is quite an incredible high, the atmosphere has changed and I don't have to keep looking over my shoulder all the time'

Chapter 3

The Road to the Old Bailey

The ordinary men and women of the West Riding woke to bright sunshine streaming from a clear blue sky which lasted all day, as if symbolising the end of a dark age of fear.

Daily Express January 1981

By 4.00 pm on Monday, 5 January 1981, the Victorian Town Hall in Dewsbury had attracted a crowd of more than 2,000 people waiting to see the Ripper. Many of them had gathered outside the building that housed the Magistrate Court since the early hours of the morning.

Two hours before the hearing, and the police were hard pressed enough to contain hundreds of children who had made up a large proportion of the crowd. Vantage points were sought on walls and windowsills in the hope of catching a glimpse of the Ripper as he was taken the few hundred yards from Dewsbury police station to the courtroom.

The town itself was still sporting Christmas decorations and had an almost carnival atmosphere. Local housewives declared they had not seen such a busy Monday for years and curious drivers drove at a snail's pace through the streets. Police and the press appeared to be everywhere and not a telephone kiosk in the town centre was vacant for more than a second at a time as a hundred journalists recorded the events of the day

Meanwhile, inside the building, three magistrates had taken their place at the head of the Court. Sonia Sutcliffe, along with her father, had already taken their seats. They were accompanied by a policewoman. The oak-panelled court number one on the first floor was packed with 200 reporters from all over the world, there was no room for the public. The county prosecutor, Mr Maurice Shaffner, addressed the court to say there had been a delay, but no sooner had he made this statement that there was tremendous roar from the crowd outside. This clearly signalled the arrival of Peter Sutcliffe.

Outside, the police van swung into the street adjacent to the court house, the crowd went wild, they booed and jeered and surged forward trying to get near, their screams growing louder. Cries of 'Hang the bastard!', 'Killer!' and 'Die Die Die!!' could be clearly heard from both outside and inside the court. Sonia Sutcliffe would later recall, 'it was an appalling spectacle, it was jungle law'.

But if the mob had hoped to catch a glimpse of the most wanted man in the history of crime, they were sorely disappointed. Sutcliffe was ushered out of the van and into court under the cover of a grey blanket. Fifty officers rushed in to form a human wall between the baying crowd, some of whom had clambered on to car roofs hoping to catch a glimpse of the accused as he entered the side door of the hall. Several others tried to break through the police line which was now four deep and some spectators began throwing pebbles and stones.

Sutcliffe was led into the court, handcuffed to a guard.

The man who had battered thirteen women to death and given nightmares to millions now stood in the dock. This short, slight, dark-haired man fitted no picture drawn up by police artists, nor did any image conjured up by the minds of detectives, soothsayers, psychiatrists, or cranks with hazel twigs and crystal balls. **Sutcliffe:** 'Pete' to all who ever knew him – was the ultimate invisible man. Four paces in any direction from his place in the dock and he would have melted into any crowd of three.

Court Clerk Dean Gardener asked: 'Are you Peter William Sutcliffe of 6 Garden Lane, Heaton, Bradford?' After an affirmative response, he continued:

> You are accused that between 16 November and 19 November 1980 you did murder Jacqueline Hill against the peace of our Sovereign Lady the Queen. Further, you are charged that at Mirfield, between 13 November and 2 January, you stole two motor vehicle registration plates to the total value of 50p, the property of Cyril Bamforth.

No sooner had the press and legal representatives taken their seats than it was over. Maurice Shaffner addressed the court, stating that Sutcliffe was not at this time legally represented and asked the magistrate, Mr John Walker, to remand him in custody for eight days. Sutcliffe confirmed that he was not represented and answered 'no' when asked if he wanted reporting restrictions lifted; that basically marked the end of the proceedings at that time.

The hearing lasted no more than five minutes before Sutcliffe was taken back out to the frenzied crowd and placed in the back of the police van to be whisked back to Armley Prison. Press men gathered inside were not allowed to leave the court building until the van carrying Sutcliffe had left the area.

Meanwhile, over in Bradford, Peter and Sonia's house in Garden Lane was besieged by reporters and curious onlookers all hoping to get a scoop on the Ripper's arrest. A parade of cars all queued up from one end of Garden Lane to the other, all hoping to catch a glimpse of the 'Ripper's House'. It became so bad that residents petitioned the council to block off the street from the public. Sonia had rather wisely moved out to stay with her parents. One angry resident spoke to the press:

Now we cannot get to sleep at night for cars crawling past our homes and stopping and peering at the house. It has been difficult enough to get our children to sleep without all this. We are asking the police and the council to close the street to non-residents and to stop these odd people from staring at the house. Garden Lane is not a vital through road and we think this would be possible without any inconvenience to local people.

As Sutcliffe arrived back in Armley Prison, plans were set in place to have his mental health assessed by several doctors to determine his state of mind before any plea could be entered. It also gave the police some much needed time to try and question him further regarding other attacks. It was nearly two months before Sutcliffe appeared before the court again – at 7.47 am on Friday, 20 February. This time he would be charged with the full catalogue of the Yorkshire Ripper crimes. His second appearance was a much quieter affair with only three members of the public seeing him arrive in court. The police had learnt their lesson from the first media circus and had decided that this time they would seal off the street leading to the court with huge metal barriers. Even though the crowd were kept well back from the proceedings, sixty officers were still drafted in to keep the peace.

Within a couple of minutes of his arrival, Sutcliffe was standing in the dock once again; he wore a pale pink open necked shirt, a dark green velvet jacket, and dark grey trousers. Sonia was nearby in a green corduroy overcoat. There was no obvious communication between her and Sutcliffe

The clerk of the court this time was Mr Stuart Baker, stood to face Sutcliffe and read out the charges:

The attempted murder of:
Anna Patricia Rogulskyj, 39, at Keighley, on 5 July 1975;

Olive Smelt, 51, at Halifax, on or about 15 August 1975;

Marcella Claxton, 23, at Leeds, on 9 May 1976;

Maureen Long, 46, at Bradford, on 10 July 1977,

Marilyn Moore, 28, at Leeds, on 14 December 1977;

Upadhya Nadavathy Bandara, 34, at Leeds, on 24 September 1980;

Teresa Simone Sykes, 16, at Huddersfield, on 5 November 1980.

The murder of:
Wilma McCann, 24, of Scott Hall Avenue, Chapeltown, at Leeds, on 30 October 1975;

Emily Monica Jackson, 42, of Back Green, Churwell, Morley, at Leeds, on or about 20 January 1976;

Irene Richardson, 28, of Cowper Street, Leeds, at Leeds, on or about 6 February 1977;

Patricia Atkinson, 33, of Oak Avenue, Manningham, in Bradford, on or about 23 April 1977;

Jayne Michelle McDonald, 16, of Scott Hall Avenue, Chapeltown, at Leeds, on June 26 1977;

Jean Bernadette Jordan (Royle), 20, of Lingbeck Crescent, Hulme, Manchester, at Manchester, between 30 September 1977 and 11 October 1977;

Yvonne Ann Pearson, 22, of Woodbury Street, Bradford, at Bradford, between 20 January and 26 March 1978;

Helen Maria Rytka, 18, of Elmwood Avenue, Birkby, Huddersfield, between 30 January and 4 February 1978;

Vera Evelyn Millward, 40, of Grenham Avenue, Hulme, Manchester, at Manchester, on or about 16 May 1978;

Josephine Anne Whitaker, 19, of Ivy Street, Halifax, at Halifax, on or about 4 April 1979;

Barbara Janine Leach, 20, of Grove Terrace, Bradford, at Bradford, between 1 September and 4 September 1979;

Marguerite Walls, 47, of New Park Croft, Farsley, Leeds, at Farsley, on or about 20 August 1980;

Jacqueline Hill, 20, of Lupton Flats, Headingley, at Headingley, Leeds, between 16 November and 19 November 1980.

The charges took eight minutes to read out. Sutcliffe gave no response pending an evaluation by psychiatrists.

David Kyle, acting for the director of public prosecutions, then informed the court that the prosecution did not intend to proceed with the theft of licence plates from a garage in Mirfield, Leeds. He also made an application for Sutcliffe's committal for trial under a procedure where the accused person can be committed for trial without oral evidence being given.

Defending counsel, Kerry Macgill, accepted committal without oral evidence. In the proceedings Macgill did not make any applications for bail or for the lifting of reporting restrictions. He did apply for two counsel to represent Sutcliffe at his trial, but fearing a fair trial would be almost impossible if held locally, he argued the case should not be held at Leeds Crown court but rather the Old Bailey in London. The hearing lasted just fourteen minutes, after which Sutcliffe was escorted back out to the van, this time to the jeering of only 150 onlookers. Sonia left escorted by plain clothes detectives, her coat collar pulled up high to cover her face, and was driven away, weeping, in a blue Hillman Avenger.

Kerry Macgill's motion for a London trial was granted on Tuesday 14 April 1981, when it was put before Leeds Court. The case of the Yorkshire Ripper would take place at the Old Bailey on 29 April. The stage was now set, but the impending trial of the Yorkshire Ripper had created its own problems behind the scenes with the West Yorkshire Police. Yes, they had apprehended the Ripper – but there was now the very real possibility that their five-year investigation would come under the closest scrutiny if a lengthy trial was to follow. Everyone behind the scenes knew the Ripper case had been seriously mishandled for most of the five-and-a-half years it took to catch Sutcliffe.

Six years before Sutcliffe had killed anybody he had been arrested in the early hours of Tuesday, 30 September 1969, hiding in a garden just off Manningham Lane, in Bradford's red-light district.

He was spotted by a police officer on routine patrol sitting in an old Morris Minor at the side of the road. The engine was running but the lights were off. As the officer, PC Bland, approached the car, Sutcliffe put it into gear and sped off down the road. A short while later the same officer noticed the car in the Manningham area again, parked up next to a row of terraced houses. This time there was no occupant in the vehicle. PC Bland started to check the gardens of the nearby houses and found Sutcliffe hunched behind a privet hedge with a hammer in his hand. He told the officer that a hubcap had flown off his front wheel and he was looking for it. When quizzed about the hammer, he claimed it was to help him secure it in place. Quite rightly the policeman thought 'what a load of bull', and arrested him for being in charge of an offensive weapon.

However, he arrested Sutcliffe on the charge of going equipped for burglary or theft and not for being in possession of an offensive weapon. A police van was summoned to come and collect Sutcliffe but, shamefully, he was never searched before getting into the van. Searching a suspect at the scene of a suspected crime would have been a routine task and this was instilled into officers at training school. He should have been searched to obtain evidence of a crime and prevent injury to the officer or offender. Had such a search taken place, the officer would have revealed the presence of a knife. Twelve years later, Sutcliffe would claim that he slipped the long-bladed knife down a gap between the side of the police vehicle and the wheel arch cover inside the police van that came to collect him.

At Bradford Police Station, he was photographed and fingerprinted and appeared at the magistrates' court two weeks later. He was fined £25 for possessing housebreaking equipment, a conviction which was noted on criminal records. The fact he was armed specifically with a hammer was never included in his arrest details.

Police also later discovered that they had interviewed Sutcliffe in the same year about an attack on a Bradford sex worker. The attack had been committed while Sutcliffe was in the company of his best friend Trevor Birdsall. On this occasion Sutcliffe had put a stone in a sock and hit a sex worker over the head with it before running off back to the car and driving off. Birdsall's car licence plate was noted and he eventually gave police Sutcliffe's name and address.

By the autumn of 1979 West Yorkshire Police had fifteen unsolved Ripper-style murders and attacks on their hands and were appealing to other forces for help, asking for facts on men who had assaulted sex workers, or any woman, without causing serious injury; for ten years that precise information about Sutcliffe lay forgotten and undiscovered somewhere in their own system.

1. To a large extent, Sutcliffe matched descriptions given by two of the seven women who had miraculously survived his savage attacks. Other women who had been attacked by Sutcliffe also gave near perfect descriptions, but were their stories either ignored, or dismissed as a Ripper attack.

2. Mrs Olive Smelt told the police in August 1975, two months before the first murder, that the man who had followed her had spoken briefly in a Yorkshire accent.

3. Sutcliffe's car registration number was logged in red-light areas on forty-six different occasions and he was interviewed nine times during the manhunt.

4. The tyre track enquiry set up after the murder of Irene Richardson was stopped before the list could be completed. Sutcliffe was on the remaining list of vehicle owners still to be questioned.

5. Sutcliffe was stopped for a spot check while driving his lorry on the A1, one of the interviewing officers was holding a copy of boot prints found at the scene of the Josephine Whitaker murder, in April 1979. Sutcliffe was wearing the exact same boots during the interview. Sutcliffe would later say 'if he wasn't going to catch me then, nobody was'.

6. Little or any importance was attached to report by a 28-year-old detective who recommended Sutcliffe should be questioned further by senior officers; his report was marked to file, simply because Sutcliffe did not have a Wearside accent. Three more women would die as a result.

7. On 25 June 1980, Sutcliffe was stopped and breathalysed when he was driving through Bradford red-light district at night. When officers radioed to check on their suspect they were told he had been eliminated from the enquiry.

So much about Sutcliffe's past had already been recorded by the police, yet the 200 strong elite Ripper Squad never listed him as a major suspect. If only they had scratched the surface of his police record, it would have almost certainly lead them to Trevor Birdsall, who knew Sutcliffe had committed two attacks before any woman had died and who held strong suspicions that his friend could be the Yorkshire Ripper

Government Ministers, senior officials at the Home Office and the West Yorkshire Police certainly would have wanted to avoid an embarrassing inquiry into the mishandling of the five-year investigation. Most of the public probably considered Sutcliffe to be mad anyway, and should he be sent to an asylum then they would never know the full extent of what he had done; the medical evidence would never see the light of day and many of the mistakes made could be brushed under the carpet.

By mid-April of 1981 it was well known around medical, legal and journalistic circles that a deal had been struck between the prosecution and the defence to put Sutcliffe away quietly. His appearance at the Old Bailey was to be a formality that would occupy a day or two at most before sentence. No jury to be called, no hearing of the masses of evidence.

Meanwhile over in Clayton, Bradford, Sonia had been in hiding out at her parents' house. Scores of reporters had descended on the property trying to get that all-important exclusive from the wife of the Yorkshire Ripper. Each newspaper fought to outbid their rivals by pushing scraps of paper through the letter box with large money offers written on them.

One letter that came through the door was from the Bradford Metropolitan Council educational authority. Sonia had been employed as a Pottery Relief Teacher with them and inside the letter was her P45. She had been sacked following Peter's arrest.

Sonia's mother finally came to the door and confronted the reporters, criticising the press and public for the harassment. She stated that Sonia had:

> already turned down millions of pounds worth of offers from the press and book deals. She has had to face all the people and go through hell, she has to think of that more than any money. She has no plans at the moment, she does not know what she is going to do, I don't know whether she will continue to live here or not, but the pressure on her has been so great she has never talked about Peter or any of the events of the last few months. She has not been able to sleep at night and when she heard she had lost her job it made matters worse.

Fearing a law suit for unfair dismissal, Gordon Moore, chief executive of Bradford Metropolitan District Council backtracked and said:

Mrs Sutcliffe has not been sacked and we are certainly not anxious to get rid of her. What happened was, after the arrest we wanted to know if she wanted to continue being called out on temporary teaching jobs. For obvious reasons we couldn't contact her direct and we did ask through other contacts and were told she didn't want to return. In case she wanted to find another job we sent her P45 to her address and removed her name off our list immediately. This is what we thought she wanted and if we are wrong then I'm sorry.

In the early hours of 29 April, despite telling friends that she would not be attending the trial, Sonia made a last minute, early morning dash to London to support her husband. At 1.00 am Sonia, wanting to avoid the reporters that were now camped outside her parents' home, decided to climb out of the kitchen window and cut through a neighbour's back garden and into a side street. Here her mother was waiting in the small family saloon. Together they drove through the night to London.

Behind them they had left a note for Sonia's father, Mr Bodhan Szurma, who, stressed out by all the unwanted attention the previous few months had brought upon him and his family, had gone out for a walk to gather his thoughts.

Sonia had written a note hastily on the back of a used envelope and addressed to him affectionately as 'tato'. It read, 'if anyone rings tell them I'm tired and have gone to bed, if someone rings or arrives early in the morning tell them to leave me alone in peace. I have had enough harassment'

As they arrived into London they found the area around the Old Bailey like something from a carnival. Hundreds of people had gathered to what many papers were describing as the trial of the century. There were of course the usual professional trial attenders and the plain curious who have been queuing since Tuesday evening for a chance to view the man behind the dark smoke glass of the police van. One wanted a story to tell her grandchildren, one rushed out on impulse having heard about it on the radio, another never missed a big murder trial and had taken the week off work.

By 10.00 am many had realised there were no public seats left in the courtroom and had decided to give up waiting, but for the rest of the day a queue of around 100 people still remained, in the optimistic hopes of trying to get one of the thirty-four public gallery seats. At the head of the queue, three budding entrepreneurs were turning profitable deals on their seats with Continental magazines who'd been unable to get one of the eighty-two press seats. Several newspaper reporters were also in a similar situation and offering £50 to anyone who would give up their seat, only to be told that they were not even in the running. A few Post Office workers from the nearby sorting office loitered around in the street opposite the Old Bailey but were easily outnumbered by foreign television crews who eventually resorted to filming each other.

Mrs Doreen Hill, mother of Sutcliffe's final victim Jackie Hill, sipped her coffee and stared out of the second-floor window of the Old Bailey cafeteria, but the air of excitement among the crowds in the street below was lost on her. 'Who are they waiting for? I suppose it's his wife they'll want to see, it's all very strange.'

The oak panelled courtroom in which Sutcliffe would appear had dealt with the country's most notorious men in its seventy-eight year history. The infamous dock had accommodated people like Dr Harvey Crippen, executed for the murder of his wife; John Reginald Christie, who was hanged for murdering six women; and Lord Haw Haw, William Joyce, found guilty for high treason during the Second World War.

Inside court number one and leading the prosecution was 58-year-old Sir Michael Havers, the Attorney General. The son of a High Court Judge, he had achieved fame as the defending counsel for the Rolling Stones – he had represented Mick Jagger and Keith Richards in a drug case. That case was later quashed on appeal. As the Attorney General he was often in the public eye; he was also a published author, and the father of acclaimed actor Nigel Havers. Assisting him in the prosecution was 47-year-old, Harry Ognall, a brilliant cross examiner and member of the Queen's council. With the appointment of both Havers and Ognall, it showed how serious the Crown viewed this trial.

For the defence was 50-year-old, James Chadwin, a larger-than-life character with a reputation as colourful as the fictional Rumple of the Bailey; he was known for smoking cheroots and possessing a sparkling wit. It was said he had a gift for influencing Juries with his ingenious mind that frequently produced surprising results.

As the courtroom filled up with crowds, Sutcliffe remained out of sight around the top corner of a narrow twist of stairs which went steeply to a block of half tiled cells two floors under the Old Bailey's number one court. The women in the public gallery who had queued half the night to be at the edge of the balcony, bent forward. Their arms dangled down towards the court and their heads turned towards the opening beyond which Sutcliffe stood with his guards.

Alongside the dock, sitting quietly next to her mother, was Sonia, wearing a brown cardigan belted at the waist over a floral pink blouse, a light blue denim skirt and granny-style shoes. She had the best front-row view in the court of the judge, in his blood red robes, under the carved lion and unicorn coat of arms which represents the Crown Court of the United Kingdom.

Nervously, Sonia looked around once at the public galley then looked away and wrapped her brown cardigan tightly around her. She no doubt felt the eyes of the entire court staring down at her. She stared straight ahead, fingering the small diamond of her engagement ring.

Then the footsteps as Peter Sutcliffe and his guarded escort climbed the stairs up into the dock. There were no gasps or deep breaths, just an eerie silence. He walked calmly into dock number one from cells below.

When he strolled into the dock the public onlookers, who had been lucky enough to sit right at the front of the balcony, all leaned forward. Women nudged each other as he stood there in silence below them; he had an air of casual ordinariness about him, average height, wearing a light grey wool and fibre suit and pink shirt, his long black sideburns brushed out into an untidy beard and a rough bundle of curls spilled out over the collar of his open-neck blue shirt. There was no hint of the monster everyone expected. Once in the dock Sutcliffe went to grab the rail in front of him then stopped and decided to let his hands fall by his side. Built up heels on his brown shoes made him look taller than he was.

Both he and Sonia glanced at each other when he first appeared, but once he sat down in the wooden dock he was shielded from her view. Sonia now lowered her head again and stared at the floor. According to one newspaper, 'she was so pale she looked like she was covered in flour'.

As Sutcliffe glanced down towards the middle of the courtroom, he would see the evidence that lay before him. On a long table sitting between him and the counsel, between the 12-inch-high pile of witness statements on the desk in front of the dock, guarded by detective Alan Foster, were the terrible tools of the Ripper's trade. Seven ball-pein hammers, a claw hammer, a hacksaw, a long thin kitchen knife, several carving knives, a cobbler's knife, eight screwdrivers and a length of cord. All were attached to yellow labels with reference numbers on them. Just a selection of the 7,000 items which had been gathered up during the case. Items ranging from a bus ticket to Sutcliffe's brown Rover.

The clerk of the court, 38-year-old Michael McKenzie rose to his feet. 'Peter William Sutcliffe,' he began reciting from a charge sheet that would take eight minutes to read, 'you are charged with the attempted murder of Anna Rogulskyj ...', he then tailed off into a brief description of the events surrounding her attack ... 'how say you Peter Sutcliffe, are you guilty or not guilty?'

Sutcliffe, in his lowest most nervous voice, looked into space and said 'Guilty'. The clerk read out a further six charges of attempted murder and Sutcliffe replied 'Guilty' to each one.

Now it was time to deal with the murders themselves.

'How say you Peter William Sutcliffe to a charge of murdering Wilma McCann in Leeds in October 1975?'

Sutcliffe remained silent for a brief moment, as did the entire courtroom, before he finally answered, 'Not guilty to murder, but guilty to manslaughter on the grounds of diminished responsibility.'

Sutcliffe had rehearsed his answer but the legal phrases tangled on the end of his tongue and he stumbled to finish the sentence. He stumbled again on the second charge of murder and once again when the third was read out. By the fourth (that of Patricia Atkinson) he got it right and the awkward sentence was spoken without error. There was now a rhythm to his replies and as the clerk went through thirteen murder charges Sutcliffe's replies became starkly perfect. By the tenth murder he seemed almost bored but his piercing eyes with huge black pupils still stared fixedly at the clerk talking to him.

Sitting across the room in the prosecution section, Sir Michael Havers crossed his legs and turned occasionally to look at Sutcliffe, seventy-five pages of typed notes were in a blue folder beside him.

Once a plea had been entered for all the murders, Sutcliffe was seated stiffly in a chair which was then pushed forward to the front of the dock. He turned and whispered briefly to one of the two guards sitting alongside him. The officer nodded and said nothing.

Attorney General Havers rose to address Mr Justice Boreham. He stated that the Crown Prosecution had accepted the pleas by Mr Sutcliffe. He then went on to say during his time at Armley Prison awaiting trial, Sutcliffe had been visited by three psychiatrists, including Dr Hugo Milne from Bradford, a man who had interviewed over 200 murderers. 'I have met with them to discuss their reports with the greatest care and anxiety and at great length. The general consensus of the doctors is that this is a case of diminished responsibility, the illness being paranoid schizophrenia.'

Sir Michael then started to read extracts from a 35-page report by Dr Hugo Milne. During eleven interviews Dr Milne had gained background information on Sutcliffe's early life, including several events through his young adult life and his married life. The courtroom remained deathly silent as Sir Michael went onto say that Sutcliffe had shown all the signs of schizophrenia including hearing voices from God during his early days as a gravedigger. He spoke of how the voices drove him on a mission to rid the world of prostitutes. This mission began when he was robbed of some money from a prostitute in 1969. Dr Milne's report also stated that Sutcliffe was not a sexual deviant and the murders showed no sign of sexual motivation, instead Sutcliffe was a mentally unwell man, extremely dangerous and needed to be placed in an asylum, possibly for the rest of his life.

Sutcliffe's trial, the unfolding of a horror story that had gripped the cities of West Yorkshire since 1975, was always going to be a sensation. But within an hour of its start, the trial ran into a legal tangle that made Old Bailey history. It soon became clear that the trial – like almost every aspect of the Ripper case – was not going to be straightforward. Although a deal had been reached between the defence and prosecution, and no doubt several ministers behind closed doors, there was one man they had all forgotten to take into consideration. The judge.

Mr Justice Boreham: 'I have very grave anxieties about Sutcliffe and his pleas. I would like you to explain in far greater detail than usual any decision that you are going to make about the acceptance of these pleas.'

For the next two hours the judge sat listening to Sir Michael as he put forward legal arguments and read from all the lengthy doctors' reports. Bizarrely, to everyone in the courtroom, the prosecution counsel had now morphed into a pretty convincing counsel for the defence.

Further reading of the doctor's report revealed for the first time that Sutcliffe had come from a disturbed family background, which included his parents' affairs and breakups; plus his own marriage to Sonia was marred with hostile ups and downs. In Dr Milne's report Sutcliffe had described his wife as 'over excited, highly strung, unstable and obsessed with cleanliness'. According to the report:

> She shouted at him so that he was embarrassed in case the neighbours heard, she would not allow him into the house with his shoes on, spent hours cleaning specks from the carpet with dust pan and brush, refused to let him use the refrigerator to make himself a meal, and would pull the plug out of the television set if he was sitting waiting for his tea.

The report said the couple had an 'intense relationship – on one hand loving, but on the other extreme, becoming very angry'. On the night of his arrest Sutcliffe claimed that he had left the home because he was 'fed up with his wife's constant nagging'.

But perhaps the most significant and revealing part of the report was that Sonia had suffered a schizophrenic episode back in 1972, while studying in London. She too had heard voices and believed she was the second Christ. She thought she had stigmata – the marks of the crucifixion nails – on her hands. She was taken back to Bradford for compulsory treatment in a psychiatric hospital which lasted three weeks, followed by a period as a voluntary outpatient. Sutcliffe took care of her throughout this time until her recovery.

What became perfectly clear to all in the courtroom was that Sutcliffe could quite easily be mimicking his wife's previous symptoms. Her mental breakdown had lasted nearly three years. Long enough for Sutcliffe to be able to copy and repeat these symptoms to eager and gullible doctors who, in all likelihood, felt he was probably mad before they had even interviewed him. The chances of deception now appeared fairly high.

There was also the matter of the discrepancies between what Sutcliffe was telling the doctors and what he told the police at the time of his arrest. It seems the defence and prosecution had ignored all of this in favour of a quick trial.

'Where is the proof?' asked Mr Justice Boreham.

Sir Michael said he felt satisfied, following discussions with the doctors, that the experts had not been deceived by Sutcliffe. All the doctors had expected to find a sadistic killer with a personality disorder, a man who had started a life of crime at a young age and escalated to murder, but none of these things were present at all.

Mr Justice Boreham:

> The matter that troubles me is not the medical opinions because there is a consensus. It seems to me that all of these opinions – and I say this without criticism – all these opinions are based simply on what this defendant has told the doctors, nothing more. Moreover what he has told the doctors conflicts substantially with what he told the police on the morning of arrest. I use the word 'conflict' advisedly. In statements to the police he expressed a desire to kill all women. If that is right – and here I really need your help – is that not a matter which ought to be tested? Where lies the evidence which gives these doctors the factual basis for these pleas? It seems to me it would be more appropriate if this case were dealt with by a jury.

Author's Note: It is not uncommon for a judge to refuse to accept a plea of guilty to less serious crimes than charged. The judge, having complete discretion, can insist that the trial continue on the more serious charge, even if the prosecution is willing to accept a guilty plea to the lesser.

Pleading guilty to manslaughter on a charge of murder on the grounds of diminished responsibility is a relatively common occurrence, and if the plea is accepted or if there is a trial and the jury finds the accused guilty of manslaughter, the judge has the power to sentence him to any term of imprisonment including life imprisonment. However, there is one difference between life sentences for murder and manslaughter. With murder the judge has the power to make a recommendation that the accused not be released for a specific number of years, he does not have that power on a conviction of manslaughter.

The judge could make a hospital order under the Mental Health Act 1959 provided he is satisfied on the medical evidence that the accused is suffering from one of a number of specified mental conditions; that order can be made at the judge's discretion without any limit of time. But the accused will only remain in the hospital until the Home Secretary orders a release solely based on the advice of doctors.

It was clear this judge had no intention of being part of any deal. A ninety-minute adjournment was granted so defence and prosecution could confer privately; when court resumed Sir Michael said that, in view of the judge's remarks, he would proceed with the case before a jury on Friday 1 May.

Defence counsel James Chadwin then asked for a longer adjournment until Tuesday 5 May, because he needed time to prepare his case. He said, 'I don't want to exaggerate … But there are things to be done.'

Justice Boreham agreed and adjourned the case until to 5 May.

Within minutes the whole courtroom was full of groups of lawyers all discussing the legal implications behind the judge's decision and scores of reporters outside were already describing some of the doctor's reports, despite a ban on reporting at that time.

Sutcliffe was taken back down the steps of the court and placed in the underground cell. Sonia was brought down to see her husband for thirty minutes before she and her mother left the court to run the gauntlet of sightseers, held back by crowd-control barriers. A special taxi service had been provided for them and they were taken to a secret hotel location. Fifteen minutes later the armoured police-van carrying Sutcliffe left the Old Bailey for its journey back to Brixton prison.

Doreen Hill emerged from court looking tired and gaunt. The experience of being so close the man who had brutally murdered her daughter had drained her, but she manged to maintain a brave face and spoke about her experience:

> I had to take tranquillisers to give me strength to come here and see this man, now it has been adjourned and the nightmare will go on, I don't think I could muster the strength to come down to London again. My husband is very ill and needs me. There is nothing more I can do here now… but I was immensely relieved when the judge gave his ruling and ordered that a jury should decide the issue. I think that was only fair and proper. I am pleased that twelve ordinary people will decide the issue and it has not been left to the lawyers. Of course it is all futile for me in a way. Jackie is dead and all the juries and judges in the world cannot alter that.

For something that was supposed to be nothing more than a formality hearing, it had now turned into a full trial. A jury would now hear every little detail of the Yorkshire Ripper murders and, much to the dismay of the policing authorities, so would the press.

Chapter 4

The Trial Begins

The reason for this trial is simple ... there is a marked difference between the versions Sutcliffe gave the police and the version he gave the doctors ... You have to decide whether, as a clever, callous murderer he deliberately set out to create a cock and bull story to avoid conviction for murder.

Sir Michael Havers 5 May 1981

The few hundred square yards of London that is now the Old Bailey Crown Court has witnessed stories of inhumanity for centuries – first as Newgate prison and then as the Central Criminal Court. But few greater horrors can have unfolded there than the catalogue of agony, terror and cruelty which the Attorney General began to relate to the jury of six men and six women on the morning of 5 May 1981.

A scream of police sirens heralded Sutcliffe's arrival at court in a green armoured van with darkened windows. Police quickly stopped all the traffic as the van approached at speed with one police car in front and two following swiftly behind.

The leading police car swung across the road to block any oncoming traffic as the armoured van drove straight into the internal court car park.

A number of police officers formed a human wall in front of press photographers and eager onlookers as the van moved under the motorised wood and steel barrier that protects the entrance to the Old Bailey cells, its driver almost blinded by a sea of popping flash bulbs.

For security reasons the van had taken a different route to the court than the previous week.

Immediately they were inside, the barrier was lowered again.

Bizarrely, among the noise of cameras and shouts, there was a single cry of 'Good luck Peter' from the dense crowd.

Sonia and her mother, Mrs Maria Szurma, arrived at the Old Bailey crouched on the back seat of a taxi. The gate of the judge's entrance was opened to allow the car to sweep into the courtyard.

The thirty-four seats of the public gallery was crammed, but unlike the previous week only seven women were in attendance. Below the gallery was another tier-seated area for specially invited guests, mostly made up of the VIP

Aldermen from the city of London and their wives. Their glossy appearance was suggestive of Ascot races – some were actually wearing binoculars around their neck, clearly unaware of how small the Old Bailey courtroom is.

There were no such smiles from the next group filling into reserved places at the rear of the court. Anna Rogulskyj and Olive Smelt, two women left for dead in attacks by Sutcliffe; then the parents of Barbara Leach, the student he had murdered in Bradford; and finally Doreen Hill, who was accompanied by her daughter Jackie's boyfriend, Ian.

Twenty-eight men and women were brought into the court at 10.40 am for the jury to be selected. Sutcliffe objected to the third and fifth men to be called. One of them was replaced by a woman and the other by another man so the jury was equally divided. Before the jury were officially sworn in Sonia left the courtroom escorted by an officer. I assume it was because she may have to be called as witness and thus could not be present during testimony.

For anyone accused of a crime the Old Bailey must be an awesome sight. The prisoner in the dock sees before him the judge, regal in his red robes. Even though Mr Justice Boreham was physically small with a kindly face and glasses, his presence filled the small room as he sat high above the room in his robes and wig, his dignity and authority set him apart. Behind him, sitting raised above the courtroom, the sword of justice suspended under the vaulted ceiling. The accused is left in no doubt – he is the law.

Sir Michael Havers rose to his feet and addressed the jury; he stated that Sutcliffe had already pleaded guilty to seven attempted murders and thirteen counts of manslaughter, but not guilty to murder by reason of diminished responsibility. The plea of diminished responsibility had been rejected and therefore it was now up to the jury to decide Sutcliffe's fate.

Sir Michael then told the jury that Sutcliffe had been seen by three psychiatrists who found him to be suffering from paranoid schizophrenia. 'The doctor's opinion was that Sutcliffe was suffering from an abnormality of the mind which substantially impaired his responsibility for the killings.'

Outlining the case against Sutcliffe, Sir Michael told the jury their task would now be to determine:

If at the time of the murders, Sutcliffe was actually suffering from an abnormality of the mind which subsequently impaired his responsibility. The burden of proving whether he was suffering from diminished responsibility lay with the defence and the burden of proof had to satisfy the jury on the balance of probability.

Sir Michael said, 'the facts themselves are not substantially an issue, but you must have the full background of facts so you can reach a just verdict and that verdict will be upon this evidence'.

What the jury would hear would be a series of sadistic, calculated and premeditated murders, but they would also hear medical evidence called by the defence to substantiate the defence of manslaughter.

The medical evidence is all one way, the doctors, you will hear from three of them, agreed that this man suffers from paranoid schizophrenia which is an abnormality of the mind which in their view substantially impaired his moral responsibility for the killings. So if those opinions are in fact accepted by you, then you would be entitled upon that to find a verdict of manslaughter.

Sir Michael told the jury they had to keep two things in mind – there had to be an abnormality of mind and to be such an abnormality of mind that it had to be one that impaired Sutcliffe to control himself. 'I have a responsibility to test this medical evidence, not in a hostile way, but to assist you.'

If the jury were wondering why they were trying the case, Sir Michael explained that under the legal system the jury decided the facts. 'Of course you must have regard for the medical opinions but the doctors opinions are not binding upon you.' He went on to explain:

The reason for this trial is simple … there is a marked difference between the versions Sutcliffe gave the police and the version he gave the doctors. You have to consider whether this man sought to pull the wool over the doctors' eyes. You have to decide whether, as a clever, callous murderer he deliberately set out to create a cock and bull story to avoid conviction for murder.

Sir Michael said that Sutcliffe had only mentioned his mission from God on 5 March 1981, on his eighth interview with the consultant psychiatrist Dr Milne, and after long statements and confessions with the police

It was relevant to comment that he had previously said in interviews that during two of the attacks he had run away in panic, and in two attempted murders he had similarly run away in panic. During the killing of Irene Richardson he appeared to have used a great deal of self-preservation so her body could not easily be seen and her boots had been placed neatly behind her knees

Reading from some of Sutcliffe's statements made to doctors during his assessment, Sir Michael told the jury:

God invested in me with the means to kill, I am in God's hands. He misled the police perhaps, involving the sending of tapes. I have heard

God since. I have been here. It seems like God has chosen to put me here. God knows what went on in my mind, the torment and the depression.

Sir Michael said that:

what he had said about the messages from God to kill prostitutes and about being part of a divine mission was what doctors described as schizophrenia, but none of that was told to the police. He told them he had urges and hallucinations but he didn't tell that to the police straight away.

It had taken the best part of two days to take down Sutcliffe's statement:

But that confession is curious, you may think. It is by no means wholly frank. There were twenty murders and attempted murders. He only spoke in his confession of fourteen.

He left out five of the attempted murders and he left out one very unusual killing. He had not included the murder of Marguerite Walls who had been strangled with a rope in Leeds in 1980; Sutcliffe claimed to have heard voices in his head say: 'Kill, kill, kill,' during the attack.

Pointing out the night Sutcliffe was arrested in Sheffield in the company of a sex worker which eventually led to weapons being discovered both in his car and hidden behind an oil tank, Sir Michael said:

Equally I should tell you that he didn't say, in any sense that he had a divine right or was responding to orders. In fact he told a long series of lies for why he had weapons in his car or a rope in his pocket or why he was even there in the first place.

It was these areas of conflict that would give the jury the greatest difficulty.

In our view there is nothing which can, from the outside, go to support what he said to the doctors. There is something from the outside which casts doubts on what he said to the doctors.

Sir Michael asked the jury to now reflect on the past five years:

In that time he made twenty homicidal attacks on women, thirteen died and seven lived. The women varied in ages between 16 and 47, some were prostitutes and some of easy virtue, but the biggest tragedy was the last six attacks made in 1979/80 were all on women of totally unblemished reputation.

This choice of words would create a fierce controversy in the press and among women's right campaign groups who found Sir Michael's statement insulting and degrading to all the women who had met their death at the hands of Sutcliffe.

Sir Michael went on to say:

With the exception of two attacks in Manchester, all were in West Yorkshire, Leeds, Bradford, Halifax, Huddersfield and Keighley. During his era of frenzied killings he travelled in one of five cars he had during this period, sometimes enticing women into his car and driving them to lonely and discrete places on the pretext of having sexual intercourse. Then having invited them to get into the back seat, he would attack them from behind with a hammer or some other heavy blunt instrument. In some cases he parked his car, laid in wait for his victims then followed them on foot.

With a few exceptions his crimes soon had their own badge of identity. The victims would be attacked from behind, suffer hammer blows to the head, then repeatedly stabbed in the trunk with a knife or a screwdriver.

His victims had no chance as they were either knocked unconscious or killed outright from the hammer blows to the head. Sometimes he removed clothing from the victims before stabbing them. He claimed he did this to make them look as 'cheap as they are'. On a number of occasions he was cruelly fortunate not to have been disturbed in the act and when he did he always managed to escape.

One might almost say, in happier circumstances, that he led a charmed life.

Sir Michael pointed out that Sutcliffe had acknowledged that he knew some of his victims were not sex workers but that there came a stage where it no longer mattered to him. He then preyed on people of 'excellent reputation' and four of these were killed

He has given no satisfactory explanation to his crimes, no motive has presented itself. When asked about the killings during an interview on January 5th of this year, Mr Sutcliffe said: 'All this really started when I was done out of £10 by a prostitute in Bradford. She went off to get it changed and never came back. This poisoned my mind about prostitutes.'

Sir Michael also explained to the jury that on another occasion, Sutcliffe had claimed his depressions and hallucinations might have occurred from a motorcycle accident which resulted in him hitting a lamp post and being left unconscious. He told doctors he was unconscious for hours, yet told others he was unconscious for half an hour. 'You may think he is embroidering this story' Sir Michael added.

As far as sexual intercourse was concerned, this did not appear to have played any part in Sutcliffe's conduct. Sutcliffe had asserted that with one exception – the case of Helen Rytka in Huddersfield – he did not seek to have sexual relations with any of the victims.

Sir Michael turned to the use of fake licence plates on Sutcliffe's car, in particular the night of his arrest in Sheffield. He said Sutcliffe had been due to appear before Bradford Magistrates' court over a breathalyser offence and disqualification was usually inevitable in such cases. Sutcliffe's car insurance had expired and to tide him over until he lost his licence he stole the number plates from a scrapyard in Mirfield, West Yorkshire.

> Of course there may be another motive, there was careful checking going on in all prostitute areas and Sutcliffe had been interviewed on a number of occasions. It may be he felt it safer to have false licence plates, whatever the reason it led to his arrest and saved the life of Olivia Reivers and perhaps many more women.

Turning his attention to the letters and tape that were sent to the police during the manhunt he said:

> The letters posted in Sunderland were couched in taunting tones and it appeared the writer had detailed knowledge of the attacks, but the most important communication came in June 1979 when the police received a cassette which had been posted in Sunderland and contained a sarcastic mocking message. The tape was made by someone with a North East accent. Unfortunately some senior officers became convinced that the voice on the tape was that of the Ripper and that the real killer spoke with a Wearside accent ... when police were making elimination enquires following cross-area sightings, one of the things that hampered the investigating officers when going around seeing hundreds, if not thousands of people, was that if the people interviewed did not speak with a Sunderland accent they tended to be eliminated from the enquiry.
>
> The harsh truth is that the sender of the letters and tape had nothing to do with the murders, that person's wicked behaviour had cast a shadow over many innocent lives. I cannot condemn too strongly this cruel hoax.

During the four hour opening, Sir Michael went on to explain Peter Sutcliffe's personal background.

He told the jury that Peter had come from a family of six and that he had left school around 15 years old. He had taken on variety of jobs, including labouring, factory work and grave digging, before he qualified as a heavy goods vehicle driver. At the age of 28 he married his 24-year-old girlfriend Sonia.

That was in August 1974 after having courted her for seven or eight years. She had been his only regular girlfriend. Before and after they were married they continued to live with her parents in Bradford before they finally saved up the money to buy their own house. They didn't have any children. Sonia Sutcliffe worked as a supply teacher, and also worked as a nursing auxiliary one night a week. Mr Sutcliffe had stated that many of his attacks took place on a night when his wife was working. The people who knew Mr Sutcliffe best, his family and friends, knew him as an unremarkable man who led an unremarkable life.

Next door to Sonia's parents lived two brothers, Ronald and David Barker. One of the Barkers, Ronald, kept a diary and was able to pinpoint events on certain dates.

Sir Michael told the jury that the court would hear details of how, on 28 May 1977, the Barker brothers were driven to York by Mr Sutcliffe. While there he disappeared for approximately three quarters of an hour, telling the brothers he had been with a girl. Later, on their way back to Bradford, Sutcliffe drove the car through the Chapeltown area of Leeds, telling the brothers they were 'in Ripper country'. Sutcliffe would sometimes drop the Barkers off at the end of the road where they lived and then would drive off by himself. Most of those evening were when his wife, Sonia, was at work at the hospital.

'It is for your consideration that this might well have been a reconnaissance trip. If so this shows a measure of premeditation.' Said Sir Michael.

Then came the biggest horror of all, an album containing the photos of the victims as they were found and how they appeared at their autopsy

At this point Sir Michael told the jury that counsel had considered very carefully whether they could conduct the case properly without making the jury look at the photographs of the victims. 'But I'm afraid we must … you will became immune to them quite quickly. You are going to have to steel yourselves to look at these pictures.'

The court was deathly silent as the jury turned over sets of horrific images relating to each murder. Many jurors paled and flinched as they flicked through the album and more than one them closed their eyes as they looked on the scenes of butchery.

At one point the album of pictures was taken back from the jury for one image to be removed on the judge's orders. This image related to the murder of Jean Jordan, whose body was almost decapitated and had the most horrendous mutilations inflicted upon it. 'It is a particularly ghastly sample', the judge told the jury.

Sir Michael said it was now necessary to outline each of the thirteen murders and seven attacks. He handed the jury copies of a voluntary statement made by Sutcliffe following his arrest and confession to being the Yorkshire Ripper.

The statement took fifteen hours and forty-five minutes to take down. He now offered to walk the jury through each one, pointing out the facts surrounding the murders coupled with Sutcliffe's confessions to the police.

* What follows is a mixture of information on the victims, the facts surrounding their murders, Sir Michael's courtroom comments and Sutcliffe's own confessions regarding the attacks.

A more detailed and comprehensive study of the crime scenes are available in my book *On the trail of the Yorkshire Ripper*.

Anna Rogulskyj

In the early hours of Saturday morning, 5 July 1975, Sutcliffe decided to take a drive to the centre of Keighley as he had heard it was a popular area for sex workers. He loitered around the area of the Ritz Cinema on Alice Street. That night, 36-year-old Irish-born Anna Patricia Rogulskyj had gone out drinking, taking the bus from Keighley to Bradford, and by midnight she was in Bibby's club, not far from Manningham Lane.

Later that night she managed to hitch a ride with two Jamaicans who drove her back to her home in Highfield Lane around 1.00 am. Probably worse for drink, she then decided to call on her boyfriend, Geoff Hughes, with whom she had a stormy relationship, at his home a short walk away in North Queen Street. To get there her route took her down Alice Street and around the back of the Ritz Cinema where she cut directly into North Queen Street. As she approached the cinema, she heard a man in a darkened doorway ask if she 'fancied it'. Quite startled, she replied, 'Not on your life', and quickened her pace towards the safety of her boyfriend's house, arriving around 1.30 am. But despite shouting and pounding on the front door, she could not raise him. Finally, in a fit of drunken anger, she removed her shoe and put it through a ground-floor window. She stormed off in the direction from which she had come, but with all the commotion she had probably forgotten about the strange man who still loitered close by. As she turned back onto the main street, he emerged from the shadows and again asked the same question. Anna ignored him and kept walking. He followed her a few paces before producing a ball-pein hammer from his coat and smashing it onto her skull.

Sir Michael read from Sutcliffe's confessions:

Yes, that was me. She had a funny name and I asked her if she fancied it. She said 'not on your life' and went to try and get into a house. When she came back, I tapped her up again and she elbowed me. I followed her and hit her with the hammer and she fell down. I intended to kill her but I was disturbed.

The initial assault took place out on the street with one hammer blow to the back of the head, followed by a struggle as the victim was dragged out of sight into the closest alleyway, which runs directly behind the cinema.

She was hit twice more on the head with the hammer, rendering her unconscious. Sutcliffe had probably raised her blouse before this and, at some stage, produced a knife and slashed her across her abdomen. In all probability, he was about to stab deeper into her stomach when a resident living at 10 Lord Street, which overlooked the alleyway, heard the commotion and decided to take a look. He called out and asked what was happening, causing Sutcliffe to flee and leaving his victim alive.

Anna lay unconscious on the ground for around forty minutes until she was found by a passer-by at 2.20 am. On her abdomen were several cut marks, 7 inches (17.78 cm) long below the navel, and above this a further seven deeper cuts. She was rushed to the casualty department at Airedale Hospital and then transferred to Leeds General Infirmary where she underwent a twelve-hour operation, which included the removal of splinters of bone from her brain. At one point she was given the last rites. When she came round, she had no idea what had happened to her and out of confusion came to the conclusion it must have been her boyfriend who had attacked her after she smashed his window. It would be a further three years before she would discover she had survived an attack by the Yorkshire Ripper.

On 22 January, nearly three weeks since his first confession, Sutcliffe admitted to attacking Anna Rogulskyj. When asked if this attack was his first, he replied: 'Yes, I'm sure of that. I hit her on the head and I think I intended to kill her.'

He then went on to suggest an early head injury be the reason behind his though process.

I had this inner complex which I think started back in 1965 when I had a motorbike accident. I ran into a telegraph pole and went into it with my head. Since then I have had severe bouts of morbid depression and hallucinations. My mind goes into a haze and I don't know what was right or wrong, or if I was acting rationally or not.

Sir Michael pointed out to the jury that, 'You will notice that he makes no mention of any voice from God, simply hallucinations and depressions.'

Olive Smelt

On Friday, 15 August 1975, 46-year-old Olive Smelt left her small terraced house at 16 Woodside Mount, Halifax for a night out in Halifax town centre with her friends, having a few drinks in several pubs, including the Royal Oak at 3 Clare Road. Just before closing time, Olive and one of her friends met two men that they knew, who offered to give them a lift home. Olive was let out of the car in a lay-by in Hayley Hill just before the Boothtown Road, next to a fish and chip shop. She was hoping to get a late supper for her and her husband Harry and their family. From here she could nip round the back of the shops and cut through the dividing alleyways, which ran from Woodside Grove to the rear door of her house in Woodside Mount.

As she approached the end of the ally she noticed someone walking on her right side.

It was a man, 'Weather letting us down', or 'weather been playing us up' he said as he got close to her. The next thing she knew she was waking up in hospital. She had been felled by a hammer blow to the head.

Sutcliffe: 'I saw her in the Royal Oak. She annoyed me, probably in some minor way. I took her to be a prostitute. I hit her on the head and scratched her buttocks with a piece of hacksaw blade or maybe a knife. My intention was to kill her but I was disturbed by a car coming down the road.'

The car lights turned out to be courting couple sitting in their car at the near end of Woodside Road. They had caught a glimpse of the woman falling half out onto the road and, after a short pause to consider what they had seen, decided to turn the car headlights on. Sutcliffe was forced to flee the scene.

Olive was rushed first to Halifax Infirmary and later to Leeds General Infirmary, where she had brain surgery and spent the next ten days under medical care. The infirmary more or less told her husband Harry that they didn't expect her to survive as her 'skull had been crushed like a coconut shell'. But survive she did and she was able to give a description of her attacker. She described him as about 30, 5ft 10ins in height, slightly built, with dark hair and some beard or growth on his face.

Wilma McCann

Regarded as the first victim to be murdered by Peter Sutcliffe, Wilma McCann, aged 28, was attacked in the early hours of 30 October 1975. She had left her house 65 Scott Hall Avenue, Leeds around 7.30 pm the previous evening. She was wearing slack white trousers, a pink blouse, a dark blue bolero jacket and her hair fashioned up in a beehive. She said goodnight to her four children:

Sonia 9, Richard 7, Donna 6, and 5-year-old Angela. Leaving Sonia in charge, she slipped out the back of the house, as she always did and went down the side of the playing fields.

In court she was described as 'someone who drank too much, was noisy and sexually promiscuous – someone who distributed her favours widely.' Other than the account Sutcliffe gave the police, there is no evidence that she engaged in prostitution.

Following her separation from husband Gerald a few months earlier, heavy drinking had become an everyday norm for the fiery Scotswoman from Inverness. She was well known to have a fondness for nightlife, with convictions for drunkenness, theft and anti-social behaviour. Her life bore all the hallmarks of spiralling out of control.

On the night she was murdered Wilma was drinking primarily in the Kirkgate area of Leeds – in the Regent Inn at 109 Kirkgate, the Scotsman at 106 Kirkgate, the White Swan at 37 Call Lane and eventually the Royal Oak at 29 Kirkgate. There she got chatting to two friends before closing time forced her to head north along Vicar Lane and towards the Room at the Top Club, located at 215–219 North Street, Sheepscar. She stayed there until 1.00 am before deciding to call it a night. Around this time, about 50 yards from the club, she was seen near Rakusen's food warehouse in Meanwood Road. She was clearly drunk and holding a white plastic container of curry and chips, while trying to thumb a lift.

Sir Michael then read from Sutcliffe's confession:

That was the incident that started it all off, I was driving through Leeds late at night I'd been to somewhere having a couple of pints … I was in a Ford Capri K registered, a lime green one with a black roof with a sun grill in the back window. I saw this woman thumbing a lift where the Wetherby Road branches to the right but you can carry straight on. She was wearing some white trousers and a jacket. I stopped and asked her how far she was going. She said 'not far, thanks for stopping' and she jumped in. I was in quite a good mood and we were talking on the way. She said something, just before we stopped, about did I want business. To me, I didn't know what she meant by this. I asked her to explain and straight away a scornful tone came into her voice which took me by surprise because she had been so pleasant. She said, 'Bloody hell, do I have to spell it out', she said it as though it was a challenge. My reaction was to agree to go with her.

Within a short while they had arrived in Scott Hall Avenue, a narrow street aligned on both sides by well-to-do-suburban houses. Half way up the street Sutcliffe took another left and found himself in the rectangular car park of Prince Philip Playing Fields. It was now around 1.30 am.

Sutcliffe: 'She told me where to park the car. It was just off this road we turned left we came to this field which sloped up. I parked near the field. Before we stopped she had said that it would cost a fiver. I was a bit surprised I was expecting it to be a bit romantic. I think she had been drinking because she was being irrational. I couldn't have intercourse in a split second I had to be aroused. At this point she opened the car door and got out. She slammed the door and shouted "I'm going, it's going to take you all fucking day." She shouted something like "You're fucking useless." I suddenly felt myself seething with rage.

Author's note: Although Sutcliffe has never admitted as much, it was fairly obvious from this statement (if Sutcliffe is to be believed) that there was some attempt to have sex in the car and that he was having difficulty gaining an erection. As we will read later, this would not be the only example of sexual impotence in the case and may provide a crucial insight into the motives behind the murders.

Sutcliffe's statement continued: 'I got out of the car wanting to hit her to pay her back for the insult. I went to her and said "Hang on a minute don't go off like that." She was only 3 or 4 strides away she turned and came back to me. She said something like "Oh you can fucking manage it now can you?" She sounded as though she was taunting me. I said "There's not much room in the car, can we do it on the grass?" This was with my idea of hitting her. She said, "I'm not going to do it here, bloody well next to the car." With that she stormed up the hill into the field. I had a tool box on the back seat of the car and I took a hammer out of the tool box I followed her into the field. I took my car coat off and carried it over my arm I had the hammer in my right hand. I put my coat on the grass. She sat down on the coat. She unfastened her trousers. She said "Come on then get it over with." I said "Don't worry I will." I then hit her with the hammer on her head. I was stood up at time behind her. I think I hit her on the top of the head I hit her once or twice on the head. She fell down flat on her back and started making a horrible noise like a moaning gurgling noise.

He hit her once more on the head and then exposed her body, which he stabbed at repeatedly. Later he claimed he went back to the car after striking her with the hammer, sat for a while and then decided to grab a knife and go back to finish her off. There is evidence to support this, as we see with the attack on Marcella Claxton.

Sutcliffe: 'I took a knife out of the tool box it had a wood handle with one sharp side the blade was about 7" long about ½ –¾" wide. I went to her. She was still lying on her back. I thought that to make certain she was dead I would stab her in places like the lungs and the throat. I stabbed her at least four times once in the throat. Before I stabbed her in the body I pulled her blouse or whatever it was and her bra so I could see where I was stabbing her.'

After he was finished, and he was quite sure she was dead, he climbed into his car and drove back to his mother-in-law's house at 44 Tanton Crescent, Clayton, Bradford. He quietly let himself in, went to the bathroom to wash his hands and went to bed.

Six hours later, local milkman, Alan Routledge, of Prince Edward Grove, Leeds, entered the car park on his rounds. He was accompanied by his 10-year-old brother Paul. It was Paul who first noticed Wilma's lifeless lying face upwards on the sloping grass just to the right of the old stone sports club. She was positioned with her head pointing uphill and her feet towards the car park. 'It's a body!' cried the younger brother in fright, and they ran over to the caretaker's house and banged on the door.

Sir Michael now read from the doctor's report to the jury:

When her body was found, her jacket and blouse was torn, her slacks were down to her knees and her bra lifted, exposing her breasts and she had numerous stab wounds... One in her neck was two and half inches deep, going through the main artery. She had nine stab wounds in her stomach and some in her chest which were four inches deep. There were also stab wounds in her umbilicus region, her red handbag strap was still looped around her left wrist.

He went on to explain that McCann had received a total of fifteen stab wounds. One to the throat, two stab wounds under her right breast, three stab wounds below the left breast and nine stab wounds around the abdomen. Later forensic tests and a vaginal swab would confirm that no sexual intercourse had taken place at all. However there were semen stains on the back of Wilma's trousers and underwear. Forensic scientists at a Harrogate laboratory were unable to identify a blood group from the semen.

Author's note: It should be noted that Sutcliffe was a Blood Group B, non-secretor. This means a person will not secrete blood cells in their bodily fluid.

Further examination at the mortuary found that the back of Wilma's head had been smashed in by two deep blows from a blunt instrument which penetrated the full thickness of the skull.

Sir Michael said Sutcliffe had been asked during his confessions why he had disarranged her clothes. He replied 'when they find them [the prostitutes] they will look as cheap as they are'. He said Sutcliffe admitted stabbing the women in the heart, lungs and throat because 'you can kill them quicker that way'.

Sutcliffe later admitted, 'After that first time I developed and built up a hatred for prostitutes in order to justify within myself the reason why I had attacked and killed Wilma McCann.'

In the weeks to follow Sutcliffe would add to this confession by saying, 'I wanted to pick up a prostitute with the intention of killing her. I realised she was a prostitute because she wanted business. I may have given her the impression that I wanted to have sex, but this was not so.'

Sir Michael pointed out that this statement conflicted with what he had originally told the police. In his first confession, he made no mention of going to Leeds with the sole aim of killing a prostitute. If anything, the murder was the result of him seething with rage when Wilma decided to walk off after he failed to gain an erection.

Emily Jackson

Sir Michael moved on the Sutcliffe's next victim, 42-year-old part-time sex worker, Emily Jackson; a married woman who used to drive into Leeds with her husband where he left her to carry out prostitution.

Beginning his analysis of the murder, Sir Michael read from Sutcliffe's statements: 'The next one I did was in Leeds not long after McCann. This time I drove to Leeds looking for a prostitute because I felt I could not justify what I had done previously and I felt an inner compulsion to kill a prostitute.'

Emily and Sydney Jackson had been married since 1953. They had three children, Neil 18, Christopher 10, and 7-year-old Angela. A fourth, Derek, had died tragically five years earlier at the age of 14 when he fell out his bedroom window and onto the pavement. The Jacksons lived nearby in a neat semi-detached house at 18 Back Green, Leeds. Sydney was a local roofing contractor, Emily was 41, slightly overweight, and looked older than her years. She helped Sydney with his paperwork and drove him from job to job in their old Commer van, since he did not drive. To the outside world everything about the Jacksons appeared to be normal. However, they were leading a strange double life.

In the autumn of 1975, financial pressures meant Emily had taken to prostitution in an effort to survive. This was supported by Sydney and the pair set about making money from Emily's night-time activities. He would often accompany her to pubs and clubs, primarily the Gaiety at 89 Roundhay Road at the junction of Gathorne Terrace. Here he would wait patiently at the bar while she took strangers out to the car park and into the back of the van. If customers could not be found in the pubs, she would step outside to take part in the more lucrative business of attracting kerb crawlers.

On the night of Tuesday, 20 January 1976, Emily and Sydney left their house at 6.00 pm, with Emily driving the van into the car park of the Gaiety fifteen minutes later. She was wearing a blue and white striped dress, white cardigan, strappy heeled shoes and a green, blue and red chequered overcoat. As soon as they arrived, Sydney went to the bar and Emily looked around to see what business could be had.

Sutcliffe: 'I drove to Leeds in my Capri about 8.00 pm – 9.00 pm. I saw a woman dressed in an overcoat trying to stop drivers from the pavement on the road that leads to Wetherby Road, it was near some phone boxes. I stopped and wound the window down. I said "How Much?' She said "Five pounds." She got in the car I remember when she got in there was an overpowering smell of cheap perfume and sweat, this served all the more for me to hate this woman even though I didn't even know her, looking back I can see how the first murder had unhinged me completely. She had an overcoat on and she was heavily built and had brown hair. She said she knew where we could go. I knew from the outset I didn't want intercourse with her. I just wanted to get rid of her. At that time I think I was dressed in my working clothes, at that time I used to wear wellington boots at work. At her direction I turned the car round and drove back the way I'd come, we had just gone about 400 yards and she told me to turn left. I turned in and then turned left again and drove behind some old buildings, it was a cul-de-sac.'

The pair had entered the Manor Street Industrial Estate which lies just off the Roundhay Road and was only a stone's throw from where Wilma McCann was last seen alive after visiting the Room at the Top nightclub. In the 1970s it was a very rough, dirty area consisting of dilapidated buildings and factories, many of which stood boarded up on the cobbled streets. Waste ground, burning-tyre yards, dark cul-de-sacs, tiny alleyways and courtyards were littered with rubbish and discarded office furniture. During the hours of darkness, it became a hangout for sex workers who found the deserted side streets and waste ground perfect sites for alone time with their clients. With the busy Gaiety pub just 400 yards up the road, it was the nearest spot away from the public gaze.

The cobblestoned cul-de-sac where Sutcliffe parked his car was isolated and private. A large brick wall lay at the far end, on the right-hand side was a flat-roofed factory building belonging to Hollingworth & Moss bookbinders, and on the left-hand side was a row of scruffy, redbrick buildings, which were boarded up and awaiting demolition.

Sutcliffe: 'I couldn't bear even to go through the motions of having sex with this woman. On the journey she told me that she could drive. I wanted to do what I'd got in mind as soon as possible ... I remember turning on the ignition again so that the red warning light came on and pretended that the car would not start I said I would have to lift up the bonnet to sort it out. I asked her if she would give me a hand. We both got out of the car I lifted up the bonnet of the car.'

Author's note: There is a break in Sutcliffe's confession between what happened after the car stopped in the cul-de-sac to when he then went to restart the car. The police did not ask him for these details and he never volunteered it. Could there have been a failed attempt at sex, similar to Wilma McCann?

Sutcliffe: 'I had picked up a hammer which I had put near my seat for that purpose. I told her I could not see properly without a torch. She offered to use her cigarette lighter to shine under the bonnet. She was holding her lighter like this, I took a couple of steps back and I hit her over the head with the hammer I think I hit her twice she fell down onto the road.'

Sir Michael paused from his reading of the confession to address the jury himself: 'Can you imagine an account which sets out a more carefully, deliberate way in which he manoeuvred her into position where he could hit her? Everything was so well planned.'

He hit her once more, fracturing her skull, then grabbed her wrists and dragged her into a narrow alleyway which ran between the red brick buildings. The alleyway was littered with rubbish, scrap metal and burnt timber, it made a makeshift shortcut into the adjacent street.

Sutcliffe: 'then I made sure she was dead by taking a screwdriver and stabbing her repeatedly. I pulled her dress up and her bra before I stabbed her to make it easier.' When asked why he had disarranged her clothing he said: 'To be truthful I pulled her clothes up in order to satisfy some sort of sexual revenge on her as on reflection I had done on McCann, I stabbed her frenziedly without thought with a Phillips screwdriver all over her body... I was seething with hate for her. I remember picking up a piece of wood from the yard about 2–3ft long and 3" × 1" and pushing up against her vagina with it as she lay on her back.'

Sir Michael reminded the jury that this is not what Sutcliffe had said to the police regarding the McCann murder. In that case he said he had pushed her bra up and exposed her breasts because it was easier to see where he was stabbing.

Sir Michael said, 'Sutcliffe had pushed a piece of wood against Mrs Jackson's vagina. Asked if he had opened her legs first Sutcliffe had replied "no I don't think so. I may have positioned her to show her as disgusting as she was."'

As for the murder itself, it was a horrific sight. She was lying on her back and her legs had been clearly pushed wide apart, with her right leg bent upwards and outwards and her left leg bent at the knee. To crime scene investigators it looked as though she had been deliberately posed in a lewd manner. She was still wearing her red, blue and green overcoat but her striped dress had been pushed up. Her tights, which were torn at the knee, were crudely pulled down on the left side revealing black knickers. This suggests an attempt was made to pull the tights down, or they were pulled down and an attempt was made to put them back into position later.

Emily was barefoot, with one shoe lying next to her right foot and the other a few feet away against the wall. Her light yellow handbag lay open close to her head (its contents would later help detectives identify her). There were blood stains on her right arm and hands, along with a larger pool of blood above and beneath her head, some of which had already congealed into clumps. The front of her body, including her face and thighs, were scratched and heavily soiled by mud and dirt. There were also marks on the ground leading from the street into the passageway, showing how Sutcliffe had dragged her body to the spot where it was found.

On this occasion Sutcliffe had left behind a noticeable shoe impression in the mud from a size 7 heavy-ribbed wellington boot. A similar boot print was also found on Emily's inner thigh.

Two savage blows had fractured the skull and she had sustained a total of fifty-two stab wounds to the torso, neck and back, clustered together in separate small areas, giving an almost 'pepper pot' look to the injuries. There were thirty stab wounds to the back, twelve to the abdomen, eight to the neck, and the heart had been penetrated twice from the front and the back. The pathologist found it impossible to see the individual track of each wound.

A vaginal swab did yield a sample of semen, but the laboratory felt this was from sexual activity prior to the attack.

Sutcliffe: 'I left her lying on her back I never took anything from her. Just as I was about to get into my car, a car came round with its lights on and stopped a few yards from where my car was. I don't know what make of car it was but it scared me. I put the hammer and screwdriver on the car floor and drove away. I went straight home to my mother-in-law's house. At that time I had a feeling of satisfaction and justification for what I'd done.'

Emily's disappearance was not reported by her husband at the time. He had assumed she had gone on to another pub and went home in a taxi around 10.30 pm. Having been drinking most of the night he went to bed, assuming his wife would make her own way home in the van.

Emily Jackson's body was discovered at 8.10 am the next morning when an employee of Hollingworth & Moss bookbinders arrived for work and noticed two legs protruding from the rubble which lay about 15ft inside the alleyway.

Marcella Claxton

Marcella Claxton, aged 23, was attacked in Roundhay Park, Leeds, in part of the park known as Soldiers Field, in the early hours of Sunday, 9 May 1976.

Marcella lived in one of the many terraces of back-to-back houses off the Roundhay Road in the red-light district of Leeds. She was a West Indian single mother-of-two but her children had been placed in care the year before. She was now three months' pregnant with her third child. On Saturday, 8 May, Marcella had been drinking at a late night party in Chapeltown, not far from her home and had set off for home at around 5 am.

Earlier that night, Sutcliffe had been cruising through Chapeltown in his white Ford Corsair. He was now parked up on Spencer Place with the lights turned off and the engine running.

Author's note: Marcella Claxton has always maintained that she was not a prostitute and consequently stories differ, depending on which account you read.

Sutcliffe: 'I picked her up in the Chapeltown area. She asked me if I was the police, I said, "No, do I really look like a policeman?" She decided to get into the car, and suggested where we go. We ended up in what I knew later as Soldiers Field. We got out of the car at my suggestion and she took off her trousers while leaning against a tree, and she sat down on the grass.'

As Sutcliffe got out of the car he dropped his hammer, Marcella claimed to have heard a clunk noise. She said, 'I hope that isn't a knife' and he may have replied, 'It's my wallet.'

Sutcliffe: 'She suggested that we "start the ball rolling on the grass." I hit her once on the head with the hammer, but just couldn't bring myself to hit her again. For some reason or another, I just let her walk away and I went back to the car.'

In fact Sutcliffe had struck Marcella eight or nine times on the head with his ball-pein hammer. She collapsed, but miraculously although stunned she remained conscious. She would later claim she had only pretended to pass out, but lay there without moving as Sutcliffe stood over her, masturbating. When he was finished he wiped himself with a tissue and threw it on the grass, then he pushed a £5 note into her hand and told her not to call the police. He then casually walked back to his car and drove up back towards the Roundhay Road, leaving Marcella sprawled out on the grass. Marcella's statement is of paramount importance in the Yorkshire Ripper case as it clearly shows the driving force of Sutcliffe's actions.

Remarkably, she still had enough strength to get herself back on her feet and, using her knickers, managed to stem the flow of blood from her head. She staggered to a nearby phone box to call for help, but to her horror she noticed Sutcliffe's car returning up the road. She said later: 'After I had dialled 999 and was sat on the floor of the telephone box, a man in a white car kept driving past. He seemed to be staring and looking for me. It was the man that hurt me.' She watched him as he stopped the car: 'He got out and began searching the spot where he had left me. He must have come back to finish me off.'

'Mercifully, she had managed to move away and get help.' Sir Michael Havers later told the jury.

Marcella required extensive brain surgery and fifty-two stitches to close the eight laceration wounds in her head. Despite her appalling injuries, her description of Sutcliffe was fairly accurate; she said he was a young, white man with crinkly black hair and beard, a Yorkshire accent, who said he didn't live in Leeds and was driving a white car with red upholstery.

Bizarrely, despite detectives looking closely at the circumstances behind this attack, it was never linked to the Yorkshire Ripper murders until Peter Sutcliffe confessed to it following his arrest.

Irene Richardson

Sir Michael moved on to Victim number 6, Mrs Irene Richardson, 28, whose body was found by a jogger among trees in Soldiers Field on 6 February 1977.

Author's Note: The body was discovered at 7.40 am by Mr John Bolton, a 47-year-old accountant from nearby Gledhow Lane, passing on his pre-breakfast jog.

Originally from Glasgow, Irene had run away from home in 1965 to live in London, and over the next five years had two children – a boy and a girl – who were raised by foster parents. By 1971 she had married 31-year-old plasterer, George Richardson, and had two more children, Amanda and Irene. By this time the family was living in Balmer Grove, Blackpool. Not long after the birth of their second child, Irene moved out of the family home and went to London. George found her and moved in with her around June 1975, but in April 1976 she ran away again. Eventually the marriage failed completely and

Irene ran away once and for all. George reported her missing and later recalled the day it happened: 'I went out to work one morning and when I came back, she was gone. I never saw her again.'

She had no proper accommodation and moved between various boarding houses; occasionally, she was found sleeping in public toilets. With a lack of money and food, she turned to prostitution in an effort to survive and was often seen on the corners of Chapeltown looking for customers.

Her final residence was 1 Cowper Street, a large Victorian mansion that had been converted into bedsits. It's worth noting that Cowper Street is only a three-minute walk from the Gaiety where Emily Jackson had last been seen on the night she died.

At 11.15 pm on 5 February 1977, Irene mentioned to a fellow resident that she was going to Tiffany's nightclub, located at the Merrion Centre in Leeds. When she left the house she was wearing a yellow skirt and brown jacket, blue and white checked blouse, brown cardigan and imitation suede coat. She left the house at around 11.30 pm.

This was the last recorded sighting of Irene alive.

Sutcliffe: 'The next one I did was Irene Richardson ... I drove to Leeds after the pubs shut. It was my intention to find a prostitute to make it one less. I saw this girl walking in some cross streets in the middle of the vice estate near a big club. I stopped my car and she got in without me saying a word. I told her I might not have wanted her, she said "I'll show you a good time, you're not going to send me away are you?"'

They drove up Roundhay Road and onto Park Avenue then turned left onto West Avenue. They parked next to the stone pavilion on Soldiers Field (used by local football teams as a changing room and toilets) located at the far end of West Avenue on the left-hand side. It was a secluded spot, surrounded by beech trees.

Sutcliffe: 'She wanted to use the toilets so she got out and went over to them. She came back and said they were locked. Before she went to the toilet she took of her coat and placed it on the ground. When she came back she said she would have a wee on the ground. She took her boots off and placed them on the ground then she crouched down to have a pee. By this time I was out of the car and I had my hammer in my hand. As she was crouching down I hit her on the head from behind at least twice maybe three times she fell down.'

The force of the attack had been so powerful that parts of her skull were driven nearly an inch into her brain. The hammer had actually got stuck in the skull with the force of one blow and marks in the bone showed it had to be levered out to remove it. Measuring the circular fracture, it was 1½ins in diameter, the precise dimension of a hammer head. Death would have occurred in seconds.

Sutcliffe then dragged her out of sight behind the pavilion. He pulled down her tights and knickers, at which point one sock came off. He pushed up her bra and exposed her breasts. Here, he produced a Stanley knife which he had concealed in his pocket and began attacking the body.

Sutcliffe: 'I then lifted up her clothes and slashed her in the lower abdomen and also slashed her throat. I left her lying face down and I covered her up with her coat I put her knee boots on top of her before I covered her up.'

Sir Michael read from the doctor's report – 'She had been viciously stabbed in the side of the neck and front of the throat, causing a gaping wound which exposed the larynx. She had also been stabbed three times in the left-hand side of the abdomen. All of these cuts were downward strokes 6–7ins long, which had caused her intestines to spill out of her body.'

Author's Note: Due to the presence of semen on the back of her knickers and tights, similar to the Wilma McCann murder, it's highly likely that Sutcliffe masturbated and ejaculated at some point during this attack. This unfortunately cannot be proved unless a modern cold case team ever decide to look again the evidence.

Sutcliffe also told police that he had left the murder scene after he heard voices, but couldn't tell where they came from. He also heard a car being driven away from the entrance to a block of apartments. It was later that he learnt that the apartments were where disc jockey Jimmy Savile lived.

Sutcliffe: 'I then got into my car and drove off the field. I cannot remember whether I drove off or backed off. When I got to the road I saw a couple sitting on a bench near the toilets. I was living with my wife at 6 Garden Lane, Heaton. I drove straight home. I looked at my clothes before I went in I did not see any blood stains.

By this time after [Irene] Richardson, killing prostitutes became an obsession with me, and I couldn't stop myself, it was like some sort of a drug.'

Sir Michael once again reminded the jury that there was no mention of a divine mission to kill prostitutes.

Patricia Atkinson

Mrs Patricia Atkinson, 32 was victim number seven. Her body was found by a male friend on 24 April 1977, in bed at her flat covered in bedding. The killing was unusual in that it took place in the victim's home in Bradford.

Patricia, or Tina as she was known, had grown up in the Thorpe Edge district of Bradford. In 1960, when she was 16, she met her husband, Ramen Mitra, a Pakistani, at a dance hall in the town. By then she was working as a 'burler', removing loose threads, knots, and other imperfections from cloth, at a mill in Greengates, Bradford. By early April 1961 the pair were married and they lived for a short time with Tina's parents before moving to their own home at Girlington, an area of Bradford next to Manningham, where they went on to have three daughters. Unfortunately the marriage was not to last. Tina grew bored of her life and perhaps having married so young, she felt she had not done any real living. She was good looking and enjoyed attention from men. This eventually put a strain on the marriage, which ended with Tina leaving the family home and her husband being awarded custody of the children. Over the next few years, Tina's lifestyle deteriorated. She advanced from casual promiscuity to full-time prostitution and alcoholism.

On 12 April 1977, just ten days before she was murdered, Tina rented a small bedsit at 9 Oak Avenue, Bradford. This put her one step ahead of most of the girls working the red-light district who served clients in dark corners, up against walls, on patches of waste ground or in the backs of cars.

On Saturday night, 23 April 1977, Tina had been out drinking heavily in her regular haunts, including the Perseverance Pub on Lumb Lane and the Carlisle Hotel – located at 86 Carlisle Road and only a ten-minute walk from Oak Avenue.

At 10.15 pm and 10.30 pm the staff at the Carlisle pub remembered her announcing that she was leaving and watched her stagger towards the exit. She set off in the direction of what appeared to be her next destination, the International Club in Lumb Lane. She was dressed in tight blue jeans, a largely unbuttoned blue shirt and a short leather jacket.

She was last seen by another street girl at about 11.10 pm, weaving and staggering her way down Church Street towards St Mary's Road.

Sutcliffe: 'The next one was a couple of months later in Bradford, this was Patricia Atkinson. It was a Saturday night late on. I drove off Lumb Lane into Church Street I knew this was a prostitute area. I was in my Corsair. I saw this woman in St Pauls Road at a junction with another road, she appeared drunk and was banging on the roof of a white Mini and was shouting and bawling 'Fuck Off' and such things to the driver who then drove off at speed. I pulled up to her and stopped and without me asking she jumped in the car. She said 'I've got a flat, we can go there. She told me where to go. We turned right at the junction with Manningham Lane, turned left down Queens Road. Left into Oak Avenue and turned second left and stopped at her flat. She told me she lived alone. I parked up outside her flat and she got out and went in. I picked up a hammer as I got out of the car.'

Patricia lived in Flat 3 of 9 Oak Avenue. It could only be reached via the main front entrance of the apartment block, then down the staircase directly opposite the entrance to the ground floor and then left along a wide corridor into the side wing of the building. Turning left once more, Number 3 was on the right-hand side. Inside the flat there was a small bathroom straight ahead and an equally small kitchen. Next to that was a door to the joint living room and bedroom. The room was fairly basic. A double wooden bed was on the right and a small dining table covered with a white tablecloth was on the left of the bed, against the chimney breast. An oak dressing table with mirror was in front of the large, rectangular window, along with two dining room chairs. There was also a two-seater sofa and a small electric heater plugged into the wall next to the door. In the far corner, there was a small fire escape door, which led directly outside the block. A large oak wardrobe had been pushed directly in front of it, probably to add a bit more security.

Sutcliffe: 'I followed her into the flat, she closed the curtains and I hung my coat on the hook on the back of the door. She took her coat off and sat on the bed, her back was slightly towards me I went up to her and hit her on the back of the head with the hammer she fell off the bed onto the floor.'

He struck her on the head once again before picking her up under her arms and hoisting her back onto the bed. In doing this, he left a boot print on the bedsheet between the wall and the body. The size 7 Dunlop Warwick Wellington boot print would later be matched to the one found close to the body of Emily Jackson just over a year earlier in Leeds. Once he had positioned her lying on her back in the centre of the bed, Sutcliffe pulled her blue bell-bottomed jeans and white knickers down below the knee, exposing her genitals and legs. He pushed up her T-shirt and black bra to expose her abdomen and breasts.

He then savagely attacked her body with the claw end of the hammer, targeting the breasts, abdomen and pubic region. He then turned her over onto her front and unfastened her bra strap before repeating the attack with the claw end of the hammer. Her body was smeared with blood as she was manoeuvred by Sutcliffe's bloody hands. The blood distribution on the bed indicated that he inflicted two more blows to the back of her head while she lay on the bed.

There were four major depressed fractures to the skull caused by the hammer blows, which left crescent-shaped wounds on her skull.

Sutcliffe: 'I hit her several times on her stomach and back with the claw part of the hammer and I saw that I was making marks on her body doing this.'

The pathologist report mentioned 'oblong marks, cuts and abrasions to the chest, abdomen and pubic region ... severe puncture marks on the vagina [and] several lacerations to the left-hand side of her body.' Horrifically, Patricia was still alive during the attack and continued to make 'gurgling sounds'.

Sir Michael then paused from reading Sutcliffe's statement and proceeded to walk over to the exhibits table. There among the different weapons he picked up a claw hammer and held it up to show to the jury. He then invited them to closely examine the weapon by passing it between themselves. The youngest jury member, a girl in her twenties, turned visibly green when the hammer was passed to her and she swiftly passed it on to the next juror before wiping her hand on her skirt.

Sutcliffe: 'I then covered her up the bedclothes. I think she was lying face down or on her side when I left her. When I first hit her she was making a horrible gurgling sound and she carried on making this noise even though I'd hit her a few times. She was still making a gurgling noise when I left, but I knew she would not be in a state to tell anybody.'

Patricia Atkinson's body was discovered by a friend, Robert Henderson, at 6.30 pm the following evening. He had forced entry into the room when she didn't answer. He noticed a pool of blood on the floor next to the electric heater. Then a lumpy bundle on the bed, protruding from it was a bloody arm, one side of her blood-soaked face and matted dark hair on the striped pillowcase.

Sutcliffe: 'I drove home and put my car in the garage. I looked at my clothes in the garage I saw that I had some blood on the bottom of my jeans. I went in the house, my wife was in bed. I took my jeans off and rinsed them under the cold tap and hung them up. I also saw some blood on one of my shoes, or they may have been boots. I rinsed this under the tap and wiped it with a sponge. I believe I was wearing a pair of brown Doc Martens boots at that time. I'm trying to think what I did with the claw hammer, I think I used it again on a woman. I have thrown it away over a wall near Sharps Printers at Cottingley, I can't remember when it was exactly. At that time I carried on as though nothing had happened. I was then working at Clarks in Bradford.'

Jayne MacDonald

Sir Michael then moved on to the murder which would make the Yorkshire Ripper international news and the focus of an intense local hatred which had not existed during the previous four murders. 'The murder in 1977 of Jayne MacDonald was typically tragic', he said 'she was 16 and completely respectable.'

The small 16-year-old had left school only six months earlier and had been walking home alone from a night out in Leeds when she was killed. Where once he'd brought fear to the streets, the Ripper now took that fear into the homes and minds of all who lived in Yorkshire.

It was 9.45 am on Sunday, 26 June 1977, when two young children playing in an adventure playground off Reginald Street in Leeds, noticed the body of a young woman lying among the discarded rubbish by the old community centre wall.

Jayne had left Allerton High School on Kings Lane in Leeds six months earlier, and gained employment in the shoe department of Grandways supermarket on the nearby Roundhay Road. Described by her neighbours and her employer as an attractive young girl with shoulder-length light brown hair, a bright smile and sunny personality, she was soon popular in the shop and on Saturday nights she liked to go roller skating or visit the local disco.

Jayne lived with her parents, Wilfred and Irene MacDonald, at 77 Scott Hall Avenue, the same street on which Wilma McCann had lived – just six doors away at Number 65 in fact.

Saturday, 25 June 1977 was a warm summer night and, as Jayne left to go to the town centre, the streets surrounding her home were buzzing with people. She kissed her parents goodbye and made her way into town where she intended to meet up with some friends at the Hofbräuhaus, a large Bavarian-style tavern in the Merrion Centre. It was there that she met 18-year-old Mark Jones, and they danced together. At 10.30 pm, they set off as part of a crowd in the direction of Briggate, the main shopping street. They were hungry and Jayne had suggested going for fish and chips. The two parted company outside the main gates of St James's hospital at around 1.30 am.

Jayne decided to take a short cut home through the vice area of Chapeltown. She continued walking and came out of the maze of streets near the Grandways supermarket, where she worked. She continued past the Gaiety on Roundhay Road, where Emily Jackson was last seen, and walked along Chapeltown Road in the direction of the Hayfield pub, Reginald Street and her home.

Sutcliffe: 'The next one I did I still feel terrible about, it was the young girl Jayne MacDonald. I believed at the time that she was a prostitute. This was on a Saturday night. I drove to Leeds in my Corsair, I think it was the red one but I'm not 100 per cent sure. At this time the urge to kill prostitutes was very strong and I had gone out of my mind.'

Sutcliffe had spent that night in the company of Ronnie and David Barker, on the same street where he and Sonia lived with Sonia's parents. After a night of drinking in the pubs of Bradford, Sutcliffe dropped them at the end of Tanton Crescent, Clayton, Bradford, but instead of going home, he turned the car around and headed to Leeds. By 1.30 am, he had already driven up Roundhay Road and into Roundhay Park – where he had murdered Irene Richardson in February 1977, and just further along, off the Roundhay Road, he had dumped the body of Emily Jackson in Manor Street in January 1976. It was almost 2 am and now he had caught site of Jayne walking alone along the Chapeltown Road.

Sutcliffe: 'I saw this lass walking along quite slowly towards the crossing near the Hayfield pub in Chapeltown Road. She stopped on the corner before crossing over Chapeltown Road. I anticipated that she was going to walk up one of the streets up past the Hayfield.'

Author's Note: The Hayfield Hotel was a notorious drop-out centre for sex workers and all sorts of villains. It lay on the Chapeltown Road and in-between Reginald Street and Reginald Terrace.

Sutcliffe: 'I drove my car into the Hayfield pub car park and got out. I took my hammer out of the car. I think it was the claw hammer. I also had a knife with me that time, it was a kitchen-type knife with a black ebonite handle and a thin blade. I walked towards the narrow street behind the Hayfield [Reginald Street] to see where she was and just as I got there she was walking up.'

She was three quarters of the way up the street and was now parallel with the adventure playground on her left-hand side. A few more steps and she would be back into the residential side of Reginald Street, and perhaps this is why Sutcliffe struck when he did. He smashed his hammer into the back of her head and she crumpled to the floor, blood staining the ground where she lay. He hit her again with the hammer and then dragged her, face down, about 20 yards through the top entrance of the playground and into the corner behind the wooden fence and up against the boundary wall of a nearby community centre.

Sutcliffe: 'I hit her another once at least, maybe twice on the head. I pulled her clothes up exposing her breasts and I stabbed her several times with the knife in the chest. Before this I stabbed her in the back. I left her lying in the corner. I cannot remember whether she was lying face up or face down.'

He said later that her shoes made 'a horrible scraping noise' along the ground as he dragged her.

Sir Michael: 'Doctors formed the view she had been hit on the head once and fallen, hit once more where she lay, dragged to where she was found and there stabbed on the front of the body and then turned over and stabbed repeatedly in the back. Unfortunately she did not die until after some of the stab wounds had been inflicted.'

He had stabbed her in the same wound as many as twenty times, causing it to become much more enlarged. He then turned her over onto her face and thrust the knife in and out of the same wound in her back, penetrating the heart, kidneys and lungs. She had also been stabbed under the right shoulder blade. When she was found, a broken top of a bottle with a screw top had been inserted deeply into the gash in her stomach. This had either been done deliberately by Sutcliffe or it had lodged there when the body was turned over.

The image shown to the jury depicted the body of Jayne MacDonald lying face down with her head pointing towards the wall and the right side of her body lying next to the fence. Her legs were straight out but her feet were crossed, the left over the right; her left arm was bent up with the hand beneath her head and her right arm stretched out. She had been wearing a grey jacket, which was now pushed up to the shoulders to expose her bare back. Her blue and white checked skirt was also pushed up exposing the upper part of her thighs. She was still wearing one of her high-heeled yellow shoes and the other lay nearby. Her black tights had been ripped but were still in place.

Sir Michael referred the jury to photographs of the body, and pointed out marks on the ground where she had been dragged to the spot after being attacked. He also pointed out that there was evidence that the killer had wiped his knife clean on the back of her body.

He then continued with Sutcliffe's account:

Sutcliffe: 'I walked back down the same street to where I had parked my car. As I got to the car park I saw a group of people walking up the Narrow Street [Reginald Street)] from Chapeltown Road.

I got into my car and drove away into Reginald Terrace into Chapeltown Road and drove straight home. I think my wife may have been working that night. I have remembered that my wife started working some Friday and Saturday nights at Sherrington Private Nursing home in Bradford. That is why

I have done a lot of my attacks on a Saturday night. I don't think I had any blood on me following this one.'

'....When the Ripper came up in conversation at work or in a pub I was able to detach my mind from the fact that it was me they were talking about and I was able to discuss it normally. This amazed me at times that I was able to do this.'

Maureen Long

Maureen was attacked and left for dead on 9 July 1977, just two weeks after Jayne MacDonald's murder. She was a 42-year-old mother of three grown up children, who lived in Farsley, a district of Pudsey, Leeds. Sir Michael was keen to point out that, like Jayne MacDonald, Maureen was not a sex worker either: 'While she had convictions', he said, 'none were in relation to prostitution.'

At the time of her attack she was living with a man called Ken Smith at 22 Donald Street, Farsley, but she was also known to reside with her estranged husband Ronnie at 1 Rendel Street, Laisterdyke, a neighbourhood on the outskirts of Bradford.

She was described by friends as 'a friendly sort and loved to dance in many of the clubs the city centre had to offer.' At 7.30 pm on Saturday, 9 July 1977, Maureen was out on the town at 101 Manningham Lane, home to the famous Mecca Ballroom. She was seen leaving this nightclub around 2 am.

Sutcliffe had also been in town earlier in the night, drinking in several pubs with his mates, Ronnie and David Barker. Once again he dropped the Barkers home at the end of Tanton Crescent, Clayton, and drove off alone, but this time to the Manningham area of Bradford.

Sutcliffe: 'I was driving along Manningham Lane towards the City Centre one Saturday night in July 1977. It was late at night. I saw her walking on the same side as the Mecca, towards Bradford Centre. She was wearing a maxi length dress and a jacket sort of coat. She was just past the hamburger stand when I saw her. I stopped my car and said, "Are you going far?" She said, "Are you give me a lift?" I said, "If you want one." She got in. She told me she had been to the Mecca. She told me where she lived, and that she lived with a man who was an ex-boxer and that he was a spoilsport and would not take her to the Mecca. She directed me where to drive to her house, which was somewhere off Leeds Road to the left.'

Maureen had directed Sutcliffe to 1 Rendell Street, just off Leeds Road. She pointed to a row of terraced houses and said that was where she was going but asked him not to stop outside but to drive past and wait on the corner. Maureen asked whether he 'fancied her', and when Sutcliffe said he did, she said they could go inside if no one was at home. She got out and knocked at the door of the house, banging at it for a minute or two before giving up and returning to the car. She said she knew a quiet spot where they could go, and directed him to nearby Bowling Back Lane

Sutcliffe: 'She told me where to drive, and I drove eventually into Bowling Back Lane and turned right down a cobbled street. (Birkshall Lane, a side street that connects to Bowling Back Lane.) I stopped the car some way down the street. There was some spare unlevelled land on the left and a big high wall on the right. She got out of the car and said she was going for a piss first and she went to the spare land and crouched down and had a piss.'

'I had my hammer ready as she got out of the car and I also had a knife. I think it was the same knife I had at MacDonald.'

'I got out of the car while she was having a piss and as she was crouching down I hit her on the head with the hammer. She slumped down.'

Sir Michael: 'There he is, from the moment of picking her up until all that happened, holding himself back, restraining himself, waiting for the right moment when she put herself in a position where he could use the hammer from behind.'

Sutcliffe: 'I pulled her by the hands further onto the spare ground. She was not making any sound. I pulled up her clothes and I stabbed her three or four times with the knife.'

Sir Michael: 'In fact he had ripped her dress off her shoulders and down to her waist, pushed up her bra to expose her breasts and with her knickers already pulled down to her knees and her dress hitched up to her waist, he then stabbed her nine times, once on her left shoulder, four times in the side and front of her torso, with one slashing stab wound tracking down from her breast to below her navel. He flipped her over and stabbed her another four times in the back. She also sustained three fractured ribs.'

[When he was sure he had killed her, he dragged a discarded mattress that had been abandoned on the waste ground and threw it over her. In doing so, he stumbled in the rubble and lost his balance and fell. He put out his right arm to cushion his fall, but this left a bloodstained partial palm print on a discarded hand basin. At this point he heard a dog barking, so he made a hasty getaway back to his car.]

Sutcliffe: 'I did see a caravan with a light on over the spare land, but it didn't put me off what I was doing. I thought that I had stabbed her enough when I left her. I went back to the car, got in, and drove off ... I was under the impression that the street I was in may be a cul-de-sac, so I reversed my car by turning it round in the street I was in. No, I didn't, I remember that I backed out of the street into Bowling Back Lane facing towards the city. I drove along Bowling Back Lane towards the general direction of the city centre, and drove home to Garden Lane.'

As Sutcliffe pulled out onto the road, he was spotted by Mr Frank Whitaker, a night-watchman from the nearby ironworks unit, who came out to see what his Alsatian dog was barking at.

Unfortunately his memory wasn't great and he wrongly identified the car as a white Ford Cortina Mark II with a dark roof (it was really a Ford Corsair). He did note the time correctly as 3.27 am.

Incredibly, Maureen survived this attack and her cries were heard around 8.45 am that morning by two traveller women from the nearby St Mary Street Caravan Park. She was found shivering and petrified under the discarded mattress and rushed to hospital where neurosurgeons battled to save her brain from permanent damage. She was hospitalised for nine weeks.

Sir Michael: 'She was successfully treated and discharged, however, she has still not recovered and continues to receive out-patient treatment and has fits. Mr Sutcliffe claimed that when he heard the next day that his victim was still alive he got a nasty shock. He thought it was the end of the line there and then. He thought she would be able to identify him.'

Sutcliffe: 'I think it was about that time that I threw the hammer over Sharps' wall. A few days after, I read that Long was suffering from loss of memory and this made me less worried about being caught. My desire to kill prostitutes was getting stronger than ever and it took me over completely. I was in a dilemma, I wanted to tell someone what I was doing, but I thought about how it would affect my wife and family. I wasn't too much bothered for myself.'

But the attack story doesn't end there. Shortly after his arrest and eventual confession Sutcliffe was to say he had come face to face with Maureen Long in Bradford.

Sutcliffe: 'I saw Maureen just a couple of weeks ago. I was in the Arndale Shopping Centre with my wife when I came face to face with her. I recognised her immediately, she seemed to look at me, but she obviously didn't recognise me.'

Jean Jordan

The next murder victim was Manchester sex worker Jean Jordan, a 20-year-old mother of two young children. Sir Michael said, this was: 'a particularly disturbing story because she was not reported missing, so no search was mounted for her.'

Described by fellow a sex worker as, 'Pretty, with a shy smile, long auburn hair and a slim, leggy 5ft 6in frame', Jean had had arrived in Manchester at the age of 16, having run away from Motherwell, Scotland.

She had built up a relationship with 26-year-old Alan Royle, an unemployed chef, and they had two children, but by 1977 the young couple were starting to grow apart. The pressure of extra mouths to feed and growing economic hardship had taken its toll. They continued to live together in their new council house in Lingbeck Crescent, Manchester, but led separate lives.

Around this time Jean had also become friendly with a group of women who earned their living on Manchester's streets. These sex workers introduced Jean to the relatively easy money to be made on the kerbs of Moss Side and Cheetham Hill. To them, she was known as 'Scotch Jean' and they described her as 'quiet, shy and timid'.

It was shortly after 9 pm on 1 October 1977 when Jean Jordan, standing at her usual beat on Princess Road in Manchester's Moss Side, encountered Sutcliffe. He was now in a red Ford Corsair having replaced the white Ford Corsair, which had been involved in many of his attacks and murders

Sutcliffe: 'I realised things were hotting up a bit in Leeds and Bradford. People had dubbed me the Ripper. I decided to go to Manchester to kill a prostitute. I had read in a paper somewhere or a magazine of a priest chastising what went on in his parish at Manchester where there obviously was prostitutes … I had been taken over completely by this urge to kill and I couldn't fight it … One Saturday night in October 1977 I drove over to Manchester I believe it was in my red Corsair. I had a look at the map in my Road Atlas to see where Moss Side was and I drove there. I went through Manchester town centre – Princess Street I think it was – followed it all the way down past the university, which eventually came out near the Moss Side area. It was a run-down area and almost immediately on arriving there I saw several girls plying for trade. I pulled up at the kerbside and asked a girl if she wanted business. She was very slim with light coloured hair, not bad looking. She told me if I waited further along the road she would meet me there. I drove on 200 yards and made a right turn, then a three-point turn to face the main road once again. After a couple of minutes, the girl drew level. She saw my car just as she was going to get into another car which had stopped for her. I think this was an 1100, a light-coloured one, either grey or fawn. She didn't get in but came over to me, which I suppose was the biggest mistake she ever made. She came up and got into my car. She told me she was going to go with the man in the other car until she saw me.'

In the car Jean explained it would be £5 and that she knew a secluded spot, a one mile drive to a dark patch of waste ground adjacent to the allotments next to Southern Cemetery. Within a few minutes, they turned left off Princess Road and along a narrow track that ran through iron gates and into the cemetery then onto a small square patch of overgrown wasteland. Sutcliffe parked the car on the grass next to the allotments and produced a £5 note. Jean took it and placed it in a disguised compartment of her handbag.

Sutcliffe: 'I said to her "Fancy coming here, you see that greenhouse?" I pointed to a greenhouse that was about 30 yards away "That belongs to my uncle." I said this to her thinking she would get out the car to use the greenhouse for business. I told her there was plenty of room and some heating in there. She got out of the car and headed for the greenhouse I followed her and seeing there was no entrance into the greenhouse from where we were I told her we would have to climb over a low fence. While she was starting to climb over the fence I hit her over the head with the hammer.'

She fell to the ground moaning loudly and he continued to smash down the hammer, 'eleven times onto her head causing massive depressed fractures to the skull which left her face unrecognisable'. He also battered her shoulders, neck and upper trunk and continued to do so until the moaning had stopped. At that moment, another car which had been standing idle further into the allotments, switched on its headlights and revved up its engine, preparing to pull out. It would appear the murderer and his victim were not the only ones using the seclusion of the area. In a quick, desperate act, Sutcliffe dragged Jean's body into the undergrowth, out of sight, and threw away her handbag, making sure nothing could be seen as the car drove out of the allotments. More cars started to arrive and Sutcliffe had to flee the scene, but not before he managed to place a large wooden door that had been discarded in the field, on top of the body to conceal it further.

He set off in the direction of Bradford, but as he drove along it crossed his mind that he had left a valuable clue behind.

Sutcliffe: 'The hammer I used that night was the one I had found lying in my garage … I took the hammer back with me. Having driven half way back I realised suddenly that this didn't put me in the clear because I had given her from my wage packet a brand new £5 note. I was working at Clarks then. I was in a dilemma once again. I kept on driving towards home I didn't realise whether she would be found or not. I decided I could not risk going back to retrieve my £5 note and I carried on home. My wife was either working or in bed when I got home.'

Sutcliffe scoured the papers over the next few days for any mention of a body being found. There were no reports. It was quite simple, he had hidden the body too well to be discovered, the area was lonely and desolate, not visited much during the day and mainly frequented by sex workers at night, many of which would be servicing their clients inside the car and not out on the grass.

There was also the fact that Jean Jordan had yet to be reported missing by her common-law husband, Alan Royle. He had assumed Jean had taken another one of her unexpected trips to Scotland.

It would be a full week before Sutcliffe realised that her body was still undiscovered and hidden in the bushes.

Peter and Sonia had recently purchased their first proper home at 6 Garden Lane, Heaton, Bradford. The three-storey, detached house would remain their home right up until his arrest in 1981. A housewarming party he held on Sunday, 9 October 1977 would give him the ideal opportunity to go back to Manchester and provide himself with an alibi should he need it.

After the party ended around midnight, he offered to take his parents, John and Kathleen, sister Jane and brother-in-law Ian home to Bingley. After he had done this he headed straight for Manchester. In the car with him was a hacksaw he had taken earlier from his garage. He arrived at the Manchester allotments within forty-five minutes.

Sutcliffe: 'I turned right when I got into the allotments as I had done before and parked up about the same place. I found the body still hidden in the place I left it. I pulled it out from the bushes and pulled off her clothes and boots. I went through them desperately trying to find the £5 note. I just threw the clothes about as I took them off. I realised that she hadn't got the £5 note in her clothes, and that it must have been in her handbag. I roamed about all over the allotments frantically searching for the bag, but I couldn't find it. I was cursing the girl and my luck all the time. Having not found the £5 note I gave vent to my frustrations by picking up a piece of broken pane of glass and slashing it across her stomach.'

Sutcliffe made sweeping gashes, 8-inches deep, to the decomposing flesh, from the shoulder to the left knee and thigh. He stabbed and sliced at her breasts, chest, stomach and area round her vagina eighteen times. The savage cuts ripped the stomach wide open and extended deep into the abdomen and into the front of the backbone. These exposed the intestines and because of the decomposition, a stench erupted when her stomach opened up.

Sutcliffe: 'When I did this there was a nauseating smell which made me reel back and immediately vomit, it was horrendous.'

Her already flattened head made Jean Jordan the most badly mutilated body he would ever leave. But he wasn't done yet. Picking up the hacksaw, he attempted to cut through the dead woman's neck. The hacksaw was blunt however, and try as he might, even by using a broken piece of glass which lay nearby, he could not get through the bone.

At this point, Sir Michael paused in his speech and held up a hacksaw, retrieved from Peter Sutcliffe's garage following his arrest. He approached the jury to show them the tool used in the horrendous attack on Jean Jordan, inviting them to examine it closely.

Sir Michael: 'that account was very much an account of someone terrified that they had left a piece of damning evidence behind … are these the actions of a man who was a paranoid schizophrenic or a man angry and frustrated because things had not gone his way?'

Author's Note: Multiple slash wounds across the body and an attempt to remove the head may have been in frustration, anger at being thwarted in his mission to find the £5 note, or they could also have been a clever desire to disguise the killing as the work of another. If the latter was true it would still show Sutcliffe to have been a very clever and calculating individual.

Sutcliffe: 'I then drove away realising I should stay looking for the fiver, but I thought I had been there long enough. I got home and went to bed. When I got home I was very surprised to see I had not got much blood on me just a bit on my shoe and at the bottom of my trousers on one leg and some on the back of my hand. I washed my hands. I was wearing a pair of casual grey trousers one of my old pair, the blood wouldn't come off these I put them in the garage in a cupboard to dispose of later. I was wearing my soft slip-on shoes, dark brown. I wiped these clean. I don't think I have got them now. I later burned my trousers with some garden rubbish at the other side of our garden wall on the field.'

Sutcliffe told police that he had read a magazine article about a priest complaining about the amount of prostitutes in his parish. Sir Michael said Sutcliffe had later added to the confession by saying that this was God's way of instructing him to go to Manchester to kill prostitutes. A point he failed to mention in the original confession.

Jean Jordan's decomposing body was found around noon that day. Two allotment holders, a Mr Morrissey and 23-year-old Bruce Jones (who would later play Les Battersby in the long-running soap opera, *Coronation Street*), were helping a friend in the adjoining new allotments and went to get some discarded house bricks from the disused land. They had not initially noticed the body lying in the grass but on one of the return trips, Bruce Jones' wheelbarrow ran over a part of the corpse and he noticed the naked woman lying on her back, her arms spread apart and in an advanced stage of decomposition. It was a sight that he later admitted would stay with him for the rest of his life.

Another allotment holder later found her green handbag which contained a new £5 note.

Sutcliffe: 'I read about the body being found and sat back waiting for the inevitable as I had assumed that the line of enquiry about the £5 note would follow. I read about the note being traced to a Shipley bank. I knew Clarks got the wage money from a Shipley bank and that a local enquiry would be made and by some miracle I escaped the dragnet.

Sutcliffe – employed by T. & W.H. Clark (Holdings) Limited in Bradford, one of the firms that could have received the note – was visited at home by detective constables Edwin Howard and Leslie Smith at 7.45 pm on 2 November. He said he had been at home the night of the murder, a month earlier, and had gone to bed around 11.30 pm. Sonia confirmed his story. When questioned about the second date, when the killer had returned to the body, Sutcliffe had an apparently solid alibi – he and his wife had been having a housewarming party.

Detectives did not probe his alibis harder. Had they done, they would have discovered that the excuses did not account for all his movements on the days in question. But police were overwhelmed with information in an increasingly desperate, sprawling investigation. 'Not connected', was the conclusion drawn in regard to the Jean Jordan murder.

Sir Michael: 'The £5 note was the "key". This was the reason Sutcliffe went back to the body several days after he killed her. That £5 note was traced to the Midland Bank at Shipley, West Yorkshire. The police are to be congratulated on their most careful endeavours made to try to trace where this £5 note had gone. In fact Sutcliffe was one of those interviewed, and although he agreed he had been paid, he said this note was not one he had been given. Some 6,000 people were interviewed, and any one of them could have had it, but all 6,000 denied it. That inquiry took something over 27,000 hours of police time. A most important lead if you could have proved to whom it went.'

Marilyn Moore

Marilyn Moore was the next victim; she was 25 years old and had been working as a sex worker for six years. The attack occurred on 14 December 1977. Marilyn survived and would provide a very accurate description of her attacker.

Marilyn Moore had been conducting business on the small side street of Gipton Avenue, which lies just of the main Roundhay Road in the red-light district of Leeds.

Sutcliffe: 'I went to Leeds one evening in December 1977 to try again. This is where I found Marylyn Moore. I drove into the red-light district at Chapeltown. I was driving along a street I now know as Leopold Street, where I saw her walking along along Spencer Place, from the phone boxes at the end. I saw her reject a man in a car who had stopped and she carried on. I turned left into Spencer Place, turned first left and left again into a narrow street and stopped near the corner of the road I had just been on. It was my intention to get her into my car with the minimum of fuss. I knew she had refused to get in one car so I got out of my car and walked to the corner. She was only a few yards away walking towards where I was stood. I walked back to my car and as she came into view I shouted "Bye now", and "Take care", and I waived towards the houses on my left. I did this to give her reassurance that I was alright. I got in and started the engine and opened the passenger window. I asked her if she was doing business. She glanced at the house said "yes" and got in.'

Agreeing on a price of £5, they were on their way to a quiet place she knew behind Brown's Mill on Buslingthorpe Lane in the Scott Hall area of Leeds. In the car, Sutcliffe said that his name was Dave. Marilyn now directed him to turn into narrow dirt track called Stonegate Lane, which ran down behind the back of the old mill. It was a notorious spot for sex workers and their clients.

Sutcliffe: 'I parked up. I suggested she got into the back of the car. She agreed and she got out and she went to the rear passenger door nearside. When she got out I got out with my hammer which I had on the floor at my side. I went round the front of my car and up behind her. I took a swing at her with the hammer but I slipped on the mud and lost my balance. I only caught her a glancing blow on the head.'

She screamed but Sutcliffe managed to regain balance and hit her harder with a second blow, which felled her. Still conscious, she covered her head as hammer blows rained down, hitting her hands and wrists. She grabbed his legs and continued to scream as all the while Sutcliffe hit her – but suddenly, he stopped.

Sutcliffe: 'I saw some people walking along about 40 yards away on the narrow road at the top. I jumped in my car and started it up. I put my foot down but the back wheels started spinning and I couldn't drive off at first. When the car got a grip I slewed round to the right and I drove away with a lot of wheel spin. I drove straight home.'

When Marilyn regained consciousness, she staggered towards the road to get to a telephone and call for help. When she reached the road, a teenage couple saw her and one of them ran to phone for an ambulance. She was taken to Leeds General Infirmary for emergency surgery which included relieving pressure on her brain from a depressed fracture of her skull.

Sir Michael: 'She was suffering from seven to eight laceration wounds between one and four inches long on the side of the head and a 4-inch depressed fracture of the skull. This required fifty-six stitches. She also had severe bruising and several cuts on her hands from where she had tried to protect her head. After being operated on to release pressure on the brain, she told police her attacker was a white man about 28 years of age, 5ft 7 to 5ft 8ins tall, of stocky build with dark wavy hair, a medium-length, neatly trimmed beard and a "Jason King" moustache … Unfortunately, despite tremendous inquiries, Sutcliffe was not discovered.'

Yvonne Pearson

'The murder of prostitute, Yvonne Pearson, on Saturday, 21 January 1978, was somewhat of an ad-lib killing,' said Sir Michael. This murder, according to Sutcliffe, had not been planned but occurred on the spur of the moment.

Sir Michael told the jury that despite the killing taking place in January, her body wasn't found until 26 March 1978, when a man out walking discovered a decomposing arm protruding from beneath a discarded sofa on waste land, in Bradford. A comb was crudely placed between her thighs. Her head had been smashed into seventeen fragments with a walling hammer. Sutcliffe also admitted stuffing the filling from the decaying settee down her throat.

With her bleached blonde hair, 22-year-old Yvonne Pearson was described by those who knew her as someone who always made sure her makeup was perfect. With her lissom figure and page-boy style haircut, she had a passing resemblance to Joanna Lumley's character Purdy in *The New Avengers* TV series, and plenty of interest and custom came her way. She was based in Bradford, but had a habit of travelling to big cities across the country where she gained clientele from the wealthy business community. She was well-liked and well-known by most of the women on the game in Bradford.

In early January 1978, she was arrested for soliciting. She was due at Bradford Magistrate's Court to answer that charge on 26 January. One of the conditions of her bail was a curfew between the hours of 7 pm and 7 am. She had already been fined twice for soliciting and as this was her third arrest, a custodial sentence looked likely; so likely in fact that she had already arranged for a friend to look after her children should she be sent to prison.

On the evening of Saturday 21 January 1978, Yvonne left her two young daughters in the care of her 16-year-old neighbour, Selma Turley, and went out for the night. As she left her home at 4 Woodbury Road, Heaton, she dressed in a black polo neck jumper, black trousers, green and black wavy striped woollen jacket with wide sleeves, and black shoes.

She drank in several of the pubs in the area and was later seen, for the last time, leaving the Flying Dutchman pub on lamb lane around 9.30 pm.

Sutcliffe: 'I was driving along Lumb Lane in my red Corsair from the city centre. A light grey or fawn Mark II Cortina started backing out of Southfield Square [a side street just off Lumb lane] on my left as I approached, so I slowed down to let it out. That's when I saw Yvonne Pearson; she was blond and was wearing dark trousers. On reflection it was a very fateful moment for her, me just slowing down as she came along. She stepped straight up to the car as I stopped and tapped on the window. She asked me if I wanted business. This was one time when I was genuinely going home as it happened, but I still had a hammer in the car on the floor, under my seat. I told her to get in. She suggested that I turn the car round and she told me where to drive. I drove back along Lumb Lane past Drummond Mill, turned right down a road onto White Abbey Road and I was directed to turn by Yvonne left into a street behind Silvios Bakery.'

Arthington Street was a derelict area with a tract of wasteland used as a rubbish dump and an unauthorised children's playground, and flanked by a bakery and a motor mechanics' garage. It was one of several short dead-end roads that ran at right angles to the main B6144 road, Whetley Hill. On either side was rough waste ground, created by the demolition of a row of terraced houses several years before. Towards the far end was a large open space covered in long grass. To the back was a steep bank and, closer to Arthington Street, there were piles of burned rubbish and discarded household items, including a broken sofa. The dark waste ground was a favoured spot for sex workers.

Sutcliffe: 'I asked her how much she wanted. She said "It depends on how much you can afford. A good time £5, more than a good time £10." She had very few words to say after that, the last words she said was "Shall we get into the back?" We both got out and she went round to the back door of the car on the nearside; she tried to open it but it was locked. I opened the front passenger door reached in and opened the rear door catch. As she opened the door I hit her from behind twice on the head with the hammer. She fell down and started to moan loudly. I dragged her by the feet on her back about 20 yards or so to where there was an old settee lying on its back on some spare land. When I got her to the settee she was still moaning loudly.'

Almost immediately, another car appeared and pulled in alongside Sutcliffe's car. He quickly ducked down behind the sofa and hid from view. But Yvonne was still moaning loudly.

Sutcliffe: 'To stop her moaning I took some filling from the settee. I held her nose and shoved the straw into her mouth, then I shoved it down her throat. I was kneeling behind the settee hiding from the motor car keeping hold of her nose. I let go after a while to see if she was still making a nose through her nose, but when I did she started again so I took hold of her nose again. The car seemed to be there for ages before it drove away. I stayed still petrified with fear while the car was there.

'When the car had gone I was seething with rage. Her jeans were nearly off because she had undone them at the car and when I was pulling her by the feet I nearly pulled them off. I pulled her jeans right off. I think I kicked her hard to the head and body. I was senseless with rage and I was kicking away furiously at her.'

Sir Michael held nothing back from the jury as he went through the medical reports, explaining how Sutcliffe had used the wall hammer again resulting in Yvonne's skull being smashed into seventeen pieces on one side and four on the other. He kicked and jumped down on her bare chest with the weight of both feet, fracturing her ribs and damaging the internal organs. Such was the violence shown to the body that the pathologist, who would later carry out the autopsy, initially thought Yvonne had been involved in a road collision.

As one reporter later stated:

The evidence although presented in a clinical and matter of fact manner would seem to lessen the horror and pity one feels for the victims, but it doesn't. Listening to the senseless catalogue of killing, even read out in the plummy, unemotional tones of Sir Michael havers, makes me shudder. For two hours while he read Sutcliffe's confession, unbelievable brutality was piled upon brutality, it was difficult not to be sick.

Author's Note: again we have an incident where Sutcliffe is seething with rage, along with an absence of what occurred prior to Yvonne getting out to go into the back of the car. By Sutcliffe's own admission her jeans were already unbuttoned by this point. Had there been another failed attempt at sex which left him humiliated?

Sir Michael: 'Obviously this was a chance killing. You will notice that on this occasion there were no messages from God, or maybe was God just telling him to kill at any opportunity? ... or was he doing this intentionally despite the fact that this was his first off the cuff attack? ... from the moment that car arrived, do you think he behaved yet again in a cool collected way, making sure he was silencing her so that she could not call out?'

Sutcliffe: 'After this I remember acting very strangely, I talked to her and apologised for what I had done but she was dead. I put the settee on top of her. I was very distraught and I was in tears when I left her. This was the first time I had apologised to someone I had killed ... I remember stopping on the way home and I just sat in the car trying to work out why I had done this killing my mind was in a turmoil.'

Sir Michael told the jury that it would be a further two days before Yvonne was finally reported missing and although there was concern for her safety, some officers felt she may have fled the area to avoid the certainty of a jail term with the court case looming. The police conducted a search in some known red-light areas and places frequented by Yvonne but no new information could be found to explain her disappearance.

Elena Rytka

Sir Michael: 'Before Yvonne Pearson's body was discovered Peter Sutcliffe had already moved and killed again committing a murder on Tuesday 31 January 1978. This time his victim was 18-year-old Helen [Elena] Rytka and he later told the police, "the urge inside me to kill girls was now practically unendurable".'

This time Sutcliffe set his sights on Huddersfield. Its red-light district wasn't as well known to Sutcliffe as Leeds and Bradford. However, the area around Great Northern Street where the sex workers plied their trade was on Sutcliffe's delivery route for work.

In early January 1978, two new faces appeared on the Huddersfield prostitution circuit: 18-year-old twin sisters, Rita and Elena Rytka (who was

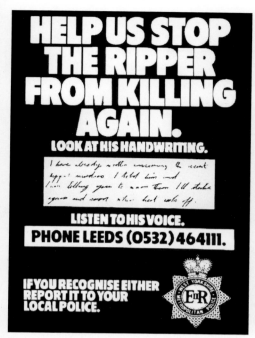

Public campaign advert to help track down the Ripper.

Information stall set up in the Kirkgate centre, Bradford.

Between 1975 and 1981, 13 women were brutally murdered by the Ripper.

Peter and Sonia Sutcliffe pictured at their home in Garden Lane, Bradford.

Peter Sutcliffe aged 12 at Cottingley Manor School and aged 23 when he was arrested for going equipped for burglary in 1969.

Peter Sutcliffe, pictured around 1976 in the cab of his lorry at the Bradford engineering firm TW Clark.

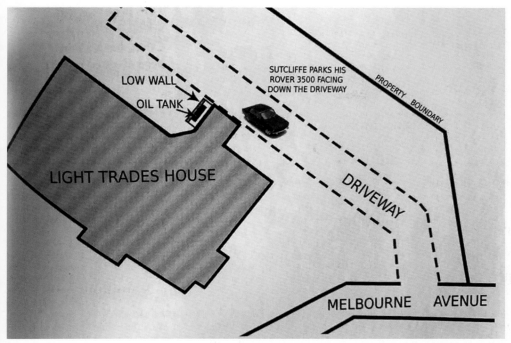

Diagram showing where Sutcliffe's car was parked at the time of his arrest in the grounds of Trades House, Sheffield.

The brown Rover 3500, owned by Sutcliffe from June 1979 until his arrest in January 1981.

On the night of his arrest, Sutcliffe first attempted to pick up Denise Hall (right). After being turned down, he moved on to pick up Olivia Reivers (left).

Peter Sutcliffe at the time of his arrest. Aged 35.

Author at the driveway where the Yorkshire Ripper's reign of terror came to an end on 2nd January 1981.

Hammerton Road police station.

Arresting officers, Sergeant Robert Ring (left) and Police Constable Robert Hydes (Right) became overnight celebrities following the arrest of Peter Sutcliffe.

Newspapers from all across the United Kingdom and the wider world, rejoice at the Ripper's capture.

Officers keeping guard outside the front of the Sutcliffe family home at 6 Garden Lane, Bradford.

Crime scene investigators examining the rear of 6 Garden Lane.

A Jubilant George Oldfield (left), Chief Constable Ronald Gregory (centre) and Jim Hobson (right) smile for the cameras at a celebration style press conference.

Crowds gather at Dewsbury town hall to catch a glimpse of the Yorkshire Ripper.

Head covered in a blanket, Peter Sutcliffe is escorted into Dewsbury magistrates to be charged with murder.

The Yorkshire Ripper peers out to the crowds as he makes his way to his trial in London.

The prison van carrying Peter Sutcliffe sweeps in through the gates of the Old Bailey court, London.

Angry mobs of protestors arrive to greet Sutcliffe.

Many people came from all over the country in the hopes of gaining a seat in the public benches to watch the Ripper trial.

Chief Superintendent Jim Hobson arriving at the Old Bailey on the opening day of the Ripper trial.

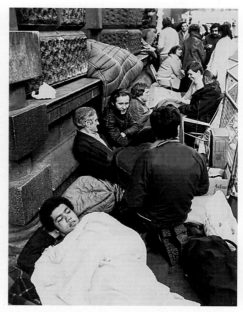

Some members of the public had camped out all night to obtain one of the public gallery seats.

Lead prosecution council, Sir Michael Havers.

Overseeing the entire Yorkshire Ripper trial.
Judge, Leslie Kenneth Edward Boreham.

Court room sketch depicting the court proceedings as they occurred.

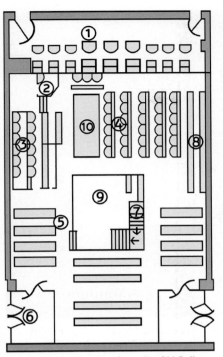

Layout plan of court room number 1 of the Old Bailey.

Plan of Court Number One, the Old Bailey.

1. Judge's chair
2. Witness box
3. Jury box
4. Counsel's rows
5. Press benches
6. Main entrance
7. Staircase from cells below
8. Seating for victims, family, Police observers
9. The Dock
10. Exhibits table

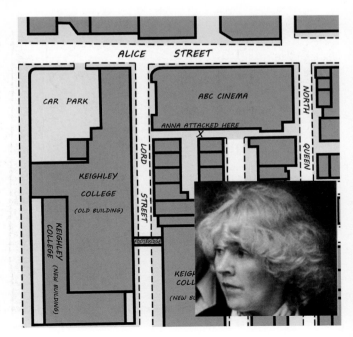

Crime Scene diagram of where Anna Rogulskyj was attacked in July 1975, Keighley.

Crime scene location image of where Olive Smelt was attacked in August 1975, Halifax, including her husband Harry, showing reporters where she was found.

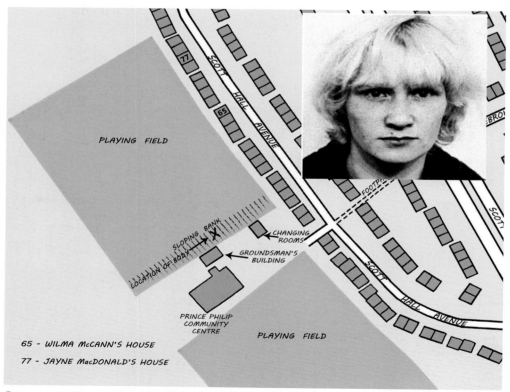

Crime scene diagram showing where the body of Wilma McCann (murder victim number 1) was discovered in October 1975, Leeds.

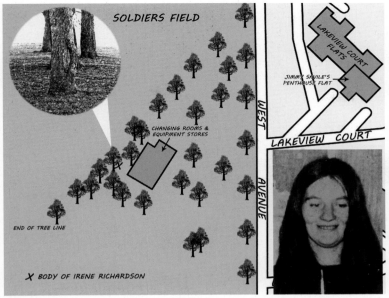

Crime scene diagram showing where the body of Irene Richardson (murder victim number 3) was discovered in February 1977, Leeds. TV presenter Jimmy Saville was one of the people questioned as he lived only 100 yards from the murder site.

SOLDIERS FIELD

CHANGING ROOMS & EQUIPMENT STORES

END OF TREE LINE

X BODY OF IRENE RICHARDSON

WEST AVENUE

LAKEVIEW COURT

LAKEVIEW COURT FLATS

JIMMY SAVILE'S PENTHOUSE FLAT

WASTE GROUND

MOUNT STREET

BIRKSHALL LANE

LAY-BY

MAUREEN ATTACKED HERE X

BIRKLANDS INDUSTRIAL ESTATE

WASTE GROUND

LANE

BACK

PARRY LANE

BOWLING

TANKS & DRUMS LIMITED

Crime scene diagram showing the waste ground in Bradford, where Maureen Long was attacked and left for dead by the Ripper in July 1977.

Crime scene diagram showing where the body of Jean Jordan (murder victim number 6) was discovered in October 1977, Manchester.

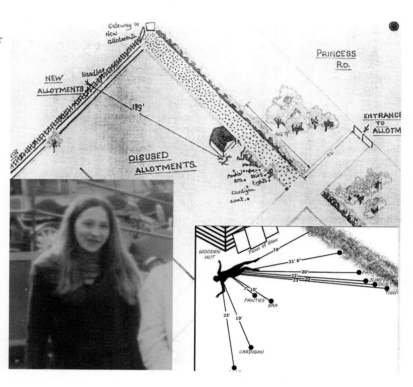

A vital clue. Discovered in Jean Jordan's handbag was a brand new £5 note, given to her by her killer. Serial number AW51 121565.

The hacksaw used by Peter Sutcliffe in an attempt to remove the head from Manchester victim, Jean Jordan.

Sonia Sutcliffe leaving the Old Bailey under police protection. She was not permitted to stay in case she may have been called as a witness.

Olivia Reivers arriving to give evidence at the Ripper trial.

The downstairs window of 6 Garden Lane boarded up following an arson attempt.

A handcuffed Peter Sutcliffe leaving court following another day of testimony.

The Sutcliffe house at Garden Lane became a grim tourist attraction during the trial and continues to do so at the time of writing.

The derelict flats of Oak Avenue Bradford (2020) Patricia Atkinson (murder victim number 4) was murdered in her room, in April 1977. Landlord, Jack Robinson was photographed outside the window to her bed-sit on the day she was found murdered.

Crime Scene diagram showing where Yvonne Pearson (murder victim number 7) was killed on waste ground in Bradford, January 1978. Her body was hidden under a sofa and wouldn't be discovered for a further 2 months.

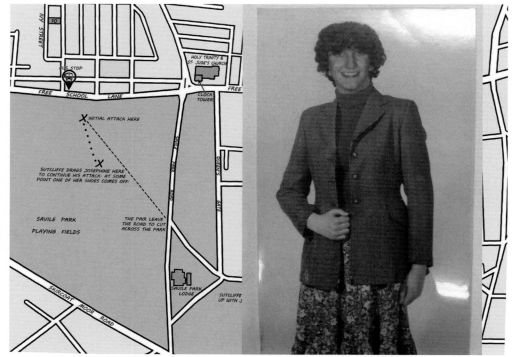

Crime scene diagram showing where Josephine Whitaker (murder victim number 10) was discovered in April 1979, Halifax.

Artist impression, at the time, of Peter Sutcliffe giving evidence in the dock.

The only known photograph in existence of Peter Sutcliffe in court room number 1 of the Old Bailey as he is lead down to the cells below the court room.

This rare photograph of Peter Sutcliffe was taken by a freelance photographer from Germany who managed fly back home before he could be prosecuted for illegally photographing inside the Old Bailey.

A young Peter Sutcliffe in his years as a grave digger in Bingley cemetery.

The grave of Bronislaw Zapolski, where Sutcliffe claimed to have heard the voice of God whilst working in Bingley cemetery.

Dr Hugo Milne arriving at the Old Bailey to give evidence.

Sonia Sutcliffe leaving the Old Bailey on the final day of the trial, she was allowed to return once it was clear her testimony wouldn't be needed.

Ripper survivor Anna Rogulskyj leaving the Old Bailey following the verdict.

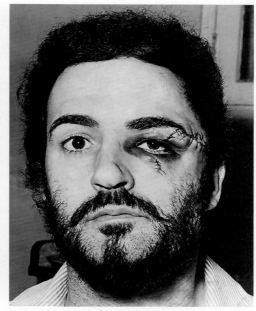

Peter Sutcliffe showing off his scars following a stabbing attack whilst in prison.

Nab Wood crematorium, near Bingley, West Yorkshire.

The garden of remembrance at Nab Wood, Bingley. The last resting place of Peter Sutcliffe?

known as Helen). Originally from Leopold Street in Chapeltown, Leeds, Rita and Helen's mother was Polish and their father West Indian; they had not had a pleasant upbringing and most of their lives had been spent in a succession of children's homes.

They had moved to Bradford and had a flat together in Granville Road, Frizinghall five minutes from the red-light district of Manningham, but with the mounting Ripper investigation and the ever-increasing police presence, it was becoming more and more difficult. Rita opted to go to Huddersfield in November and Helen followed in December.

At 8.30pm on Tuesday, 31 January 1978, Rita and Helen Rytka left their flat and took the short walk down to the viaduct archways of Great Northern Street. Within forty minutes Rita had seen her sister off with a client in a dark coloured vehicle, Rita then took a client driving a Datsun. She would never see her sister alive again.

Sutcliffe: 'The urge inside me to kill girls was now practically uncontrollable. I drove to Huddersfield in my red Corsair one evening. When I got to the red-light area I came across one or two girls walking round the street. I stopped and asked one girl if she was doing business. She said yes, but I'd have to wait as her regular client was picking her up at any minute. She was a half-caste girl. I drove off and after going about 50 yards round the corner I saw another half-caste girl. I stopped and asked her and she got in. She told me she shared a flat with her sister but she was quite willing to have sex in the car. She said it would cost £5. She told me where to drive which was only about 80–90 yards away in a timber yard. I drove straight into this yard and parked in it.'

The timber yard was located in Lower Viaduct Street, a dark seedy lane lined with deserted railway arches. It was the rear yard of Garrards Timber on the corner of Great Northern Street. The sprawling maze of wood was ideal for sex workers and their clients to conduct their business between the rows of sawn timber stacked 8–10ft tall.

Sutcliffe: 'She undid my trousers and seemed prepared to start sexual intercourse right away in the front of the car. It was very awkward for me to find a way to get her out of the car. For about five minutes I was trying to decide which method to use to kill her. She was beginning to arouse me sexually. I got out of the car with the excuse that I needed to urinate and managed to persuade her to get out of the car so that we could have sex in the back. As she was getting in I realised that this was my chance, but the hammer caught on the edge of the car door frame and only gave her a light tap. She said, "There is no need for that, you don't even have to pay." I expected her to immediately shout for help. She was obviously scared and said, "What was that?" I said, "Just a small sample of one of these," and hit her on the head hard. She just crumbled making a loud moaning noise.

'I realised that what I had done was in full view of two taxi drivers who had appeared and were talking nearby. I dragged her by the hair to the end of the wood yard. She stopped moaning but was not dead. Her eyes were open and she held up her hands to ward off blows. I jumped on top of her and covered her mouth with my hand. It seemed like an eternity and she was still struggling. I told her that if she kept quiet, she would be all right. As she had got me aroused a moment previous, I had no alternative but to go ahead with the act of sex as the only means of keeping her quiet. It didn't take long. She kept staring at me. She just lay there limp and didn't put much into it.'

The taxi drivers left and Sutcliffe retrieved his hammer. Helen Rytka staggered to her feet and towards his car.

Sutcliffe: This was when I hit her heavy blows to the back of the head. I dragged her to the front of the car and threw her belongings over the wall. She was obviously still alive. I took a knife from the car and stabbed her several times through the heart and lungs. I think it was a kitchen knife which I believe the police later retrieved from my home.'

The medical evidence showed he had in fact hit her a further four times. In all she suffered six lacerated wounds to the head; one in the centre of the forehead, three to the right side and two to the back. After producing an 8-inch knife that he had taken from his kitchen, he stabbed her in the chest. Although initially there appeared to be three stab wounds in the chest area, it was apparent at the autopsy that he had thrust his knife through the same two wounds at least thirteen times, piercing the heart, lungs, aorta, liver and stomach.

Sutcliffe now decided to hide the body.

Sutcliffe: 'I dragged her by the arms to where I thought she would not be discovered which was behind some bushes in a gap between a woodpile and a wall. There wasn't much room I had to part lift, part pull her in. I stayed in the wood yard for some minutes and when I looked the taxi drivers had gone. I reversed out of the yard and drove off.'

Sir Michael informed the jury that Sutcliffe told police that he had pulled Miss Rytka a few yards away and covered her body with sheets of asbestos or corrugated metal. Sir Michael then asked the jury: 'if it was Gods will, did it matter when the body was found?...a great deal of time had been spent hiding some of the bodies.'

Helen's sister Rita had returned to the designated meeting spot by the toilets. She stayed for a while in the cold waiting for her sister, but when it became obvious she wasn't coming, she headed back to their flat in Highfields, thinking she may have taken a client back there. It would be a further three days before Rita overcame her fear of the police and reported her sister missing. 'Being a prostitute, this immediately caused a wide search.' Sir Michael told the jury.

At 3pm on Friday, 3 February, a police dog handler arrived at Garrards Timber and was greeted by foreman Melvyn Clelland who informed the officer about the some blood on the ground that had been discovered a couple of days before.

Within ten minutes, the dog had picked up the scent and discovered the body of Helen Rytka. She had been wedged into a narrow 18-inch gap behind a pile of timber and a disused garage, next to the steep railway embankment.

Vera Millward

On 8.15 am, Wednesday, 17 May 1978, two yellow work vans belonging to a Rochdale landscaping firm, arrived in the grounds of Manchester Royal Infirmary. A team of six gardeners, hired to maintain the grass and flowerbeds, parked in the corner of a bricked compound near the junction of April Street and Livingstone Street, close to the private wing of the infirmary. As he exited the van, Jim McGuigan, one of the gardeners, noticed what looked like a discarded doll or mannequin lying against the wire fence acting as a temporary barrier where part of the wall had collapsed; as he drew closer however, he recoiled with horror. The 'doll' was a slightly built woman, whose head had been smashed in and whose body had been mutilated by stab wounds.

Vera Millward was born in Madrid during the Spanish Civil War and brought up during the lean years of the Second World War; Vera Evelyn Millward arrived in Britain during the 1950s as a domestic servant. She married soon after and went on to have five children. By the 1960s, when the youngest child was 15, her husband had died and the children under the age of 18 were taken into care. In desperation, Vera turned to prostitution – gravitating to the seedier areas of Hulme and Moss Side in Manchester's notorious red-light district. The 40-year-old went under the aliases of Anne Brown and Mary Barton. Despite this, she did not avoid the long arm of the law and by the time of her death, had racked up several convictions for soliciting.

By 1978 she was living with her common-law husband, a 49-year-old Jamaican by the name of Cy Burkett, in a ground-floor flat in Grenham Avenue, Hulme – not far from the home of Ripper victim Jean Jordan. The couple had two children, a boy aged 6 and a girl aged 8. In constant pain from a stomach ailment and weighing less than 8½ stone, Vera's face was prematurely lined with suffering. She had only one lung and had undergone three operations in 1976, 1977 and May 1978. A desperately ill woman, she ignored police warnings and, for the sake of her children, regularly joined the 400 sex workers who made their living on the streets in Manchester, loathing every minute of what she was forced to do for money. It was common knowledge that the women who worked the back streets and alleyways around Moss Lane and Denmark Road in Moss Side would take their clients to one of two discreet places. It was either a patch of ground next to the Southern Cemetery and allotments, where Jean Jordan was murdered, or a section of waste ground near the grass and flowerbeds of the car park at Manchester's Royal infirmary. Both afforded the women and their clients privacy from public eyes. On Tuesday, 16 May, Vera left her home at around 10.00 pm, telling Cy that she was going out to buy some cigarettes and pop to the chemist to buy some drugs for her stomach pains. Knowing what she really meant, he did not expect to see her for a few hours. The truth was that on Tuesdays and Thursdays she had a regular client who would park outside her flat and flash his headlights. This man was well-to-do and drove a 1963 maroon Mercedes. For about five years he had been meeting Vera every week – 'Just for a chat', he would later tell police – and would give her small gifts of food and money. Popping into the local shop, she bought two packets of Benson and Hedges and went to wait on the corner of the street for her regular. That particular Tuesday, however, he didn't turn up. Vera decided to hang around for other business.

Sutcliffe: 'When I got there, there was no sign of any girls, so after reaching a nightclub on a corner in a small labyrinth of terraced houses about three-quarter-mile square, I took the third left after the nightclub, which was a long street running from one end to the other of this area. I drove down to the bottom end and there I saw a woman obviously waiting to be picked up … I stopped and asked her if she was doing business. She said yes, but it would have to be in the car. The price was £5. She got in and I drove off.'

They made their way along Upper Brook Street, took a right onto Hathersage Road and another right which took them into Livingstone Street and the grounds of the Royal Infirmary. It was a familiar route used by many of the sex workers. As they approached the junction of April Street, there was an opening in the wire mesh fence which formed the perimeter of a section of waste ground that was used as a car park, just behind the private patients' wing. He drove through the gap, took a sharp right then reversed the car until his bonnet was pointing towards the exit, ready for a quick getaway.

Sutcliffe: 'I parked up the car and suggested to her that it would be better in the back. I don't think I'd payed her. She got out of my car and went to the back door. I picked my hammer up from under the seat and walked round the back of the car. As she was opening the rear door I hit her on the head with the hammer and she dived backwards past where I was stood. She was on her hands and knees when I hit her again at least once. She fell flat on her face. I pulled her by her wrists over to the edge of the area where there was either a fence or bushes. I took out my knife I was carrying, I think it may have been the same one I used on Rytka but I'm not sure. I pulled her clothes up and slashed her stomach either vertical or diagonal. It opened up her stomach. Then I rolled her over onto her stomach and left her lying there. I drove away. I think I had to reverse out to get back again.

Following Millward, the compulsion inside me seemed to lay dormant but eventually the feeling came welling up and each time they were more random and indiscriminate. I now realised I had the urge to kill any woman.'

When Vera was found the next morning, she was lying on her right side, face down, arms folded beneath her, and her legs were straight. Her face was covered by a large paper sheet. Like the murder of Irene Richardson, her blue and brown reversible checked coat had been draped over her body and now covered her from knees to neck. Her blue canvas wedge-heeled shoes had been placed neatly on her body. The heavy hammer blows to the skull created three savage wounds and caused many fractures, including a laceration of the brain. Vera's blue cardigan, floral-patterned, yellow, sleeveless dress and underskirt had been raised to expose the abdomen and she had been slashed so viciously across the stomach several times that her intestines had spilled out of the wounds and onto the ground. Her white bra was still in place, and she been stabbed in the chest repeatedly, cutting through to her ribs and penetrating the left lung, liver and stomach. The weapon had been thrust into the wound three times in different directions without being withdrawn completely. A similar multiple wound was located on her back; her right eyelid had been punctured and the eye bruised.

Josephine Whitaker

The 19-year-old Halifax Building Society clerk had left her home at 10 Ivy Street, only 250 yards from Savile Park, where she lived with her mother, Avril Hiley, stepfather Hayden Hiley and two younger brothers, David and Michael. She took a fifteen-minute walk to visit her grandparents, Tom and Mary Priestley, at their home at 294 Huddersfield Road. She was eager to show them a new silver cocktail watch for which she had just paid £60 from a mail order firm. When she arrived, she found her grandfather watching TV, but her grandmother was out at a church function. Jo waited patiently with her grandfather and after her grandmother returned home and she showed her the watch she said she'd walk back home. Her grandparents were reluctant to let her walk back in the dark and offered her a bed for the night, but Jo refused. She had to get home, she said, because she was wearing her contact lenses and wanted to clean them before putting them away in their special case. The case in question was sitting on her bedside table at home. Tom Priestley had been suffering from a chest complaint, so when he offered to walk Jo home she declined the offer, knowing that his condition would be aggravated by the walk. Besides, she was a healthy girl, 5ft 8in tall, and was not afraid of the dark – and this was Halifax, which was not part of the Ripper territory. She left around 11.40 pm and started on the route that would take her across Savile Park. Although her parents had always advised her to stick to the longer route along well-lit Main Street, she opted for the short cut, walking across the park's dark sports' pitches towards Free School Lane and the suburb of Bell Hall, Halifax, and then onto Ivy Street. It was a route she was familiar with and it would slice a few minutes off her journey.

Meanwhile Sutcliffe, who was circling the park in his car, caught a glimpse of Jo making her way home. She was wearing a skirt, with a multi-coloured pattern on a black background and white lace trimming, a pink jumper, a light brown checked hacking jacket and brown heeled shoes.

Sutcliffe: 'I saw Josephine Whitaker walking up this street. She was wearing a ¾ length skirt and a jacket. I parked up in this street with terraced houses and started to follow her on foot and I caught up with her after a couple of minutes. I realised she was not a prostitute but at that time I wasn't bothered I just wanted to kill a woman.'

Unlike with Jayne MacDonald he didn't strike her right away, but started a conversation. He asked her if she had far to go and she said, 'It's quite a walk.' The pair continued along the road and all the while Sutcliffe waited for his moment to strike. His short height and high, weedy voice had probably reassured Jo and she started to converse with him. She told him she'd just left her grandparents' house and that she had considered staying there but had decided to walk home. As they talked, she and Sutcliffe made their way along the street that bordered the park where they were spotted by a man out walking his dog.

Sutcliffe: 'She said she normally took a short cut across the field. I said you don't know who you can trust these days. It sounds a bit evil now, there was I walking along with my hammer and a big Phillips screwdriver in my pocket ready to do the inevitable. We both started to walk diagonally across the grass field, we were still talking when we were about 30–40 yards from the main road I asked her what time it was on the clock tower which was to our right. She looked at the clock and told me what time it was. I forget the time she said. I said to her she must have good eyesight and I lagged behind her pretending to look at the clock. I took my hammer out of my pocket and hit her on the back of the head twice, she fell down and she made a loud groaning sound.'

He looked round and spotted a figure in the near distance walking along the main road. The man, who had been walking home, would later claim to have 'heard a strange noise, a wail, the sort that makes your hair stand on end'. Sadly, despite hearing this noise more than once, he continued on his way, oblivious to the fact the Yorkshire Ripper was committing another murder less than 30 yards away.

Sutcliffe took hold of Jo by the ankles and dragged her face down away from the road and further into the park. When he thought it was a safe distance from the road, he stopped. Then he heard voices from somewhere behind him to his left. At least two people were walking along the path across the park towards Huddersfield Road. Jo was still moaning loudly. To shut her up, Sutcliffe pulled out the sharpened screwdriver, pulled some of her clothing off and, in a frenzy, stabbed her repeatedly in the chest and stomach. There were twenty-one stab wounds to her torso, with further multiple stab wounds to her back and six wounds to her right leg. He also stabbed her several times in the vagina, with some of the thrusts showing clear signs of reinsertion through the same wound. This had been carefully and methodically done, in the dark, with almost no injury to the external parts of the vagina. When he'd finished, he left her face down in the wet grass and doubled back the way he had come, back to his car, and made a quick getaway to Bradford. It would be a further five hours before anyone in the Bell Hall suburb would learn about the murder on their doorstep.

Barbara Leach

Barbara Janine Leach – 'Babs' to her student friends – was a 20-year-old studying for a Bachelor of Arts degree at the university. Two years earlier she had left her parents, David and Beryl Leach, in Kettering, where her father worked for Barclays Bank. They lived in a modest pre-war, semi-detached house close to the two schools Barbara attended growing up: Henry Gotch School and Southfield Girls' School. Her mother worked in the local telephone exchange until she took a higher education course and became a teacher. The extra income helped put Barbara and her brother Graham, who was two years older, through school and university. With her A levels in English and Religious Education, Barbara had a choice of several universities available to her and decided to study Social Sciences at Bradford University. She told her family she wanted to mix with 'real people'. She was a bright, lively and outward-looking young woman with a wide circle of friends; she enjoyed pop and classical music, horse riding, reading and growing indoor plants. She threw herself into university social life, which took up almost all of her time. She shared a big house, which had been divided up into flats, with six other students – four men and two women.

It was a warm evening on 1 September 1979, when she set off with three friends to walk round the corner of the terrace to their favourite pub, The Mannville Arms, at 31–33 Great Horton Road. Here Barbara and her flatmates, 20-year-old Lynn Johnson, 21-year-old Paul Smith and another 21-year-old called Walter, enjoyed a lively night over a few pints before finally leaving together at 1.00 am. The group debated about whether to go for Indian food in one of the many nearby restaurants that normally stayed open until 2.00 am, but then decided to call it a night and go home. Despite the mist-like drizzle that had started, at the corner of Grove Terrace Barbara announced to Paul Smith that she was 'just going for a little stroll'. She said she didn't have her front door key and asked him if he would wait up for her. 'I shan't be long,' she said. She bade her friends goodnight and strolled off up Great Horton Road.

On that fateful Saturday night, Sutcliffe had been cruising the streets in his dark brown Rover 3.5, registration plate FHY 400K. Presumably mindful of the police presence in his normal haunts of Lumb Lane and Manningham, he moved over to the West End of the city to try his luck there. He had spotted Barbara Leach walking up the left-hand side of Great Horton Road, just up from the Mannville Arms and opposite the entrance to the university. He drove ahead of her and turned right into Ash Grove, parking a few doors away from Number 13. He was about to exit the car when he saw Barbara turn the corner and walk towards him. He waited until she passed before he got out and followed her. In his hand, he had a ball-pein hammer and in his pocket was the large screwdriver that he had carefully fashioned into a point; it was the same fiendish weapon he had used on Josephine Whitaker five months earlier in Halifax, leaving a distinctive 'Y' mark instead of the usual 'X' crosshead mark. As she reached the front of Number 13, he swung the hammer down onto her head causing a large laceration. Barbara collapsed in a heap, moaning loudly.

This all took place in full view of the living room window of 16 Ash Grove, where the engineering students were holding a party. Sutcliffe had either not noticed the open window or not cared. He took hold of her wrists and dragged her up the driveway of Number 13 and round to the right side of the house, through the narrow walkway and into the bin area at the rear. She was still moaning as he pushed up her shirt and bra and undid her jeans, partly pulling them down to expose her crotch and stabbed her repeatedly with the screwdriver. In total, there were seven stab wounds in her trunk, four in her chest and three round her navel. The weapon had been reintroduced to the same wound in the chest fifteen to thirty times, just as he had done with Jean Jordan, Yvonne Pearson and Helen Rytka; when he was finished, he moved the metal bins out of their place between the house and the low brick wall and put Barbara's body there instead. He took some time to manoeuvre it into a distorted jack knife position to make sure it was concealed in the small gap. Before leaving he dragged over a discarded carpet, probably left in the overgrown alleyway, and draped it over her body, weighting it down at the edges with stones from the garden wall. Exiting via the front driveway of 13 Ash Grove, he got back in his car and drove straight home. Later he would dispose of the screwdriver by throwing it over the embankment on the westbound side of Hartshead Moor services on the M62 near Bradford.

Barbara's body was discovered during a police search by PC Simon Greaves on the Monday morning, following her housemate's reports of her not coming home.

Following his description of the Leach murder, Sir Michael then explained to the court that Sutcliffe's original confession had skipped out Marguerite Walls, Dr Bandara or Theresa Sykes, a short description of their attack is mentioned in the first chapter of this book.

Jackie Hill

Jacqueline 'Jackie' Hill was to be the final victim in the Yorkshire Ripper murders. She was a young and gifted third-year student. Those that knew her say she was gentle and caring, a selfless person who was loving towards others; a genuine good Samaritan who had planned to devote her life to the community but never got the chance. She had high hopes of becoming a probation officer after leaving Leeds University. When she wasn't in Leeds studying, Jackie taught children at Sunday school at the family's local village church, where later she would be buried. On the night of her murder she decided to put in extra study time by journeying into Leeds city centre to attend a seminar in Cookridge Street for probation officers. It would normally take forty minutes to walk to her student residence in Alma Road, but as it was wet that night, Jackie decided to take the Number 1 bus from Beeston to Holt Park. This would drop her off opposite the front of the Arndale Centre. From there it was only a two-minute walk to Lupton Flats.

Arriving in Otley Road just before 9.00 pm, Sutcliffe parked his car and bought some Kentucky Fried Chicken from the outlet attached to the Arndale Centre. He returned to the car a short while later and ate his meal while scanning the street ahead for passers-by. At 9.23 pm, the green and white Holt Park bus pulled up in front of him and Sutcliffe watched as five people disembarked, going off in different directions. One of them was Jackie Hill. He watched her cross over by the lights and go in the direction of Alma Road. Sensing his opportunity, Sutcliffe fired up the ignition, drove up past the bus stop and turned right into Alma Road. As he did so, he overtook Jackie who had just turned the corner, and stopped about 40ft in front of her on the left-hand side of the street. He sat and waited for her to draw level with the car, a ball-pein hammer in his hand. Within a minute Jackie passed the car. Sutcliffe jumped out and quickly crossed over to the other side of the road to position himself behind her. As she passed by the opening of the waste ground next to the Arndale Centre, he struck her on the back of her head and, like so many of his victims, she crumpled to the floor. He bent down to drag her off the path and into the undergrowth, but he had only got her half way in when a car turned onto Alma Road and drove towards him. He ducked down and, amazingly, the occupants of the vehicle failed to see him – or if they did see him, they failed to comprehend exactly what was going on. After the car had gone, Jackie began to move and moan. Sutcliffe bent down and hit her again with the hammer, then he picked her up into a standing position, grabbed her under her armpits and dragged her into the waste ground. Sutcliffe had managed to move the body a full 30 yards into the undergrowth and was now hidden by trees and shrubs, just below the car park ramp of the Arndale Centre. He began stripping off Jackie's clothes and tossing them aside. He pushed her bra up and her knickers down before producing a yellow-handled screwdriver from his pocket and thrusting it repeatedly into her chest and lungs. As he did so he stared at her face and noticed her open eyes staring back at him. This angered him for some reason and he stabbed the screwdriver into her eye, piercing part of her brain. When he was finished he left her lying on her back with her head pointing towards the car park ramp, legs spread open and feet pointing towards the entrance to the waste ground. He draped Jackie's checked coat partially over her body. After leaving the scene he got back into his car and made a U-turn before driving back down to Otley Road. As he got to the bottom, a passer-by signalled to him that he was going the wrong way on a one-way street. He ignored the man and drove on.

After he had listed all the murders and attacks, Sir Michael paused a while to let the jury reflect on every word he had said. He casually walked over to his table then turned to address the jury once more.

Sir Michael: 'All this finally ended on the night of January 2 this year. [referring to the night that South Yorkshire police officers, PC Robert Hydes and Sergeant Robert Ring, were on routine patrol in Sheffield] The area they were in was regularly used by prostitutes … They saw a Rover parked without its lights on. They decided to investigate and found both the defendant and "a well-known prostitute" sitting in the car. A further investigation at the scene uncovered that the licence plates were false and belonged to a Skoda. The man and the woman were both arrested and transferred to Hammerton Road police station.

'It was a routine procedure which at first sight gave no indication there was about to be an end to a five year reign of terror, which became the largest , most expensive and most protracted manhunt in British criminal history.'

Chapter 5

'This Is Ripper Country'

'He pulled a sock out of his pocket. There was brick or a stone inside it and he wound down the window and threw the stone out. I think he said he had hit the women over the head with it'

Trevor Birdsall

On 7 May 1981 among the crowds of onlookers and those queuing up hoping to grab seat in the public gallery, another much noisier group had descended upon the Old Bailey.

A crowd of women from the protest group 'The English Collective of Prostitutes' had descended upon the Old Bailey. Among the thirty placard-waving demonstrators, many of whom were sex workers, was the former MP Maureen Colquhoun.

Voicing her outrage she declared:

The Attorney General almost gave the impression that prostitutes deaths did not matter, he said of the Ripper's victims, that some were prostitutes but perhaps the saddest part of this case is that some were not. The last six attacks were on totally respectable women. We are demanding that Sir Michael Havers apologise to relatives of the Ripper's prostitute victims.

This was echoed by the leader of the English Collective group, Anne Neale, but she went further to also attack the police for their part in the whole sorry affair. Standing on the steps of the Old Bailey she said: 'The Ripper said his mission was to clean the streets of prostitutes – the same aim as many police forces in this country. It was only when non-prostitutes began to die did they decide to hunt this man. Until then, they did not care.'

The protest, understandably, made the evening news but West Yorkshire Police were quick to hit back with a statement clarifying that 'as much effort is put into the murder of a prostitute as any other murder enquiry'.

Meanwhile inside Courtroom Number One, Peter Sutcliffe was about to come face to face with his onetime best friend Trevor Birdsall, a man who actually named him twice as a likely suspect in the Yorkshire Ripper murders.

But before proceedings could officially begin, Mr Justice Boreham made a statement to the court. He announced he was immediately excluding from the room, all journalists from the German Magazine *Quick*. He went onto say that it had come to his attention that the editor of the magazine had 'printed a picture of Sutcliffe standing in the dock'.

Photographs are forbidden from inside British courts but it appeared a mini-camera was smuggled into the press benches behind the dock and had been used to snatch shots of Peter Sutcliffe as he was escorted out by prison officers at the end of the other day's proceedings. It was later established that the image was captured by freelance crime journalist Mr Armin Zipzer. Lucky for Mr Zipzer he had recently returned to Germany and thus escaped prosecution.

It was the first published photo of the Old Bailey court proceedings in sixty-nine years. The only time it happened previously was a photo published in 1912 showing the convicted poisoner Oliver Seddon being sentenced to death.

Mr Justice Boreham made it known that 'the act was totally contrary to long standing British traditions'. He went on to say legal proceedings on the matter would follow shortly and that from now on all journalists would be searched thoroughly before being allowed entry to the court.

Author's Note: This story grew even more spicier when it was revealed that the London editor of the magazine, who later had to stand before the bench to receive a legal rebuke, was Lady Gowrie, the 37-year-old wife of Lord Gowrie, minister of state and department of employment. She would later announce her resignation.

Once the matter of the illegal photographs had been dealt with, Mr Justice Boreham instructed Sir Harry Ognall to continue proceedings.

Trevor Birdsall, an unemployed van driver, from Bingley, entered the witness box as Sutcliffe stared at him from across the dock flanked by warders. But Birdsall did not once look at the man who had been his mate for last fifteen years.

Ognall opened up the questions by asking Birdsall if he had been paid for his story by any newspapers. He admitted he had been paid £500 plus £65 expenses from the *Sunday People* newspaper.

Mr Justice Boreham, still upset at the revelations surrounding the illegal court photo, abruptly interrupted Mr Ognall to address Trevor Birdsall personally. He said:

You are here to give evidence, whatever arrangement you may have made with anyone else. Your duty here is to give evidence to the best of your ability. Whatever has gone on in the past, from this moment on, you will not discuss your evidence with anybody else, whether from a newspaper or from any other source. If you break that injunction then my powers are very wide and immediate.

Ognall asked Birdsall to explain his relationship with Peter Sutcliffe. Birdsall told the jury that he had met Sutcliffe in 1966 at the age of 18 and came closest to witnessing first-hand the beginning of Sutcliffe's reign of terror,

Author's note: In the course of the day Trevor Birdsall would be the first of three drinking companions who would give evidence against Sutcliffe. He was also one of three witnesses that had been paid off by the press. Others included Ron Barker and Olivia Reivers, between them they have been promised £5,600 by TV and press. Eventually this would lead to a public outcry which in turn coined the phrase, chequebook journalism.

Sutcliffe's friendship with Birdsall had blossomed by 1969 and they were regular drinking partners. On the nights when he did not see Sonia, Sutcliffe would call at Birdsall's home in his car and they would go out to Bradford, Keighley, Halifax, even as far as Manchester or York on occasions.

After questioning him about his early life and friendship with Peter Sutcliffe, Ognall now wanted to probe deeper, and in particular the nights that the pair were out and about in Bradford. These outings took place between 1967 and 1969.

This caused great distress to Birdsall; as he stood in the witness box, he turned pale and began shaking, so much so it appeared he was about to collapse.

Sir Michael Havers stood up and stopped Ognall mid-sentence, obviously noticing Birdsall was struggling, and said 'If you do not feel well then say so, this is not a torture chamber.' A glass of water was put into his shaking hand before an usher sat him on a chair.

Author's Note: Trevor Birdsall's nervousness was quite understandable. He would be present in some of Sutcliffe's early attacks on women, yet remained strangely silent when the whole world was later asking what kind of man the police could be looking for. It probably crossed his mind, when faced with the reality of being in a courtroom, that perhaps some blame for the murders might come his way.

Slowly he began to describe one particular night in the red-light district of Bradford shortly after his 21st birthday in September 1969.

He told how he and Sutcliffe had been driving along Manningham Lane in Birdsall's Mini, when Sutcliffe suddenly ordered him to stop his car at the junction of Manningham Lane and St Pauls Road. 'He then quickly got out and up a side street.' Said Birdsall.

About twenty minutes later, Sutcliffe 'suddenly reappeared fairly quickly. He looked a bit excited and was not breathing normally. It looked as if he had possibly been running.'

Ognall asked whether Mr Sutcliffe had said anything.

Birdsall: 'He just told me to drive off. I asked him where he had been and he said he had followed a woman to her house somewhere. I think he said he had hit her. Pete said she had screamed and I asked if she was alright. He said, "Of course she is, the old cow. I just wanted the money." He pulled a sock out of his pocket. There was brick or a stone inside it and he wound down the window and threw the stone out. I think he said he had hit the women over the head with it'

Ognall: 'Did you get any impression as to what sort of woman he had followed?'

Birdsall: 'I would imagine the lady was a prostitute – but that was just my guess – because of the area.'

Author's Note: It's unknown if her screams had scared Sutcliffe away, or perhaps attracted others who chased him from the scene, but he didn't stick around for long. Surprisingly, someone managed to take a note of Birdsall's registration plate as the pair drove off. This could have been the woman he attacked or perhaps someone who had given chase following the assault.

A few days later, two police officers knocked on Birdsall's door and he promptly gave them Sutcliffe's details and address at 57 Cornwall Road, Bingley. Sutcliffe admitted hitting the woman but failed to reveal he used the makeshift cosh as a weapon, instead saying he hit her with his hand. Luckily for Sutcliffe, the woman probably did not want to draw attention to her lifestyle so she did not press charges.

Author's Note: Her identity, remains unknown to this day.

Birdsall then spoke of another time in 1969 when he and Sutcliffe had been out in the Otley Road area of Bradford.

Birdsall: 'Peter had spotted a woman looking drunk staggering up the street. He said he was going to go talk to her and got out – crossed over and disappeared. He was away twenty minutes. Later, when he returned, he said he had been talking to her and that her husband or boyfriend had beaten her up and thrown her out. He then said he had taken her to a derelict building and made love to her.'

Sir Michael asked Birdsall if Peter ever spoke about prostitutes in his company.

Birdsall: 'He'd comment if he saw a particular young woman with big knockers on'

He also said that although he had never actually seen his friend go with any prostitutes, Sutcliffe had told him he had been with prostitutes more than once. He also mentioned that sometimes he did not pay.

Birdsall was then asked about the night 51-year-old Olive Smelt was attacked in the Boothtown Road area of Halifax on 15 August 1975.

As he spoke of the incident Mrs Smelt sat listening at the back of the court.

Birdsall: 'We went out to Halifax in Peter's car and went to a few pubs. We probably saw about half a dozen or so unattached women. I remember Peter leaning across and chatting to them. I think Peter had remarked that it was a prostitute pub … on the way home we passed through Boothtown. Peter stopped, then stopped the car and got out and said he was going to speak to somebody. I didn't notice if he had anything with him but I did notice he seemed to put his hand down the side of the seat. I remember seeing a woman. She was walking very quickly. Peter went round the back of the car and disappeared. He didn't seem to be going in the same direction. He was away for about ten to twenty minutes, I was getting impatient. When he returned he said he was talking to someone but was quiet, unusually quiet.'

Interestingly, Birdsall told the court that Sutcliffe then told him roughly the same story as he had in 1969, when he followed a drunk woman on the Otley Road in Bradford.

'He said he had went to comfort a woman who had an argument with her boyfriend and then had sex with her.'

The next evening Birdsall read in the *Telegraph & Argus* a report about a brutal attack on a woman in Boothtown. At first it never crossed his mind that Sutcliffe had committed the attack because 'it seemed contrary to his nature', but over the next few days the more he thought about it, the more he was concerned because Sutcliffe had been away from him in the area of Boothtown in Halifax at the time. 'It then crossed my mind that Peter might be connected with it.'

Mr Ognall now moved onto the hoax tapes and letters that were sent to the police during the manhunt. He asked Birdsall if he had heard the tape recording.

Birdsall: 'Yes, I think I heard it.'

Ognall: 'Did you think, after hearing that tape, that there might be a connection with what Mr Sutcliffe did [in 1969] and the attempted murder of Olive Smelt? What effect did it have on you?'

Birdsall said he kept his suspicions to himself but confessed that when he then heard the hoax tape playing on the radio it eased his mind because Peter clearly didn't have a Wearside accent.

Birdsall: 'I thought there was no chance at all that it could be him. It destroyed the link.'

Ognall: 'At the back end of last year, in late November, you went to the police and gave them certain information which had been in your possession for a long time and had done nothing about.'

Birdsall then told the jury how his suspicions came back following the murder of Jackie Hill and that descriptions of a dark Rover car seen in the area matched Sutcliffe's. He had only recently been out drinking with Sutcliffe in the exact same car.

Birdsall: 'The paper gave a description of the car thought to have been used by the murderer – a dark Rover saloon. I thought it was possible it was the same as Peter's car. I sent an anonymous note to police on 25 November last year. I was worried more about it, and very shortly after that I went to see the police myself.'

Trevor Birdsall's letter was then read out in court.

> 25 November 1980
> To whom it may concern
> I am writing to inform you that I have very good reason to believe I know the man you are looking for in the 'Ripper Case'.
>   It is an incident which happened in the last five years. I cannot give any date, or place, or details without myself being known to the Ripper and you if this is the man.
>   It is only recently that something came to my notice and a lot of things fit into place. I can only tell you one or two things that fit for example.
>   This man has always had dealings with prostitutes and always had a thing about them. Also he is a long distance lorry driver, collecting engineering items etc. I am quite sure if you look up on dates etc., you may find something.
>   His name is Peter Sutcliffe, 5 Garden Lane, Heaton Bradford.
>   Clark trans. Shipley

He said Sutcliffe had never shown any hostility towards prostitutes.

James Chadwin for the defence addressed the court and explained that in Sutcliffe's confessions to the police he had deliberately left out the attack on Olive Smelt because he was protecting his friend.

Chadwin read out a line from the confession which said, 'I have been hanging back on that one. There was somebody else involved. Have you had an anonymous letter? I think the person I was with sent one.' Chadwin also pointed out that Sutcliffe had later confirmed to the police that Birdsall had nothing to do with the attack and had sat in the car the whole time during the attack.

Birdsall was now asked about Sutcliffe's attitudes towards prostitutes. Birdsall stated that in all the time that he had known Sutcliffe he had never indicated a hatred for prostitutes.

Chadwin then asked him whether he actually believed the stories told by Sutcliffe about going with prostitutes.

Birdsall: 'I don't know whether it was true or whether he was showing off. I half did and I have didn't.'

Chadwin asked about Sutcliffe's manner following the Olive Smelt attack. He wanted to know if Sutcliffe was calm and collected or showed any signs of aggression or frustration. He also asked Birdsall whether, in all the time he had known Sutcliffe, he had ever seen any signs which would point to him being a sadistic and cruel killer?

Birdsall said that Sutcliffe was a very quiet individual. He had always been very quiet and calm ever since he'd known him. As for the Olive Smelt attack, he said: 'for someone who had, only moments before, apparently struck a woman on the head, he was not agitated or concerned.'

Turning to the £5 note that was found with the body of Manchester victim Jean Jordan in 1977, and subsequently traced to a payroll batch in West Yorkshire, Chadwin wanted to know if Birdsall had ever discussed this with Sutcliffe. Birdsall said that Sutcliffe had told him he was one of the employees interviewed by police but didn't seem worried about it at all. 'He appeared surprisingly unworried about the incident and exceptionally clam about the whole thing.'

Birdsall finished his testimony by telling the court, 'I now know Peter has admitted what happened in the last five years, but I still find it difficult to fit that in with the man I have known for so long, a rather quiet, unaggressive person.'

As Trevor Birdsall left the witness box the next of Sutcliffe's companions was being ushered into the court.

Insurance agent Ronald Barker lived next door to Sonia Sutcliffe's parents in Clayton, Bradford. He and his brother David had known Peter and Sonia before they were married in August 1975 and had spent many nights out drinking with Peter, usually when Sonia was working or babysitting.

The trial had come at a very inconvenient time for Ronald Barker as he was standing for local elections as a Liberal candidate in Bradford's number seven district. It became even more inconvenient when he had to now reveal in court that he and his mother had both been paid £700 by the press for several wedding photographs of Peter and Sonia. He would later claim that the taking of 'Blood Money' destroyed his political hopes.

The most interesting aspect of Ron Barkers testimony is the revelation that he kept a diary. Several of these diaries dating between 1975 and 1980 were brought into court. They provide an intriguing insight into Sutcliffe's fascination with prostitution and possible planning of the attacks.

Sir Michael asked Mr Barker to look at his diary for 28 May 1977, and to tell the jury about a trip to York. He said he remembered making the trip with his brother, David, and Sutcliffe.

Ronald Barker: 'It was Saturday night and we wanted to go to York, I remember Peter wanted to go to Manchester but it was too far, we had already dropped Sonia off at her part time job. We called at several pubs in York, and while playing pool Peter disappeared. We were a bit annoyed, because we didn't know how to get back. But at closing time, we walked back to the car and Peter was standing near it. It was about three quarters of an hour since we last saw him and he told us he had followed a lass out of the pub. I can't remember him saying anything else.'

Mr Barker said he expected to be taken back home to Bradford, but he and his brother had fallen asleep in the car. With Sutcliffe at the wheel, the three of them set off towards home.

Ronald Barker: 'when I woke up, we were in Chapeltown, Leeds. It was not necessary to pass this way and I may have asked what we were doing there. Peter was just driving around [the streets] and I think he said something about this being 'Ripper Country'. The car stopped at Chapeltown, and Peter got out. He didn't say where he was going and we didn't ask him. He walked off and was away fifteen to twenty minutes. When he returned he never said where he had been. He just drove back to Bradford.'

Mr Barker then consulted his diary for Saturday 25 June 1977 – the night that 16-year-old Jayne MacDonald was attacked and murdered. He said he and his brother went to three or four pubs in Bradford with Peter.

Ronald Barker: 'I think Peter drank three or four bottles of brown ale. We left about closing time.'

He was asked if Sutcliffe appeared to be under the influence of drink.

Ronald Barker: 'I had never seen him [Sutcliffe] under the influence before. He always appeared quite normal to me. We went for fish and chips and then he dropped me and my brother at the end of our street. It was about 1.30 am.'

Author's Note: This is extremely significant, if Sutcliffe had dropped the Barker brothers off at 1.30 am he must have immediately driven to Leeds. It's a forty minute drive to Reginald Terrace, which only gave him a five or ten minute window to see and attack Jayne Macdonald at 2.15 am. The window is so tight he would, theoretically, have had the Barker brothers as a good alibi. At other times he may have parked up and left the car with both the brothers still asleep. If, under the influence of alcohol, they didn't wake up until they finally got to Bradford, then he would have had a seemingly perfect alibi.

Ronald Barker also told the court of other trips through red-light districts with Sutcliffe after they had drinking sessions together.

Ronald Barker: 'I always wanted to go home, but Peter always wanted to go around the red-light districts, these trips would last around half an hour. Peter never said why he wanted to go, it happened three or four times in 1977. He once stopped in the King's Road area of Bradford, got out of the car and went for a walk. He later said he had followed a girl back towards her flat.'

Author's Note: Could this be linked to the later murder of Patricia Atkinson in her flat, at 9 Oak Avenue, in April 1977? Oak Avenue to the junction of Kings Road is only an eight minute walk.

On 9 July 1977, the date Maureen long was attacked, Mr Barker said he, his brother and Sutcliffe had gone to Halifax in Sutcliffe's car for a night of drinking. It was a similar night, with Sutcliffe drinking a few bottles of brown ale. They all grabbed some fish and chips before Sutcliffe left the brothers back at their house. 'This was about 11.30 pm or 12 midnight.'

Mr Ognall then asked Barker if he knew a nightclub called Tiffany's on Manningham Lane (the club where Maureen Long was drinking before she was attacked.) Barker said that he had been there several times with Sutcliffe. He also stated that Sutcliffe often boasted about girls he had been with.

Ronald Barker: 'He says he went with a nurse at one time, and about the time two girls followed him back to his car the previous night. He claimed he had one in the back and one over the bonnet. He told me that in 1977.'

Mr Ognall: 'What did he mean when he said, "Had one"?'

Ronald Barker: 'he meant intercourse.'

Author's Note: These boasts are in stark contrast to what we know from the confession statements and eye witness testimony (Olivia Reivers) regarding Sutcliffe's sexual inadequacies. These could suggest Sutcliffe had a massive ego which needed protecting and he would no doubt be at his most dangerous following a blow to his self-esteem. We have already seen evidence of this with the Wilma McCann murder and will later hear from Sutcliffe himself when he describes the night he was cheated out of money by a prostitute.

Barker said Sutcliffe had never shown any aggression towards women and admitted he was astonished when he heard what he was being accused of. 'With all the publicity given to the Ripper attacks it never once crossed my mind that Peter was responsible.'

Barker admitted that Sutcliffe had once stopped at some traffic lights in the red-light district and shouted to a couple of women across the street. He said 'How much?' before speeding off. Barker said that Sutcliffe had only said this in jest and it was all very light hearted.

Chadwin then focused on the payments he had received from the press. Barker said that the week after Sutcliffe's arrest the *Sun* newspaper had contacted him about photographs of Peter and Sonia Sutcliffe's wedding. He then learned of the 'massive amounts' that were being offered for photographs.

Chadwin asked him if this was why he had decided to contact the press in the first place. In answer to that Barker said that he had assumed there would be some obvious interest from the press about his account of how Sutcliffe had got out of his car in Chapeltown.

Chadwin: 'You see, Mr Barker, I put it to you that, although the car may have passed somewhere near Chapeltown on its way through Leeds, that car did not stop and Peter Sutcliffe did not get out of it.'

Ronald Barker: 'You can suggest what you like. I have said what happened.'

Chadwin: 'You entertain some hope or expectation that there may be some more money available to you if your story is published in the press?'

Ronald Barker: 'Yes'

Chadwin: 'You must be very glad you kept your diaries?'

Ronald Barker: 'I gave one to the *Sun* newspaper. The one for 1977.'

Mr Justice Boreham then interrupted Chadwin to question Barker himself. 'You mean to say a newspaper man asked to see your diaries and took one away?'

Ronald Barker: 'Yes, but it was returned eleven days later.'

Sir Michael: 'My Lord, it is my understanding that the Sun newspaper drew the attention of this diary to the police.'

While Ronald was giving his evidence before the court, his brother David was waiting outside in the main hall, accompanied by two police officers. David had been given a special day release from prison as he was serving an eighteen-month sentence for grievous bodily harm. He was to be the next witness in the box.

David Barker told the same story as his brother Ronald. He talked of times he and Sutcliffe went out drinking and then drove round the red-light areas in the early hours of the morning. He spoke of trips to Halifax and pubs such as the Bull Ring or the Continental club. He also admitted that he had received £20 from ITN Television and £10 from the BBC on 23 March 1981.

Asked what Sutcliffe had said about the pubs they visited David replied, 'I was told this is where the prostitutes hung out.' Asked by Mr Ognall what business he and Sutcliffe wanted with prostitutes in the area he said, 'we wanted to go just for a laugh'.

Ognall: 'Did Sonia Sutcliffe ever know where you and her husband went to on your nights out?'

David told the jury that Sutcliffe used to tell Sonia that they were going to play snooker. He also said these nights out occurred when Sonia was either babysitting, or when she worked nights as a nursing auxiliary. Often the three men would drop Sonia off at work before going out.

When Sir Michael asked him if he or Sutcliffe had ever used the services of prostitutes on these nights out, David replied that Sutcliffe had admitted showing interest in prostitutes but denied they had ever picked any up. He would also add that at no time could he remember Sutcliffe being mocking or insulting towards prostitutes.

When further questioned, David confirmed it was all Sutcliffe's idea to go to the red-light districts in the first place. 'I had no idea what he thought about them [prostitutes] but he appeared to know his way around Chapeltown.'

He also recalled Sutcliffe insisting on going to Manchester in 1977. When asked by Mr Ognall why this was, he said Sutcliffe claimed he wanted to go somewhere different and they started the evening drinking at a pub by Victoria Station and then three different pubs spent at random. David also confirmed that other trips included Halifax, York, Bradford, Wakefield and Bingley.

It was now time to call another witness and this particular witness would provide crucial information on the night the Yorkshire Ripper was finally captured. The witness was Olivia Reivers and, if not for incredible luck, she would have been the fourteenth victim to be murdered by Sutcliffe.

Nervously, Miss Reivers stepped into the witness box. She had come over a bit faint just prior to her appearance and had to be given a stiff sniff of police smelling salts before entering the stand just 20ft from where Sutcliffe sat. As she grasped the smelling salts in her hands she whispered her story.

She was 24 years-old, from Birmingham and of Jamaican descent. She had moved to Sheffield seven years prior and had been working the red-light district for the last four years. She was the mother of two children and had a live-in boyfriend named Joe. They seemed to have an arrangement when it came to her night-time activities, although he much preferred her to have regular clients instead of risking the danger of strangers on the street.

Once she had given a brief description of her background, Sir Michael Havers stood up and stated that he wanted to clear a few things up before Miss Reivers could continue with her testimony. He asked her if she had received any money from the newspapers for her story.

Reivers: 'yes the *Daily Star* gave me £1,000 but I had to pay my solicitor £300 out of that.'

Sir Michael: '[have you] signed an exclusive contract with the paper and expecting more money?'

Reivers: 'Yes, there is another £3,000 to come.'

Sir Michael Havers sat back down and allowed Mr Ognall to continue.

Miss Reivers was now invited to recall events four months previous, in particular, the night of 2 January that year.

She told the jury that at 7.00 pm that night, she had made the short journey from her house in Wade Street, Sheffield, over to pick up a fellow sex worker, 19-year-old Denise Hall, who lived in Brunswick Street. Together the pair worked a similar patch in the Hanover Square area of Sheffield.

Reivers: 'It was almost 9.00 pm when I stood [in Broomhall Street] chatting for a while with another girl, Christine, who is also on the game. There seemed to be a lot more police around than usual. I found out later this was because there was likely to be trouble between two groups of West Indians. Then this little twerp stopped his car beside me.'

Unknown to Reivers at the time, Sutcliffe had already attempted to pick up her friend Denise, who was working around the corner in Hanover Square. Denise had declined.

Reivers: 'I don't know why Denise was suspicious, but she turned him down, obviously something must have warned her off. You might think you can judge people's characters by looking at them, but I can't look at a person and decide what sort they are.'

Author's Note: Denise hall would later tell the press that there was something about him that put her off. His eyes were dark, almost black and appeared to pierce through her own. This had frightened her and she said 'sorry no' then walked away from him.

Sir Ognall asked Miss Reivers if she, or Denise Hall, had been worried, or at least more cautious, because of the Yorkshire Ripper murders.

Reivers: 'We were all worried about the Ripper but no one knew what he looked like, so we wouldn't have known him if we saw him. Anyway you can't afford to turn down the chance of £10 in this game.'

Mr Ognall asked her to continue recalling the events of 2 January 1981.

Reivers: 'The driver asked me if I was doing business and I said I was. I told him it was £10 in the car with a rubber. He said that it was OK. I got into the front seat and he had dark curly hair, dark beard and moustache. He asked me where to go and I directed him to Melbourne Avenue a few minutes away. It was one of my regular places, a well-known place for prostitutes. I thought about going to a place behind Jessop Hospital [n the Brook Hill area of Sheffield] which is really quiet and only a few people know about it. Looking back I think I would have been a gonner if we went there because no police would have clocked us.'

Sutcliffe drove up Broomhall Road. Here Olivia directed him up Park Lane and then left onto Glossop Street. A further left and they were now in Melbourne Avenue.

The avenue was situated in the up-market residential area of Broomhill and contained large stone Victorian and Georgian properties with large shaded driveways. Most of these houses had been converted into office premises. At number 3 there sat a large three-storey Victorian property with a long sweeping driveway that curled round to the back of the building.

Reivers: 'I told him there may be other prostitutes there [in the driveway of number 3], when we got there. I told him to drive straight inside but he went past it and then reversed back.'

Mr Ognall asked her if this was unusual to her. Reivers said she had been to the offices more than a dozen times before, but on no other occasion had anyone backed in.

Ognall: 'You may think that the reason for this was to make a quick getaway, if he had to.'

Sutcliffe drove in through the gates but instead of going all the way up and around the back of the building, he swung the car to the right so he was now pointing towards the gate entrance and his back bumper drew level with the doorway of the house. This was probably because another car was occupying the space further up the driveway.

Once Sutcliffe had parked up and turned the light off, the other car, parked further up the driveway turned its lights on and went past them, leaving them alone. Miss Reivers explained that she recognised the other girl in the car as it drove past. She told Sutcliffe she had spotted her.

She then asked Sutcliffe for payment.

Reivers: 'He gave me a £10 note and I took a rubber out and had it in my hand putting the money into the packet. He asked "Do you mind if I talk to you a bit?" I said: "No", I asked him if he was married and he said yes. He spoke about his wife quite a lot, he seemed worried about her.'

He then told her he had a row with his wife. The argument with his wife included 'not being able to go with her'. She took that to mean the couple were having sexual problems.

Reivers: 'He asked me my name and I said "Sharron". He said his name was "Dave". He then took off his car-coat and put it on the back seat. He asked me if I would like to get into the back, I said "no it's alright". He said he might not be able to do it because of the dashboard, I said it would be ok and that I would manage.'

Mr Ognall then asked her if she felt more comfortable performing intercourse in the front seat and Miss Reivers agreed.

Reivers: 'I've had experience in having intercourse in the front of a car. I told him about a previous client that night. I told him I had a very fat bloke who smelt. He was a taxi driver.'

Unclasping her hands Miss Reivers then demonstrated how she had removed her knickers and how Sutcliffe had then moved towards her.

Reivers: 'He was supporting himself with one hand on the gear lever and one on the back of my seat.'

As Olivia Reivers gave her evidence she never once looked at her would-be killer, who sat just 20ft away in the dock. It was probably just as well as it was fairly clear to everyone in the courtroom that Sutcliffe was certainly staring intently at her. His gaze fixed but totally expressionless.

She said she had tried for about fifteen minutes to get Sutcliffe to have sex with her.

Reivers: 'I tried to arouse him but he was cold as ice; he didn't respond at all. He was very nervous. I sensed it. I said "there's nothing to worry about, why are you frightened?"'

Asked what had happened after fifteen minutes of trying, Miss Reivers explained, 'I said I don't think we will be able to do it and he said "it looks like it" He got off from across me and went to sit down in his seat.'

She then said that Sutcliffe once again suggested getting into the back seat and trying again, but Olivia wisely refused, preferring to stay where she was.

Author's Note: It was a wise move as Sutcliffe would no doubt have used the locked door method on her as he had done previously on Vera Millward, Marilyn Moore and Yvonne Pearson. He already had the ball-pein hammer lodged down the side of his seat, along with a knife he had taken from his kitchen drawer. The coat he had just placed in the back seat also contained another knife and the length of knotted rope he had used on Marguerite Walls and Dr Upadhya Bandara.

Reivers: 'It was then that I began to sense something was wrong. Drunks who don't measure up to it get angry with themselves, but this was the first guy I'd come across who couldn't manage it when he was stone cold sober. Then I noticed he became tense; frightened, like, though I don't know what of. For some reason which I still can't explain, I began to get nervous myself. He was showing no signs of wanting to drive off.

'The next thing that happened a car turned up and parked directly in front of us. It was difficult to see who it was at first because the windows [of Sutcliffe's Rover] were steamed up. I wiped and peered through the windscreen and saw it was the police.'

This was the moment Sergeant Ring and PC Hyde had arrived on the scene. Their routine patrol had spotted Sutcliffe's Rover parked up in the driveway.
Reivers: 'When I told him it was the police he said "leave it to me, you are my girlfriend", she then said, "he wound the window down and told the police it was his car and that his name was Peter Williams."'

Mr Ognall asked her if Sutcliffe had shown any emotion when he learnt it was the police parked in front of him.

Reivers: 'He appeared very frightened by the arrival of the police. I then heard the sound of the police sergeant using his radio and then the police said to him something about the plates being wrong for the car.'

Miss Reivers explained that both she and Sutcliffe were questioned in regards to their name, address and reason for being there, then both officers went back to their car, presumably to carry out further radio checks.

Reivers: [Sutcliffe turned to me and said] 'can't you make a run for it? And I said no I can't explaining that I was a well-known prostitute.'

Sergeant Ring and PC Hyde returned to Sutcliffe's Rover and asked both he and Miss Reivers to exit the car. Mr Ognall asked her if she saw how Sutcliffe reacted when they were both asked to get out of the car.

Reivers: 'No I didn't see anything, I only know he got out of the car, but he went across to where the oil bunker [tank] was.'

When asked if she saw anything of significance later on when they were both taken to Hammerton Road police station, she said Sutcliffe emptied his pockets and took a length of rope out of one of them. Sir Michael Havers stood up and went to the exhibits table and lifted up a piece of rope, it was about 2ft long, of the type used for washing lines. He then showed this to the jury and passed it around them for closer examination.

Miss Reivers then explained that she was released from custody in the early hours of the morning and heard nothing more until two days later when the police came to see her.

Reivers: 'The inspector looked me straight in the eye and said "you don't know how lucky you are, right now I could easily be in the morgue looking at your body on the slab."'

During the final questions she admitted she had first considered leaving Sheffield to get away from all the attention caused by the case.

Reivers: 'In a way it might have been better if I'd been killed, then I wouldn't have to face all the people staring at me in the street, and asking me questions. I've had so many letters and postcards from all over the world, even people writing to me to say I should join the church.'

She had decided to stay and had returned once again to working the streets, but remained extremely nervous.

Reivers: 'Believe it or not, I even get men asking if I'm the woman who was with the Yorkshire Ripper. It seems to give them some sort of thrill.'

Mr Ognall thanked Miss Reivers for her testimony and sat down. It was now turn for the defence to cross-examine, but there really wasn't much for Mr Chadwin to ask Miss Reivers about. He asked her to go to back over the night's events again to make sure everything matched up and then asked her if in the whole encounter Sutcliffe never achieved any sort of erection. She said that he hadn't.

Chadwin: 'So much so that after a quarter of an hour you told him he was not going to be able to and he agreed. Yes?'

Reivers: 'Yes.'

Chadwin: [Did Sutcliffe seem] bothered, annoyed or angry at not being able to sexually perform?

Reivers: 'It didn't seem to bother him very much, it didn't bother him at all.'

The witness testimony from Trevor Birdsall, Olivia Reivers and the Barker brothers was felt to be a significant piece of evidence for both the prosecution and the defence.

As far as the prosecution was concerned there was a now a clear pattern Sutcliffe's actions which showed his fascination with the red-light district, his aggressiveness in a previous attack on a sex worker in 1969 and, more importantly, his ability to differentiate between right and wrong by his clear attempt at hiding weapons behind the building in Melbourne Avenue.

The defence they felt they had shown that Sutcliffe had no sexual desires towards prostitutes at all. With his failure to be aroused and his calm demeanour shortly before and afterwards, they felt the evidence showed that far from being a cruel, sadistic killer or sexual deviant, he was, in fact, a quiet, calm man whose actions were totally out of character to all who knew him. Not quite the monster painted by the prosecution.

But one thing the day did reveal was the fact every witness seemed to be jumping on the bandwagon when it came to the press desire to pay money for a good story. It also raised the possibility that the testimonies may not be entirely accurate. As the public mood shifted against the press it was also revealed that members of Peter Sutcliffe's family were being paid even more to tell their stories about his early years and upbringing. One report showed that John Sutcliffe, Peter's father, had been paid £5,000 for his story. But even this was nothing compared to the story that the *Daily Mail* had struck an exclusive deal with Sonia Sutcliffe for the amount of £250,000.

Once this piece of information was leaked, Jack and Doreen Hill, the parents of murdered student Jackie Hill, wrote a strongly worded letter to Buckingham

Palace, proposing that new laws should be set up to stop the culture of 'chequebook journalism'. They asked for the Queen to intervene personally. They included in the letter that 'the money would be tainted by the blood of our daughter and other victims'.

In most cases the Queen will not get involved in political or legal matters, they are an issue for parliament and the MPs to discuss. In this case, however, I feel she certainly got the ball rolling, because within a week the Hill family had received a reply.

William Heseltine, private secretary to the Queen, wrote back on her behalf:

Her majesty can well understand about the proposal, if true, that the *Daily Mail* is planning to publish the story of the man accused of murdering your daughter, told by members of his family and paying them substantial sums of money to do so.

Although there is nothing illegal in what is being proposed and therefore no way in which Her Majesty could properly intervene, she certainly shares in the sense of distaste which right-minded people will undoubtedly feel.

The letter was published in several newspapers, forcing the editor of the *Daily Mail*, David English, to write personally to the Queen denying that any deal with Sonia Sutcliffe had been done. He claimed his newspaper was the victim of a sustained campaign of vilification, promoted by tabloid rivals.

His associate, Stephen Smith, was less apologetic when it came to paying for sensational stories. He said that all newspapers indulged in chequebook journalism, it's how they got the good stories in the first place. He went onto say the issue had only arisen because some money was paid to relatives of Peter Sutcliffe and the thought of them profiting from his crimes did not rest easy with the public. 'In this case we don't feel we have anything to be ashamed of – nothing to be ashamed of at all, but I understand that members of the public may not take such a sophisticated view as I do.'

In London, the newspapers were reporting that several of Ronald Gregory's officers from the Ripper Squad had been dancing the night away in several of the expensive London night clubs. Entertained by the press, they were being treated like celebrities – drinking free champagne and dining in some of the best restaurants in the city. One paper went as far as to suggest a female journalist had offered sexual favours in return for the possibility of an exclusive story. Ronald Gregory slapped a gagging order on all officers and everyone in the force was under no illusion that there was to be nothing but silence when it came to the media. But it was too late.

An explosive interview with a young officer had already made the papers. Detective Constable Andrew Laptew had been one of the investigating officers during the Ripper hunt and his interview would highlight the serious errors made during the five-year investigation, errors which lead directly to the deaths of three women.

He recalled how, on 29 July 1979, he and a fellow officer, DC Graham Greenwood, had visited Peter Sutcliffe's house in Garden Lane, Bradford. The reason for their visit was to question Sutcliffe about why his car had repeatedly been flagged up in the red-light districts.

It wasn't a question of just one red-light area; his car had been spotted thirty-six times in all three key areas of the investigation, Leeds, Bradford and Manchester.

Sutcliffe had been questioned before throughout the manhunt and his answers had always been readily accepted by the police. He said he drove through certain areas on his way to and from work; other times he claimed to be at home with his wife and because these questions were asked weeks or months following a murder, Sonia could not remember specific dates and unwittingly agreed with his story, providing an alibi for him.

However, this time his answers and demeanour did not allow him to avoid the suspicion of the officers and DC Andrew Laptew said, 'there was something not quite right about this man'. The first thing that stood out to Laptew was the likeness Sutcliffe had to the description given by Marilyn Moore. He would later recall: 'He had a striking resemblance to the photofit [created by] the woman who was attacked in Buslingthorpe Lane in Leeds. He had a gap in his teeth, which again was indicative of the attacker of two of the women who were killed.'

Sutcliffe was also the same height and build as the man described by two survivors; he had a beard, a 'Jason King' style moustache, collar-length black hair, dark complexion and smallish feet. He was also a lorry driver which, after the murder of Josephine Whitaker, was one of the suspected occupations of the Ripper.

Laptew said: 'He stuck in my mind. I was not ninety-nine per cent certain, but he was the best I had seen so far, and I had seen hundreds. The gap in his teeth struck me as significant. He fitted the frame and could not really be taken out of it.' Laptew would recall the coldness he felt from both Peter and Sonia when he used his tried-and-tested method of breaking the ice with couples he interviewed:

I was in the house with the Sutcliffes about an hour and a half. I remember Sutcliffe and his wife seemed to have no sense of humour. I looked at his wife and said now was a good time to get rid of her old man, meaning Sutcliffe, if she wanted to. Normally this would cause a laugh or a reaction from those I spoke to, but with them there was nothing. Just straight-faced and cold.

Sonia Sutcliffe would later express her own opinion on this conversation by saying: 'First of all, the term "old man" didn't appeal to me and secondly, because we didn't find his cheap joke amusing, it doesn't mean we were devoid of a sense of humour, it just wasn't very funny.'

When questioned about his car being seen in the Ripper hotspots, Sutcliffe claimed once again that the Bradford red-light sightings were on his route to and from work and the Leeds sightings were when he visited a nightclub with his wife. He had no good reason for being in Manchester so he denied having been there. This was a red flag to the detectives.

At one point in the questioning Sonia agreed to leave the room, giving the officers an opportunity to probe him further about his possible use of sex workers. Sutcliffe continued to deny he used prostitutes, saying that he had no need of such women since he hadn't been married very long.

The interview lasted for a full two hours but Sutcliffe was not taken into custody. There were several reasons for this: the officers did not know at the time that Sutcliffe had already been questioned about the Jean Jordan murder and that he was one of the employees who would have received that £5 note in their pay packet, and they also didn't know at the time that Sutcliffe had been arrested in 1969 in the red-light district armed with a hammer. The main reason, however, was that orders had been given that no one was to be arrested without first submitting a full report which had to be passed up the ladder to Dick Holland, who would review it before deciding whether or not to pass it on up to be given the green light by ACC George Oldfield himself. This process effectively prevented officers from apprehending suspects based on gut instinct.

All that Laptew and his colleague could do was take handwriting samples and perform a search of Sutcliffe's his car and garage. Finding nothing to connect him to the murders, they left empty handed, but were far from happy.

When he arrived back at the station, Laptew began to dig around for more information. He soon discovered that Sutcliffe could have been one of the employees to receive the £5 note in his pay packet and he also discovered, through the Regional Criminal Records Office, that Sutcliffe had been convicted for 'going equipped to steal' in 1969. Unfortunately, Laptew did not check with the Criminal Records Office at Scotland Yard, where there were two important and vital details – the burglary tool had been a hammer and Sutcliffe had also been arrested in the red-light district of Manningham

Lane. Laptew compiled a two-page report, detailing his and DC Greenwood's suspicions and noting the key points of interest:

A: The loose alibi

B: Sutcliffe's denial of having been to Manchester after a positive sighting of his vehicle

C: Sutcliffe's strong resemblance to the Marilyn Moore photofit (which they had previously been told to disregard since Moore was as an 'unreliable witness')

D: That he took size 8½ shoes (which was close to the size of prints found at the scene of the murder of Josephine Whitaker)

E: That Sutcliffe had a pronounced gap between his top front teeth

F: That for a man who was being interviewed in connection to a series of murders, Sutcliffe's attitude was almost too casual

Laptew made sure he took the report personally to Dick Holland, his superior officer and the superintendent in charge of the inquiry. What happened next beggar's belief. His report was dismissed instantly as the inquiry was now focused on the killer being from the North East. In a later TV interview Laptew would state that a quick check of Sutcliffe's handwriting showed it didn't match the letters sent from Sunderland and Dick Holland then asked: 'Has he got a Geordie accent?' 'No, he's local,' replied Laptew. 'He's from Bradford, and he's a dead ringer for the photofit.' Holland exploded into a rage. 'Photofits! If anybody mentions photofits to me again they will be doing traffic for the rest of their service.' Andrew Laptew was left feeling humiliated in front of all his colleagues and said later: 'I could have crawled under the crack in the door.'

Laptew's report was routinely marked 'to file' where it would languish with thousands of others in the massive backlog of reports not yet filed in the system, thus allowing Sutcliffe to escape yet again from further and more probing investigation. He would go on to kill a further three times.

One can only imagine the devastating impact this must have caused to the reputation of West Yorkshire Police once it appeared in the newspapers. Laptew was blacklisted by most of his colleagues and he suffered greatly for speaking out, but as more modern attitudes emerged in the years that followed there was a newfound respect for him among officers and historians; his comments were found to be fair words which highlighted the very real need for the authorities to rethink how investigations should be conducted.

Chapter 6

'I'm as normal as anyone'

'I am going to do a long time in prison, thirty years or more, unless I can convince people in here I am mad and maybe then ten years in a loony bin.'

Peter Sutcliffe

Monday 11 May, outside the Old Bailey the usual crowds had gathered once again, all hoping to gain a seat in the public gallery. One young man queued for twelve hours only to find, when he finally managed to get inside, that he couldn't hear a word of the proceedings. Rather annoyed about this he dared to stand up and shouted to prosecution counsel to speak up, before being told rather abruptly to sit down and be quiet by the court usher. The young man was hauled away before he could regain his seat. Others had a similar issue with the noise level and during the less interesting parts of the trial took to conversing with each other or reading newspapers. The judge would halt the trial several times during the day to address the lack of respect for the proceedings by some members of the public. Later, one officer would comment, 'It's like more Number One Court at Wimbledon than Number One Court at the Old Bailey.'

Another talking point was the fact that Sonia Sutcliffe had left London to return to Bradford. She was still supporting her husband, but over the weekend two unknown prowlers had smashed the windows of her house at 6 Garden Lane, then set fire to the living room. The noise of cracking glass alerted both neighbours and two police officers stationed in their car nearby. Luckily the officers had a fire extinguisher in the boot of their car for just such emergencies, and proceeded to tackle the blaze, holding it at bay until the fire brigade arrived. The house was saved from complete destruction but it had caused £1000 worth of damage. It was decided to board up all the downstairs windows to deter a repeat attack. The arsonists have never been identified.

Back at the Old Bailey, it was the turn of police officers and prison guards to take the stand and give their evidence for the prosecution. The officers explained the circumstances around Sutcliffe's arrest and subsequent confessions, but as the day unfolded it would be the prison guards who would provide the most controversial testimony – and one that struck right at the heart of the defence.

Mr Harry Ognall QC, for the prosecution, began the proceedings by reading through the statements made by Sergeant Robert Ring and Police Constable Robert Hydes, following the arrest of Sutcliffe in Sheffield. He explained how the officers had spotted Sutcliffe's brown Rover in the driveway of a large property in Melbourne Avenue on 2 January, and that they had established the licence plates to be false so confiscated the ignition key and arrested Sutcliffe for theft.

Mr Ognall then recounted how Sutcliffe had disappeared to the side of the building on the pretence of needing to urinate but was called back after Sergeant Ring heard a scuffling sound. He also explained how, twenty-four hours later, Sergeant Ring, learning that Sutcliffe was now being questioned by the Ripper Squad, went back to the scene of the arrest armed with a torch.

Ognall: 'At the corner of the building and near an oil storage tank among a pile of leaves, [Sergeant Ring] saw an engineer's ball-pein hammer and on closer examination saw the shiny blade of a wooden-handled knife, partially covered by the hammer shaft. [He] left them there and contacted his headquarters.'

This discovery eventually led to the discovery of a second wooden-handled knife hidden in the toilet cistern of Hammerton Road Police Station, placed there by Sutcliffe following his arrival and prior to being processed.

Mr Ognall then showed the jury both knives and hammer which formed part of the grim catalogue of court exhibits. The prosecution counsel pointed out that Sutcliffe had done everything he could to avoid detection: he had placed false licence plates on his car; had given a false name when questioned in Melbourne Avenue; had purposefully hidden his weapons at both the arrest site and the police station so they would not be discovered on his person and the prosecution would show that Sutcliffe continued to be evasive and untruthful right up until the discovery of those weapons by Sergeant Ring twenty-four hours later.

Detective Sergeant Desmond O'Boyle stepped into the witness box and described step by step his interviews with Sutcliffe, which eventually led to him confessing to being the Yorkshire Ripper. O'Boyle highlighted several points were Sutcliffe was particularly evasive and reluctant, and how he denied his true intentions for being in Sheffield.

When asked to give a blood test, Sutcliffe seemed concerned and did not want to cooperate, even asking the detectives. 'What if it's the same as the one you're wanting?' he was then asked if he was the Ripper, to which he replied he wasn't; if that was the case, he was told, he had nothing to worry about. 'Oh, all right then. Will you let me know the result of the blood test as soon as you get it?'

In O'Boyle's opinion the blood sample test and the fact Sutcliffe knew the weapons had been found had been the reason for his confessing to being the Yorkshire Ripper. He explained how Sutcliffe gave clear and precise details of the murders which left them in no doubt he was the man responsible.

O'Boyle said that on 16 January, Sutcliffe had taken detectives to several key areas where he had disposed of weapons used during the attacks. One of these sites was a service station about eleven miles south of Leeds City centre on the M1. Sutcliffe pointed out an embankment on the side of a lorry park and told them it was where he had thrown a screwdriver used in one of his attacks. After it was recovered he was asked why he had sharpened it to a fine point. He said he had used it as a hole punch for rivets, and he had disposed of it from his lorry because it was a horrible looking thing.

Mr Boyle was then cross-examined by defence counsel, James Chadwin.

Chadwin: 'I'm sure I will do not injustice to your distinguished career if I suggest that you have not on any other occasion interviewed a man who was admitting to killings on this scale?'

O'Boyle: 'Indeed not sir.'

The detective agreed that shortly after he first saw Sutcliffe, he admitted for the first time he had taken number plates in his car because he was thinking of committing a crime with the car. He took it that Sutcliffe was suggesting that he might have been intending to commit some other offence. Mr Chadwin mentioned the moment that Sutcliffe then admitted he was the Ripper.

Chadwin: 'I do not suppose you will ever forget that moment?'

O'Boyle: 'No sir.'

Chadwin: 'In view of what he was saying and what he was going to admit to, would it be a fair way of describing it, that he was almost incredibly calm?'

O'Boyle: 'Yes sir.'

Chadwin: 'You must have interviewed hundreds, if not, thousands of suspects in your time, some are easy and cooperative, some are very difficult and uncooperative. From that point would you say he was as easy a man to interview as you had ever come across?'

O'Boyle: 'Yes, it is fair to say that.'

Mr Chadwin remarked that Inspector O'Boyle had used great fairness when he immediately cautioned Sutcliffe after his admission, and you were scrupulous to give the opportunity from that point to have a solicitor present.

O'Boyle: 'Yes sir.'

Chadwin: 'I take it had he asked for a solicitor to be present you would have stopped the interview until a solicitor was obtained.'

O'Boyle: 'Yes.'

Chadwin: 'In spite of your scrupulous offer, he quite politely declined and said he did not need one?'

O'Boyle: 'Yes that is correct.'

O'Boyle went on to describe how Sutcliffe's only concern at this point was how the news was to reach his family.

Mr Chadwin pointed out that from the moment he admitted being the Yorkshire Ripper he said a number of things that were not in his interests.

Chadwin: 'I do not mean just the admissions of killings, but for example after the offer of a solicitor was offered, he said he would have killed that girl in Sheffield had he not been caught.'

O'Boyle: 'That is right.'

Mr Chadwin reminded the jury of DS O'Boyle's account that, despite Sutcliffe confessing to being the Yorkshire Ripper and then confessing his intention to kill Olivia Reivers, had the police not turned up, he had shown no interest in evading justice. He turned down the chance to have a solicitor present and even though he was entitled to say nothing, he was compliant and cooperative. He then addressed the fact that Sutcliffe had not confessed to several attacks and one murder.

Chadwin: 'I'm not suggesting it was a perfect match, but his detailed descriptions of the killings by himself in nearly every case tie up with the other evidence you have?'

O'Boyle: Yes.

Chadwin: 'We know it took hours and must have been a long ordeal for your colleagues, would you say for the duration of taking such a long statement that the bulk of that time he still remained incredibly calm?'

O'Boyle: 'Yes, he remained calm.'

Chadwin: 'The medical and forensic evidence, the weapons he said he used and everything seems to be consistent and when he talked about the killings he seemed to be completely frank and open?'

O'Boyle: 'Yes.'

Mr Chadwin went on to address certain aspects of Sutcliffe's confessions. The prosecution had maintained that during his lengthy interviews, Sutcliffe had never mentioned any divine mission as being the driving force for the murders. They maintained that Sutcliffe was being honest in his original statements and was now changing it for an insanity plea. It was up to the defence to show that what he had told the officers originally wasn't accurate.

Turning to the aftermath of the Wilma McCann murder, Mr Chadwin read from the confession statement: 'I carried on trying to act as normal, living with my wife. After that first time I developed a hatred for prostitutes in order to justify within myself a reason why I had killed Wilma McCann.'

Chadwin: 'Now, Mr O'Boyle, that does not make sense when you remember his other previous attacks does it?'

O'Boyle: 'Of course not.'

The divine mission may not have been mentioned at the time of his arrest, but Mr Chadwin wanted to demonstrate to the jury that Sutcliffe may have eluded to it in several references made throughout his confession. These references pointed to an uncontrollable inner compulsion which slowly built up over time and could well explain why Sutcliffe, in his poor mental condition, felt he was being guided by a higher power. Mr Chadwin began to read from the confessions. When talking about the Emily Jackson murder, Sutcliffe had said:

I felt an inner compulsion to kill prostitutes I went looking for prostitutes because I felt I could not justify what I had done before, looking back I can see now that first murder unhinged me completely … I had a feeling of satisfaction and justification for what I had done.

With the Irene Richardson killing in Leeds, Sutcliffe said:

It was my intention to find a prostitute to make it one less … Killing prostitutes became an obsession for me I could not stop myself it was like some sort of drug.

With the Jayne McDonald killing he said:

At this time the urge to kill prostitutes was very strong and I gone out of my mind.

Dealing with Jeans Jordan's murder in Manchester, Mr Chadwin said Sutcliffe had confessed:

> My desire to kill a prostitute was getting stronger than ever and took over me completely.

After the attack on Marylyn Moore:

> I had been taken over completely by this urge to kill I cannot fight it.

With the murders of Helena Rytka and Vera Millward, Sutcliffe had stated that:

> The urge inside me to kill was now practically uncontrollable ... The urge inside me still dominates my actions. The compulsion inside me remained dominant but then the feeling came welling up.

And finally, with his last murder, that of Jacqueline Hill, in Leeds, Sutcliffe said:

> I was in a world of my own out of touch with reality.

The next prosecution witness was Detective Sergeant Peter Smith of West Yorkshire Police, who went through the same statements made by Sutcliffe in various interviews.

Mr Harry Ognall QC read out the questions from police officers to Sutcliffe and DS Smith read Sutcliffe's replies. It covered much of the same ground as DS O'Boyle's testimony earlier, but a few key pieces emerged which suggested a possible motive for the start of the murders.

DS Smith said the interviews he had conducted with Sutcliffe began with discussions of a motorcycle accident which Sutcliffe had said triggered bouts of morbid depression and hallucinations. Sutcliffe claimed he started hearing strange noises in his head, humming and buzzing 'my mind was in bits'. These deep depressions would result in him thinking all kinds of things which at the time seemed irrational.

The interviews then dealt with the time that Sutcliffe said he was duped out of money by a prostitute and how he was later humiliated by her in a public bar. This humiliation led to him becoming severely depressed, and during this depression his thoughts turned to anger and resentment and a desire to inflict pain on this particular prostitute. To pay her back for the insult.

When asked by DS Smith if anything would trigger these feelings, Sutcliffe said he 'felt it was all linked with the attacks of depression'. When asked how the bouts of depression linked with the attacks on prostitutes, Sutcliffe said, 'I was out of my mind with this obsession about finding the prostitute in the original incident!'

Smith told the jury that Sutcliffe had said he had been out with Trevor Birdsall, 'looking out for this particular one and it was getting late and I just give vent to my anger on the first one I saw'.

It was a crucial piece of evidence. What the prosecution was trying to get across to the jury was that rather than a mission from God to rid the streets of prostitutes, Sutcliffe was retaliating in anger and resentment. The first attack had, in all possibility, woken a new desire to inflict pain on women, especially during times when his self-esteem was low. The attacks gave him power and a sexual dominance that he lacked in real life. A satisfaction and justification in himself after being mocked and made to feel small. There were clear signs of this in his original confessions when he talked of having a seething rage, following both the McCann and the Jackson murders. In the McCann murder this rage occurred as she stormed off, mocking him by saying: 'I'm going, it's going to take you all day, you're fucking useless.'

On cross-examination Mr Chadwin again pointed to statements made by Sutcliffe that although he had *set out* to kill, he never *wanted* to kill. Reading from a later confession Sutcliffe made concerning the attack on Dr Bandara in Leeds in September 1980, he said: 'I did not myself want to kill any of them, it was really just something that had to be done … I am not proud of doing any of the murders.'

Mr Chadwin also pointed out that at no point since his arrest had Sutcliffe shown any signs of this angry resentful man the prosecution claimed he was. DS Smith agreed that throughout the interviews Sutcliffe remained calm and polite, and never became angry. He also agreed that at times Sutcliffe did mention his disgust with prostitutes, but according to Sutcliffe there was no question of his seeking sexual gratification when seeing these women.

It was now time to call in the prison officers who had been assigned to watch over Sutcliffe in Armley Prison, Leeds, while he awaited his trial. Sir Michael Havers would lead the prosecution questions.

The first of these officers was Mr Leach. He was sworn in to the witness box before giving a brief description of his job role within the prison and the events relevant to the case. He revealed some of the internal workings that went on behind the scenes at Armley. He said all the officers kept a log book noting anything about a prisoner which they thought might be relevant.

He gave an example by reading a section of notes from the prison dated 6 January. It read: 'Has need to talk at times and boasts about his near misses with police. Example – having blood all over his hands and being chased by police. These points of information are deemed relevant as they could affect the upcoming trial.'

Leach was handed the hospital occurrence book and asked to look at a particular reference dated 8 January, he said Sutcliffe's wife had visited that day along with his solicitor Mr Kerry McGill

Sir Michael: 'Do you remember anything of significance which occurred that day?'

Leach recalled that on this particular day, the Sutcliffes and Mr McGill had chatted about general things, including the upcoming trial. At some point Mr McGill left the room.

Leach: 'Sutcliffe then said to his wife, I would not feel any animosity towards you if you started a life of your own. I am going to do a long time in prison, thirty years or more, unless I can convince people in here I am mad and maybe then ten years in a loony bin.'

Sir Michael: 'Are you sure these are the words he used to the best of your recollection?

Leach: [looking into his notebook again] 'What I have written down here. Yes Sir, I made a note of it directly after I came back into the Ward within two hours of the conversation.'

It was a potentially devastating piece of witness testimony for the defence and, if true, blew apart Sutcliffe's whole claim of diminished responsibility. What the prosecution was attempting to show was that during his original police confessions, Sutcliffe had not yet thought of the insanity plea. He then tells his wife he will attempt to convince people he is mad. After this, for the first time, he mentions the voices of God to the doctors who come to examine him. This would prove that Sutcliffe was nothing more than a cold and calculated killer who was simply lying in an attempt to cheat a lengthy prison sentence. A man who, if found to be insane, would be sent to a hospital as a patient, rather than a prisoner. At a later date no doubt, much to the success of the doctors and medical treatment, he would make a miraculous recovery and be deemed sane enough for release back to society.

It was now up to the defence to come up with a counter argument. Here, Mr Chadwin showed his skill in creating possible doubt in witness testimonies. He asked Leach if he could remember every word spoken during the conversation Sutcliffe had with his wife. Leach said that he didn't, but had made a point of recording down the crucial information regarding the insanity plea. 'When I wrote this down it would be the passage I felt would have been relevant to the visit as far as the doctors were concerned.'

Chadwin: '"I am going to do a long time in prison, thirty years or more, unless I can convince people in here I am mad." Are these the exact words or are they written up as a general description of the conversation. In other words, is it possible Sutcliffe could have said "If I can prove", rather than, "get people to believe"?'

Leach: 'Not to my record and not to my recollection.'

Mr Chadwin pointed out that it was nearly two hours following the conversation that he had decided write it down. He questioned how good his memory might have been, given his other duties and conversations within that time period. Wasn't it possible that he had forgotten or reimagined some of the words that had actually been said? He was asked to think hard and could he recall Sutcliffe ever saying the word prove?

Now beginning to doubt his own notes, Leach looked once again at his notebook.

Leach: 'I don't think he used the word prove, but I'm not 100 per cent sure.'

Chadwin: 'You're not 100 per cent sure?'

Leach: 'I always remember the gist; I don't know the exact words, but the gist is correct.'

Chadwin: 'So it's possible he did use the word prove?'

Leach: 'I suppose that could have been one of the words.'

Mr Chadwin sensed a chance to cast doubt on Mr Leach's recollections.

Chadwin: '[Could Sutcliffe have] used the word we instead of I? Meaning the conversation would have been, "If we can prove I'm mad", and by "we" I don't mean his wife, but as you know he'd already on one or more occasions seen his solicitor, maybe that is what he meant?

Leach: 'I don't think so.'

Mr Chadwin now wanted to explore the possibility that Sutcliffe had merely stated these words to save his wife further stress and to stop her worrying. He examined the prison notebook.

Chadwin: 'Your record says Sutcliffe told his wife that he was guilty of the murders and he could expect to do at least thirty years, did this have any effect on Mrs Sutcliffe when he told her that?'

Leach: 'Not that I can remember, she didn't become excited or agitated, or not more than she became excited or agitated on other occasions.'

He was then asked to read out another entry dated 9 January, the day after the 'loony bin' statement. This entry was made following another visit by Mrs Sutcliffe; it read, 'A little less frantic than previous visits from his wife but she completely overwhelms and dominates him and the situation.' The notes went onto to say that Sutcliffe was always quiet, but Sonia would never stop talking.

Mr Chadwin suggested that these notes proved that there had been a previous incident were Sonia had become quite frantic and stressed, and during these conversations she showed signs of being upset, angry and excited. His suggestion was that Sonia was a woman who had to be calmed down frequently. This would, in some way, explain Sutcliffe's attempt to appease her by claiming he might only do ten years.

Mr Leach didn't agree with this, but did say Sonia often bossed and henpecked Sutcliffe and as she was aware time was restricted, she had all her notes and questions written on pieces of paper. She took charge from the start until the end. He said she was often 'excited but not necessarily angry'.

Chadwin: 'Isn't it true that officers had been warned to be on their guard against Sutcliffe losing his cool and were warned to look out for his behaviour after visits from his wife?'

Leach: 'We knew the situation. We knew Sutcliffe, and the staff there were able to take care of him.'

Mr Chadwin then moved to questions that would suggest to the jury that Sutcliffe wasn't really normal.

Chadwin: 'Did he fluctuate from being very talkative to being very quiet?'

Leach: 'Yes. He didn't fluctuate much up or down from a normal line.'

Chadwin: 'Did he sit with a book in front of him, but not reading it – just staring into space?'

Leach: 'Yes.'

The next prison officer to step into the dock was Mr Anthony Fitzpatrick. He confirmed he was also from Armley, and his duties included maintaining a full watch over Peter Sutcliffe during the evening of 5 April 1981.

He too had been under orders to record anything of significance that the prisoner might say regarding the murders or the trial. He referred to his notebook and recalled a conversation he had with Sutcliffe following a visit by a doctor.

Fitzpatrick said they started discussing the possibility of Sutcliffe spending time in a long term prison; according to Fitzpatrick, Sutcliffe said 'I'm not going to do a long term in prison, I'm going to Park Lane [a mental hospital in Liverpool], a bed has been reserved for me there.' Sutcliffe went onto to say he had been told this by his solicitor Kerry McGill.

Sir Michael asked if Sutcliffe had said anything about how long he might expect to get, as a sentence, if he was sent to Park Lane.

Fitzpatrick: Sutcliffe [told me] that a psychiatrist said he would have to do no more than ten years to satisfy the public.

Sir Michael: 'What was his attitude during and after he had told you all this?'

Fitzpatrick: 'I think he was quite cocky about it. It was unusual for him to be so cocky but he was sure, quite adamant about it.'

On cross-examination, Fitzpatrick was asked by Mr Chadwin which psychiatrist had seen Sutcliffe in prison. Fitzpatrick said he was not sure but he thought it might have been Dr Milne or perhaps Dr Keane. Chadwin questioned why this important piece of information had not been recorded down.

Mr Fitzpatrick: 'I'm not sure.'

Mr Chadwin then went down the same path of questioning as he had done with Mr Leach; he questioned Fitzpatrick's memory and suggested it was a general description of the conversation written in Fitzpatrick's own words, rather than a 100 per cent accurate, word-for-word account. He suggested that whatever had been said was to the effect that a plea of diminished responsibility would be accepted, and that there had been no mention of an agreement. Unlike Leach, however, Fitzpatrick was quite adamant on what words were used and the word agreement had been mentioned.

Chadwin then put it to him that what he could have heard was the word agreement, but in the context that all the doctors had agreed that Sutcliffe was suffering from diminished responsibility.

Chadwin: 'If the word was used at all, it was in this context and simply meant that that the doctors had all agreed, isn't that correct Mr Fitzpatrick?'

Fitzpatrick: 'No!'

The third prison officer to enter the witness box was Mr Frederick Edwards. He confirmed he was an officer who worked in the hospital wing of the prison. He recalled from his notes that he was supervising Sutcliffe on 14 April, Between 9.00 pm and 10.30 pm. He testified that Sutcliffe had appeared 'cheerful and bright' just after hearing the news that Leeds Crown Court had moved his trial to the Old bailey in London.

Sir Michael then asked Edwards if Sutcliffe had made any mention about his case following any of the psychiatrists' visits. He confirmed that Sutcliffe had mentioned a few things of importance.

Edwards: 'He was saying to me that the doctors considered him disturbed and he was quite amazed by this and was smiling broadly leaning back in his chair.'

He described Sutcliffe as amused and cocky about it all. He was asked by Sir Michael to elaborate further and could he recall Sutcliffe's response to this news surrounding his medical condition.

Edwards: 'He said to me, I'm as normal as anyone.'

On cross-examination Mr Chadwin suggested to Mr Edwards that Sutcliffe was not being cocky at all, but rather protesting about his diagnosis. He clearly didn't agree with the doctors and felt himself to be normal and that they had got it all wrong?

Edwards: 'No, he was not protesting, he appeared amused.'

Chadwin then got Edwards to read a prison report in which it stated that: 'Mr Sutcliffe had said that the doctors thought there was something wrong with his mind because he heard God's voice.' The report said: 'But he said why should he be classed as mad because of this?'

Chadwin suggested that this was a form of protest and disagreement with the doctors and he considered himself quite normal.

Edwards was asked if Sutcliffe had shown any signs which would suggest he was not acting normal. He said he had not and that he appeared calm and collected. Chadwin pointed out sections of the prison notes which might suggest otherwise.

The 6 January notes, where Sutcliffe had boasted about his near misses with police, read:

Says does not go out intending to kill but gets into a compulsion, very confused, seems to lose track of the time and seems to think he's been here longer than he has.

18 January:

appears quieter than usual. Reading a lot. Begins talking of experiences, says it seems as if it was his purpose to do what he did.

20 January:

> talkative but only about the crimes and any possible trial outcome, has
> no intention of disclosing anything about himself when not involved in
> crimes. Says he was possessed when he committed his offences.

10 February:

> Talkative tonight especially about prisoners on D wing calling and
> shouting to each other from windows and an extremely noisy cockroach
> outside. Quite cheerfully talking about trying to rid the country of
> prostitutes and the merits of our police force. Very talkative, spoke about
> when a gravedigger and used to hear voices. Convinced voice came from
> the grave, heard voice from the headstone of the Polish tomb. Eyes open
> very wide and seemed to gleam obviously when he reached points of
> conversation interesting to him. Concerned about the long wait for the
> trial to start and commented that he wanted his 400 years.

By the end of the day's proceedings and in a somewhat devastating start to
the day for the defence, Mr Chadwin had skilfully cast doubt on some of the
prosecution's witnesses. He had managed to suggested different contexts to
which the prison officer's notes had been written down and once again shown
that there seemed to be very little evidence for Sutcliffe being an aggressive
monster – quite the opposite. Even he knew, however, that the real challenge
was only just beginning, because Mr Edwards's testimony marked the end of
the prosecution's case. It was now the turn of the defence to put forward their
own witnesses.

As the prosecution rested its case, Barbara Leach's father left the court.

He had decided he had heard enough and was unwilling to listen to yet
another recital of the particularly brutal way in which his daughter died. As
he walked through the foyer he found himself looking down at Olive Smelt,
a survivor of one of Sutcliffe's attacks, she was sat on a bench lost in her own
thoughts. They were two quite different people, the urban Mr Leach and the
hearty, earthy working-class woman. Under normal circumstances they would
probably have been at pains to avoid each other, but he walked up to her and
took her by the hand, 'I'm going now,' he said, 'I won't be back for a few days,
I just wanted to say goodbye and good luck in whatever you do.' And he bent
down and kissed her on the cheek.

Chapter 7

The Mission

'She [Jean Jordan] was in league with the devil and between them they had hidden the £5 note and I was going to do the same with her head.'

Peter Sutcliffe

As morning broke over the London skyline it was clear that 12 May 1981 was not going to be a normal day for anyone at the Old Bailey. Reports of a mystery sniper were broadcast to the news media as three people were shot by what appeared to be an air rifle outside the court building. The gunman's targets were the women demonstrators from the English Collective of Prostitutes group, who had gathered the day before to protest against violence to women. The sniper managed to hit one of them plus injure a barrister and a press photographer, Barrie Beatie, who was shot in the leg.

The lawyer who was struck behind the right ear by one of the pellets was 32-year-old William Clegg; he was knocked to the ground but not seriously hurt. 'It felt like I had been hit on the back of the head with a hammer.' he was appearing in a case at the Old Bailey, but it was not connected to the Ripper.

The women's group of protestors soon dispersed in a panic, but with crowds thronging the area hoping to catch a glimpse of characters in the Ripper trial, the police had a difficult task trying to find the gunman. Officers searched nearby offices and shops but were unable to find the sniper. The person responsible for the gun attack remains unknown to this day.

As this drama was unfolding outside the Old Bailey, an even bigger one was about to take place inside.

Seventeen minutes into the start of the proceeding, Mr James Chadwin for the defence counsel stood up and asked for an adjournment. He informed the judge that 'there have been certain events over the weekend, and I've received certain instructions which make it impossible to continue without taking more detailed advice.'

Mr Justice Boreham asked if these events would affect the case; Chadwin would not comment in open court but would need a forty-five minute adjournment. The adjournment was granted and suddenly the courtroom was alive with whispers and rumours as to what was going to happen next. By the time the court reconvened it was widely thought that Sonia Sutcliffe was about to go into the witness box.

Once the courtroom quietened down and the judge had taken his seat, Mr Chadwin stood up and announced, 'I call Peter William Sutcliffe.'

A loud gasp from the public benches and the obvious sound of whispering led Mr Justice Boreham to order silence in the court. The side door to the dock where Sutcliffe had sat throughout the trial was unlocked and he was now being escorted, by two prison officers, across the courtroom, past the jury, and into the witness box.

Until now most journalists and the public had only seen him in a sliced profile, often watching the back of his head as he sat in the dock, but now he would face everyone from across the court, his arms clasped modestly in front of him.

Upon the clerk of the court's guidance, he took the oath in a clear, slightly high-pitched voice, with an undeniable Yorkshire accent. He acknowledged he was ready to begin his testimony. Before doing so his eyes swept below to the table where the detectives all sat.

Chadwin: 'Is it right that you have admitted both to the police and by your pleas you have tendered in this court that you have killed thirteen women?

Sutcliffe: 'I have.'

Chadwin: 'You have pleaded guilty to attempting to kill seven other women?'

Sutcliffe: 'Yes.'

Chadwin: 'You are recorded as having said it was your intention to kill Miss Olivia Reivers, the girl in whose company you were when you were arrested.'

Sutcliffe: 'It was.'

[Mr Chadwin asked if, when he was caught with Miss Reivers in his car, he wanted to run away.]

Sutcliffe: 'I had an opportunity to drive away.'

Chadwin: 'That is not the answer to the question. Did you want to get away at that stage?'

Sutcliffe: 'No. I could have done. I could have literally driven away before the police knew I had false number plates.'

Chadwin: 'Did you want her to try and make a run for it?'

Sutcliffe: 'Yes.'

Chadwin: 'Were you intending to get away at that stage?'

Sutcliffe: 'I thought so.'

Chadwin: 'Why did you want to get away?'

Sutcliffe: 'I am not entirely sure that I did.'

Chadwin: 'You said you had thought of it, why didn't you make any attempt?'

Sutcliffe: 'By the time the police arrived I no longer wanted to kill Miss Reivers. The urge inside me had disappeared. I didn't feel the vengeance. I felt very little animosity at all towards her.'

He was then also asked about an event in 1969 when he was out driving in Bradford with his friend Trevor Birdsall. Chadwin asked him if he remembered leaving his friend's car armed with a stone in a sock. Sutcliffe acknowledged that he did. Chadwin asked what he had done with the sock.

Sutcliffe: 'I hit a woman on the head with it. I had to do it; it was my mission. I was told they were scum of the earth and they had to be got rid of.'

He was then asked who told him these things.
Sutcliffe: 'God. I tried to kill her, I hit her on the head once.' [He said he may have asked her the time before hitting her and that he knew she was a prostitute because she was walking slowly and looking at the passing cars.] 'I got out of the car crossed the road and hit her, the force of the impact tore the head of the sock and some of the contents came out and I crossed the road and got back into the car.'

Sutcliffe confirmed that the police later spoke to him about the attack, but he insisted he had hit the woman with his hand. The victim did not want to press charges and Sutcliffe escaped with a warning.

Chadwin: 'Did you enjoy striking that blow?'

Sutcliffe: 'No.'

Chadwin: 'What did you feel about the fact that the lady whom you had hit with the sock had not pressed any charges and nothing had come of it?'

Sutcliffe: 'I felt I was not meant to be caught or punished for the attempt.'

Mr Chadwin then asked Sutcliffe about a court conviction in October 1969 (four weeks after the stone in the sock attack). He was arrested after being found hiding in the garden of a house just off Manningham Lane. In his possession was a hammer with which he intended to kill a sex worker (he also had a knife but managed to conceal it from the police). He was later charged with going equipped for theft and eventually fined £25 in Bradford magistrates' court. Sutcliffe confirmed that he wanted to kill on that night – and would have, had he not been discovered by PC Bland hiding in the garden.

Sutcliffe was then asked about his early years as a gravedigger in Bingley cemetery. He had two spells of work which ended in 1967.

Chadwin: 'Was it in the first or the second of these spells that something occurred there?'

Sutcliffe: 'In the second term of employment.'

Chadwin: 'During that second spell, what age do you recall you were?'

Sutcliffe: '20, I think.'

Chadwin: 'What was it that happened at Bingley cemetery that you particularly remember?'

Sutcliffe explained that he had been digging a grave in the Catholic section of the cemetery. He wasn't sure whose grave it was at the time, but that he experienced 'Something that I felt was very wonderful at the time. I heard what I believed then and believe now to have been God's voice.'

Sensing this was going to be the key point in Sutcliffe's defence, Mr Justice Boreham interrupted Mr Chadwin's next question and instructed Sutcliffe to keep his voice up so that all the jury could hear him. Sutcliffe nodded and continued.

Sutcliffe: 'I was digging, and I just paused for a minute. It was very hard ground. I just heard something – it sounded like a voice similar to a human voice – like an echo. I looked round to see if there was anyone there, but there was no one in sight. I was in the grave with my feet about 5ft below the surface. There was no one in sight when I looked round from where I was. Then I got out of the grave. The voice was not very clear. I got out and walked – the ground rose up. It was quite a steep slope. I walked to the top, but there was no one there at all. I heard again the same sound. It was like a voice saying something, but the words were all imposed on top of each other. I could not make them out, it was like echoes. The voices were coming directly in front of me from the top of a gravestone, which was Polish. I remember the name on the grave to this day. It was a man called Zipolski. Stanislaw Zipolski.'

Mr Chadwin now reached down to the table and picked up a picture file folder. He approached Sutcliffe and showed him images of the graveyard, and in particular the area in question. He was asked if he recognised any particular grave. Sutcliffe said that he did and pointed to the grave from which he heard the voices calling to him, a man called Bronislaw Zapolski and confirmed it by saying, 'It is the one with the statue of Christ on the top.'

Chadwin: 'In relation to what we can see on that photograph, where had you been working when you heard the voice you described?'

Sutcliffe: 'To the left of the grave, lower down the slope.'

Chadwin: 'Up to that moment in time had you ever heard a voice which you could not identify, a voice which you could not attach to some human source?'

Sutcliffe: 'I had never heard this voice before. That was the first occasion.'

Chadwin: 'Did you look at Mr Zapolski's grave?'

Sutcliffe: 'Yes.'

Chadwin: 'Why did you look particularly at this grave?'

Sutcliffe: 'Because that is where the sound was coming from. That is what made me walk closer to it.'

Chadwin: 'What did you see on that grave when you looked at it?'

Sutcliffe: 'I remember getting a message from the grave. I looked at several graves. I was looking round to determine where the sound came from. After looking at the grave I walked back. I was kind of transfixed because of the voice. I just stepped back, and I didn't know what to think at first.' [Reading on the gravestone the Polish word 'Jejo', he assumed it meant 'Jesus'.]

Chadwin: 'Did that convey anything to you in particular?'

Sutcliffe: 'Something did, because immediately afterwards as I stepped back to the path immediately in front of the grave, I saw what I took to be a definite message about the echoing voice. I always thought it was on the same grave.'

He was asked what the message had said, he told the court.

Sutcliffe: 'I recall it as Jesus was speaking to me.' [He also remembered the phase: 'We be the echo.']

Chadwin: 'What is your recollection, not of what you heard, but of what you saw, that conveyed a message to you?'

Sutcliffe replied he read the words 'Wehvy' and 'Echo' in Polish. 'Echo' was spelt 'Ecko'.

Sutcliffe: 'I thought the message on the gravestone was a direct message telling me it was the voice of Jesus speaking to me.'

He looked at the folder which contained a close-up picture of the Zapolski gravestone and agreed with Mr Chadwin that the words he claimed to have read were not on the stone. 'I remember seeing them.' He said before acknowledging he had also looked at other gravestones in the area.

Chadwin: 'What effect did all this have on you?'

Sutcliffe: 'It had a terrific impact on me. I went down the slope after standing there for a while. It was starting to rain. I remember going to the top of the slope overlooking the valley and I felt as though I had just experienced something fantastic. I looked across the valley and all around me and thought of heaven and earth and the universe and how insignificant each one of us was, but I felt so important at the moment.'

When he was asked why he had felt such importance he told the court that he felt like he had been selected or chosen to hear the voice of God but admitted he could not understand what exactly was being said.

Sutcliffe: 'It was not the context of what was said, it was how it was said. It was so real, yet it was so unreal in quality. [When asked if he shared this experience with anyone else, including friends and family, Sutcliffe said he had not] I told no one because I thought that if it was meant for everyone to hear, they would hear. I felt I had been selected.' [Sutcliffe also said he did not know why he had been selected.]

Chadwin: 'Have you ever been back to Bingley Cemetery since then?'

Sutcliffe: 'Just once to visit my grandmother's grave a few months after I finished working there.'

Although he admitted having been back to the cemetery, he denied returning to the Zapolski grave where he had heard the voices.

Mr Chadwin then questioned him regarding his religious upbringing and Sutcliffe revealed he had been a regular churchgoer through most of his childhood and school years, but had not attended much after that. Mr Justice Boreham intervened to ask if he was interested in religion or had taken any active roles within the church. Sutcliffe stated that he had only been interested in religion between the ages of 15 and 17 and had spent a short while as an altar boy. He admitted he was puzzled to why he had been chosen to hear God's words, considering he was no longer religious and that he couldn't explain it, but he genuinely believed it was the voice of God.

Chadwin: 'At any stage from that incident until now have you changed your mind about that?'

Sutcliffe: 'No.'

It was now time to turn to Sutcliffe's personal life and in particular his relationship with Sonia. He said they had met on St Valentine's Day in 1967. It was at the Royal Standard pub on Manningham Lane, Bradford. Sonia was 16 years old at the time and still at school. He explained that at the time they met, he did not have any interests or altercations with sex workers. The couple started meeting regularly in Bradford City centre.

Sutcliffe: 'I did not go to her home for the first few months. I used to see her on Saturday and spent most of the day with her.'

Sutcliffe described the relationship as a happy one until Sonia left school and started studying for her A levels at Bradford Technical College. It was around this time that Sutcliffe heard from his brother Mick that Sonia had become involved with another man, an Italian ice cream salesman named Antonio, he was seeing her three times a week, meeting her from college then taking her out during the evening.

Sutcliffe was working on contract from the local waterworks and after talking to Sonia about her other friendship and having several rides with her, he was determined to leave work early one day to meet her from college and thrash it all out.

Sutcliffe: 'I left early but unfortunately there was a disaster at the waterworks. I left my assistant in charge and he nearly drowned several men, they said I was to blame for that and I was later called before the board and demoted.

'I caught Sonia coming down the road from college, she looked the other way as though she was shocked to see me, so I knew that what my brother had said was true. We walked all the way to her home about four miles away, arguing all the time, and when I left nothing had been settled, we just parted company.'

Sutcliffe claimed Sonia's other relationship made him depressed

Sutcliffe: 'I could not resolve the situation no matter how hard I tried because I saw her once a week and he was meeting her twice or three times during the week. When I was with her on weekends, she told me where she had been with him and because the only time I saw her was a Saturday we would always end up arguing. She would not say for sure if anything was going on with this chap and I did not know where I stood at all. I suspected something was going on that it was not just a platonic relationship, but she would not tell me if anything had happened off this nature.

'The problem was resolved eventually when she promised she wouldn't see the man anymore.'

Mr Justice Boreham inquired whether, in the end, Sonia had admitted she was seeing this other man.

Sutcliffe: 'She was seeing him, yes.'

Mr Justice Boreham: 'And you wanted her not to see him, is that the sum total of it?'

Sutcliffe: 'Yes.'

Sutcliffe then said that a further six months elapsed between the times they quarrelled until the time she gave her promise to stop seeing the man. During this time Sutcliffe claimed he had become more and more depressed. He said he did not want to blame his girlfriend for anything that might have occurred between her and his rival and decided his only way out was to find another woman, so 'I would be able to view it in a different light and not blame her, that is what led me to my first encounter with a prostitute.'

Taking his car, he patrolled Bradford's red-light district. One of the main areas for sex workers was the area around the Belle-Vue Hotel on Manningham Lane. This pub sat opposite Bradford City football ground. It was well known pre-match drinking den for supporters ,but also hosted female strippers and a topless DJ as a means of attracting custom. Directly opposite the pub was a service station located between Valley Parade and Burlington Street, it was a notorious rendezvous for sex workers hoping to capture both the passing car trade of Manningham Lane, and the Bradford City supporters in the Belle-Vue opposite. He spotted a sex worker clearly waiting for customers by the station. He drew alongside her and after confirming that she was 'doing business' they agreed on a price of £5.

Sutcliffe: 'We were on the way to her place [which she shared with her sister] and I realised what a coarse and vulgar person she was. By this time, we were practically there, and I realised I didn't want anything to do with her. Before getting out of the car I was trying to wriggle out of the situation, but I felt stupid as well. We went into the house, there was a huge Alsatian dog on a mat in front of the fire downstairs. She started going upstairs and I realised I just didn't want to go through with it. The whole thing was awful. I felt disgusted with her and myself. I went upstairs behind her and into the bedroom. I even unzipped her dress, but I told her straight out I didn't want to do anything with her. She could keep the money, just give me my change. [He drove her back to the service station to get change but] she went inside and there were two chaps in there. I don't know whether she did this regularly, but she wouldn't come back out. One of the men came banging on the car roof when I refused to go away. He said, "If I were you, I wouldn't get out of that car. You'd better get going." I would have had a go at him, but he was holding the wrench in a menacing sort of way. Then I saw the girl come out with another big-built bloke. They walked off together, having a laugh. I just felt stupid, I drove home angrier than ever. I felt outraged and humiliated and embarrassed. I felt a hatred for the prostitute and her kind.'

Sutcliffe then revealed that several weeks after this encounter, he saw the same woman again in the Olde Crown pub at 23 Ivegate in Bradford. She was in the company of another woman and he took her to be another sex worker.

Sutcliffe: 'The two were talking to men in the pub and acting in the way you expect prostitutes to act. I went and approached the one I had been with three weeks earlier and told her that I hadn't forgotten about the incident and that she could put things right so that there would be no hard feelings. I was giving her the opportunity to put things right and give back the payment I had made to her. She thought that this was a huge joke and, as luck would have it, she knew everybody in the place and went round telling them all about the incident. Before I knew what was happening most of the people were having a good laugh.'

Sutcliffe left feeling humiliated and degraded.

When asked by Mr Chadwin if it was a case of being out of pocket and having nothing to show for it, Sutcliffe said it wasn't just that, but also the fact that he felt so annoyed at not being able to resolve the situation with Sonia. That the fact he hadn't 'done it' made him feel worse than ever. He revealed that soon after this his attitude towards sex workers changed and there were times when he 'received messages' and had bizarre thoughts. He was asked to elaborate.

Sutcliffe: 'When I was depressed, when Sonia was involved with this man, I had the incident with the prostitute. It went wrong and I felt worse than ever. I went home and I was really feeling bad. I felt so depressed that I was reassured again.'

Chadwin: 'What reassured you?'

Sutcliffe: 'This is what I believe was the voice of God saying it was prostitutes who were responsible for all these problems … I did not hear any voices from God at the time of the visit to the pub, I heard it later when I was thinking all kinds of things about Sonia, perhaps not reasonable things to think about an innocent person, my mind was in turmoil and it could have passed through my mind that she too was a prostitute as well, but I had reassurances [from inner voices] that she wasn't, and she was a good girl.'

During his frequent depressions Sutcliffe said the voices returned; no longer indescribable echoing sounds from the cemetery, but a string of precise instructions to pull himself together, snap out of his gloom and above all – hide his depression from Sonia. The voices went on to tell him that the cause of all his sufferings was prostitutes, not just the woman who had cheated him, but all those of her kind. It was God's will that he, Peter Sutcliffe, should rid the world of them.

Author's note: Within a couple of weeks following the pub incident, Sutcliffe committed his first assault on a sex worker by hitting her over the head with a stone in a sock. It is possible this may have been the same one who he claimed had ripped him off.

When asked if he had a history of depression Sutcliffe claimed that it 'may have started with a motorcycle accident which occurred in 1965 or 1966.' He said he could not remember being depressed before this period. During this event, he and another group of motorcycle enthusiasts had 'been drinking in the village of Eldwick, just outside Bingley. The group had run into trouble with a coachload of engineers from Bradford. Several of the bikes had been attacked and some of the tyres partly let down.' One of these was Sutcliffe's bike and as a result, the motorcycle skidded on a tight right-hand bend on the road leading down towards Bingley. It was, and still is, a well-known accident spot. As the bike lost control, he struck a small side wall adjacent to the driveway of a house, this resulted in him being flung forward and into a lamp-post head-first. He said that luckily, he was wearing a crash helmet but was badly bruised to the face and forehead. He couldn't remember getting any medical attention at the scene but claimed he was carried into the house next to the crash point and cleaned up. He believed he had been taken home in another vehicle. He was unconscious for about thirty minutes.

Asked what effect this had on him, he told the court that he would hear a buzzing sound in his right ear and began suffering from depression and hallucinations. This continued right up to hearing the voices in the cemetery.

Chadwin: 'Have you ever stopped thinking that it was the voice of God?'

Sutcliffe: 'I have stopped thinking that on several occasions for maybe a day or two, but never more than that. Then I got very depressed, especially if I read in the newspapers where somebody was supposed to be innocent and I had killed them. I had been quite convinced by the message I received that they were prostitutes. I would be very depressed by this but had advice during the depression which lifted me out of the depression, and I thought I was all right and I wasn't wrong. God didn't make mistakes and the newspapers did.'

Moving back to Sutcliffe's personal life, Mr Chadwin asked him some more questions surrounding life with Sonia. Sutcliffe said they were married and lived first with her parents and then finally got their own home at 6 Garden Lane in Bradford. He was asked if his relationship with Sonia had involved violence.

Sutcliffe: 'No, I have taken hold of her by the wrists, but I've never hit her. When she loses control over absolutely nothing, she maybe hits me or starts kicking, but I just get hold of her wrists when she loses control quite often.'

He also said he never lost control and would never physically retaliate against her.

When asked about the period between 1969 and 1975, Sutcliffe said he had moved to London sometime in 1970. This was mainly due to Sonia attending a teacher training course at a college in Greenwich. The couple stayed with her sister Marianne and her husband, Haleem Hasani.

Mr Chadwin asked whether, during these five years, had he any doubts in his mind or asked himself about the mission.

Sutcliffe: 'Yes. Why it should be me that did it, because I found it so difficult. When I went to live in London, I saw Sonia practically all the time and it never had the chance to get on top of me. Then, I went to work nights for about three years, and this kept me busy every night, and at weekends I saw Sonia, so I was able to overcome it.'

He then said he returned to Bradford before Sonia had completed her teacher training course and got a job at Bairds Television, Lidgett Green.

But around Easter 1972, Sonia suffered a nervous breakdown.

Sutcliffe: 'It was while I was there [Bairds Television] that I got a telegram from Sonia saying, "Meet me at King's Cross station." That was all, no time, no date, nothing. I thought there was something strange about it. So, I took it to her parents. She was still their responsibility. Her father dashed off to London and found she had had a nervous breakdown and had been taken to Bexley [a mental hospital].'

Sonia was diagnosed with schizophrenia. She heard voices and believed she was the second Christ. She thought she had stigmata – the marks of the crucifixion nails – on her hands. She was taken back to Bradford for compulsory treatment in a psychiatric hospital which lasted three weeks, followed by a period as a voluntary outpatient. When Sutcliffe saw her at Linfield Mount Hospital in Bradford, all the colour had gone from her face. 'She just looked grey. She looked terrible.'

Sutcliffe said that Sonia's parents had advised him not to see her. She was taking tablets and had started to put on a great deal of weight. He had not recognised her as the person he used to know, as she had lost her personality altogether. Sonia received treatment for about two or three months, and then she suffered a relapse. Sutcliffe took care of her, but she was never the same again. She became reserved, tense, highly strung and obsessed with cleanliness.

Author's note: It was this strict hygiene code that would hinder any chance of Sonia becoming suspicious of Peter's activities in later years. He was forbidden to wash his work clothes with hers and she insisted he did all his washing out in the garage. A black bin liner was kept in the corner where only his clothes could go. Never once did she look inside the bag and, had she done so, she may have seen the bloodstained garments waiting to be washed.

Mr Justice Boreham: 'In London, when you were seeing Sonia, you still got messages and resisted them, or what?'

Sutcliffe: 'I didn't see any prostitutes.'

Mr Chadwin asked whether he heard any voices in 1975.

Sutcliffe: 'Yes. Before the attack on Anna Rogulskyj and during the time I worked on nights. They kept reminding me that I had a mission and wanted to know why I was on nights. I knew why I was on nights and stayed there as long as possible. The voice reminded me where I had to go next. I went in my car. I was told again that this was the night to go. It was about two days after hearing the first voice. I went there and it culminated in the attack on Anna Rogulskyj.'

On that night he had taken a hammer and a knife with him 'with the purpose to killing a prostitute'. He had hit Anna Rogulskyj on the head but had been disturbed by someone in a car nearby. He did not think he had stabbed her.

Mr Chadwin then asked about the attack on Olive Smelt in Halifax in 1975. He was asked why he had gone to Halifax.

Sutcliffe: 'I went with Trevor Birdsall. We went for a couple of drinks. In one of the public houses, I had seen her and on the way back, I saw her again. I said to Trevor that is a prostitute we saw in the public house.'

He told the court that he immediately stopped the car and got out, leaving his friend behind in the passenger seat, and then followed and attacked Mrs Smelt as she made her way back to her house.

Sutcliffe: 'She fell down. I was going to kill her. I had the knife with me at that time. I was going to kill her, but I did not get the chance.'

He also said that during the night he had gained a strong urge to kill a prostitute and that these feelings did not subside as he hoped they would.

Sutcliffe: 'Consequently, I did it with Trevor still in the car. I knew it was my mission. I heard voices – echoes. Sometimes it was the voice, sometimes an echo, sometimes it was very clear, sometimes not.'

Mr Chadwin began to go through each of the murders, beginning with Wilma McCann on 30 October 1975, just two-and-a-half months after the Olive Smelt attack.

Chadwin: 'This was the first time you had killed. Did you go out intending to kill a prostitute that night?'

Sutcliffe: 'Yes.'

Chadwin: Why?

Sutcliffe: 'The same reason as before. I was reminded it was my mission. It had to be done, so I went.'

Chadwin: 'This time you did kill.'

Sutcliffe: 'Yes.'

Chadwin: 'Did you enjoy striking the blows you struck?'

Sutcliffe: 'No.'

Chadwin: 'How did you feel about the physical act of striking those blows?'

Sutcliffe: 'I found it very difficult, and I couldn't restrain myself. I could not do anything to stop myself.'

Chadwin: 'Why could you not stop yourself?'

Sutcliffe: 'Because it was God who was controlling me.'

Chadwin: 'How was he doing that?'

Sutcliffe: 'Before doing it, I had to go through a terrible stage each time. I was in absolute turmoil, I was doing everything I could do to fight it off, and asked why it should be me, until I eventually reached the stage where it was as if I was primed to do it.'

Chadwin: 'Did you ever look forward to killing anyone with pleasure?'

Sutcliffe: 'No, certainly not.'

For the next hour, occasionally clasping and unclasping his hands in front of him, and sipping water from a plastic mug brought from the dock, Sutcliffe took the jury through the bare basics of each of his attacks and murders. He betrayed little emotion as he recalled how the hammer blows and stab wounds were inflicted upon each of his victims' bodies. The courtroom was silent and the jury was listening intently, hooked on every word.

Often his voice would drop into a low monotone whisper, and to most he almost appeared bored when recalling the events of the past five years. Several times the judge had to get him to repeat his answers so he could record them down into his ledger-size notebook.

Sutcliffe's defence counsel concentrated on his state of mind during each of the murders, avoiding the issue of *what* Sutcliffe had done and worked entirely on *why* he had done it.

It was here that Sutcliffe never faltered, occasionally smirking as he recounted his hatred of prostitutes, whom God had told him were scum of the earth. Here his answers all remained the same. God was the driving force behind it all. A compelling and uncontrollable urge to complete a divine mission. Asking if the attacks formed any sense of sexual excitement or satisfaction, he quickly answered 'no'.

Dealing with the circumstances surrounding the Jean Jordan murder in Manchester in 1977, Mr Chadwin enquired why Sutcliffe had hidden the body only to return to the scene later and to search for the £5 note he had given her.

Sutcliffe: 'Because I was told that this would point a finger directly at me and I would be traced, and the mission would have to stop unless I retrieved it.'

Mr Justice Boreham: 'Who were you told by?'

Sutcliffe: 'By God. I thought it would probably be found and the voices told me that I ought to get it back. I was persuaded that it was perhaps better not to go back, because there were cars going in and out with prostitutes taking their clients into the allotments. I got the message that it would probably be too risky to go back but couldn't understand why there was nothing in the news about the body being found. By the following weekend, I was getting advice again to get the £5 note back. I realised the reason it had not been found was to give me the chance to go back and get the note.'

He told the court that he had failed to find the £5 note and admitted that the police did interview him about it as he was one of the employees who could have received the money in their pay packet. He came to believe that God was protecting him.

Sutcliffe: [The voices were reassuring me constantly saying] 'If it was traced back to me, to say I knew nothing about it, and it would be all right. This did happen and as it turned out, it was all right, although I could not see why I had not been discovered. But then again, God took care of the situation. I was puzzled that I did not get advice to where the £5 was when I was looking for it. I was quite often left to work things out for myself. I was not able to do so and this troubled me.'

According to Sutcliffe one of the main signs that he was being protected by a heavenly authority was the infamous hoax letters and tape sent to the police during the manhunt, which threw them in the wrong direction and allowed him to kill a further three times.

Sutcliffe: 'I thought it was a diversion, so I could be left to carry on.'

Chadwin: 'Who did you think was responsible for this diversion so you could carry on?'

Sutcliffe: 'I thought it was an indirect act of God.'

Sutcliffe admitted he had heard the tape being played numerous times and was well aware of the huge publicity that surrounded it. The Geordie accent and the multiple enquires taking place in Wearside served him well as the police investigation was looking elsewhere.

He told the court he had no idea who had sent the letters and the tape, but he agreed that he had friends with Wearside accents and had delivered steel to the Wearside area.

Author's note: In 2005, West Yorkshire Police's Homicide and Major Enquiry Team decided to re-examine the 'Wearside Jack' mystery. They were able to extract DNA from where the sender of the tapes and letters would have licked the envelope. The results came back, and it was a direct hit. The DNA belonged to 50-year-old ex-bricklayer John Samuel Humble. Luckily for the police, he had a long career of petty crime and, after a 1991 conviction for being drunk and disorderly, his DNA was put on the database.

Humble was 23 years old when he recorded the tape on a cheap cassette recorder he had purchased from Woolworths. It was recorded in the kitchen of his family home at 15 Halstead Square, a red-brick, semi-detached house on Sunderland's Hylton Lane Estate. In March 2006, Humble was convicted on four counts of perverting the course of justice and sentenced to eight years' imprisonment. He served half his sentence before being released in 2010 and disappeared into obscurity. A recluse and chronic alcoholic, he died of heart disease and alcohol abuse on 30 July 2019 and was cremated in a private ceremony under the name John Samuel Anderson. Only four mourners were in attendance.

Mr Chadwin asked Sutcliffe about the number of times he had been questioned during the investigation.

Sutcliffe: 'I can't remember how many times the police interviewed me. So many times, I have lost count.' [He also admitted he already knew what was behind their questions and dates that they were inquiring about.]

Chadwin: 'Did that frighten you?'

Sutcliffe: 'No'

Chadwin: 'Did you think that the net was going to close in and that you would be caught?'

Sutcliffe: 'It was a miracle that they didn't apprehend me earlier. They had the facts. They knew it was me. They had the facts for a long time, but then I knew why they didn't catch me, because everything was in God's hands. The way I escaped; the way they went away satisfied. There was no chance of them getting me.'

By now Sutcliffe had woken up in the witness box, his eyes were wide and for a moment he seemed to be enjoying the tale he was telling. It was the same sense of enjoyment that prison officers had noticed when Sutcliffe told them about his near misses with the police. Sutcliffe seemed boastful, or even proud.

Sutcliffe: 'They questioned me at work and at home. One of them said they knew it was me and that he had no doubts at all, but he did go away. He must have had doubts. Another officer said that he knew it was me and he had a picture in front of him with my boot print on it. He had been in my car accusing me of being the Yorkshire Ripper. If he wasn't going to catch me, nobody ever would. The boots were new, and the soles and the heel were quite plain to see. The pattern was the same as he had on the picture. I knew they knew it was me. I expected them to come back, really, and question me again, but they didn't. I had no option but to tell them it wasn't me. Not that it was a deliberate lie, but that the mission was more important. [Because he was being guided and protected by God, Sutcliffe was not frightened by the search for the Yorkshire Ripper] 'I was intended to go on and carry on doing it all the time.'

Chadwin: 'Intended by whom?'

Sutcliffe: 'By God.'

Following more questions by Chadwin, Sutcliffe confirmed that every night he killed he had deliberately set out with murderous intent – except once, and that was the murder of Yvonne Pearson in Bradford in January 1978, when he 'heard no voice at all no instructions'. He was asked why he had killed her.

Sutcliffe: 'It was a sequence of events the way it happened, I was simply on my way home from work and a car backed out into the road. I had to stop suddenly and she came straight round the same corner the car had reversed out of. She tapped the window and opened the door. It was a complete surprise to me because I wasn't looking for a prostitute at all. She said are you having business or something, I asked her where she'd sprung from because it happened so suddenly, she said it's just good timing or you can put it down to fate. Unfortunately for her I thought this was my direct signal.'

Sutcliffe told the court that he had a walling hammer on the car floor. After he took her to a patch of waste ground in Arthington Street he used this hammer to kill her. Yet he claimed that afterwards he had apologised to her.

Sutcliffe: 'I said I was sorry and that she could get up and that she would be alright'.

Chadwin: 'Did you think she would get up and be alright?'

Sutcliffe: 'Oh yes. I thought it was if I was wrong, she would be perfectly alright and she would be able to get up, she didn't and I realised it was meant to be. I thought I may have done the wrong thing because I had no instructions. I just sat in the car with my head in my hands distraught because I didn't fully realise at that point that it was all intended and set out. It was only afterwards that I realised it was. I felt it was all fitting into the pattern and it was a message direct from God, you could put it down to fate was the message.'

Mr Chadwin then asked him what sort of woman he thought he was attacking and in all the cases Sutcliffe replied 'prostitutes every time'.

Sutcliffe said he never attacked any woman he did not think was a prostitute and 'never used violence on any people apart from those in the case'. He was asked if he remembered the first time he read in the papers that one of his victims was not a prostitute.

Sutcliffe: 'I am not sure but I do remember the effect it had on me, oh yes, it was the MacDonald woman in Leeds.'

[Mr Chadwin asked Sutcliffe how he felt when he read in the paper that she was not a prostitute.]

Sutcliffe: 'I felt utterly shattered mentally. I could not accept it. I felt terrible full of remorse.'

He went on to tell the court that at the time he killed her, he had no doubt she was a prostitute.

Dealing with some of the attacks where his victim survived, Sutcliffe pointed out that sometimes the voices told him to stop during the attack. He used the attack on Dr Bandara in Leeds 1980 as an example of this.

Sutcliffe: 'At the time I was having messages. I simply heard the word "Stop" and I felt that way about it myself, so I left the scene. I was having a conflict and found it extremely horrible, the act of strangling her. That is when I heard the word "Stop".'

[Staying on the topic of strangulation, Mr Chadwin asked Sutcliffe why he had admitted using a rope on Dr Bandara but initially denied the murder of Marguerite Walls in Farsley, Leeds in 1980, when he also used a rope].

Sutcliffe: 'This was because there was so much pressure on me. But I was aware that admitting to this would probably open lots of new lines of inquiry that were nothing to do whatsoever with me and I thought I would deal with the ones which were attributed to me.'

He then went on to deny that he had committed any other murders using the rope as a weapon.

Chadwin: 'At the time of these attacks did you think you were attacking anyone other than a prostitute?'

Sutcliffe: '[I did not.] May I just add that I thought so myself once or twice, but my feelings were completely overruled. I was persuaded that they were trying to persuade me otherwise on the occasions when I had doubts.'

Mr Justice Boreham: 'Do I understand you correctly, before killing one or two of these women you thought this woman is not a prostitute, but the voice said you're wrong, she is?'

Sutcliffe: 'Yes.'

When asked if he could give an example of such an occasion, Sutcliffe referred to the murder of Josephine Whitaker in Halifax 1979.

Chadwin: 'How did it come about that you entertained some doubt at the time but were reassured?'

Sutcliffe: 'Because I was walking along chatting to her, and she was telling me things which I thought sounded completely innocent – she had been to her grandma's, she had bought her a watch, and liked to go horse-riding. [The voices were telling me that this] wasn't true and not to believe her nonsense about visiting her grandmother, that it was a deliberate ploy [to avoid me]. She is really trying to play tricks on me. She is very clever, this one. [The voice also said] You are not going to fall for all this.'

Sutcliffe said the voice convinced him so much that he eventually gave way to it and killed her.

Mr Chadwin moved to the final night of Peter Sutcliffe's mission. His arrest in Sheffield on 2 January 1981 by Sergeant Ring and PC Hyde. An arrest which ultimately led to him confessing to being the Yorkshire Ripper.

He asked Sutcliffe why he had hidden his weapons next to a wall when pretending to urinate.

Sutcliffe: 'I should think that's quite obvious.'

Mr Justice Boreham: 'It is dangerous to allow any of us to make assumptions, it is better to come from you.'

Sutcliffe: 'I did it so that the mission would not be discovered or my purpose for being there. They were obvious pointers to what my intentions were.'

[He was then asked why it had taken him so long to confess his guilt to the police.]

Sutcliffe: 'I did not expect to be charged with murder even when I was caught with that prostitute in Sheffield. I had confidence in God. I gave a false name and address to the police because the fact that I had been caught in that situation had no bearing on the mission being terminated whatsoever. Even when I was transferred from Sheffield to Dewsbury, I told the police lies because the point had not been reached where I could do otherwise. I was waiting and hoping that I would get advice from God.'

[He was asked why, after hours of interview, he had finally decided to come clean and confess to being the Ripper.]

Sutcliffe: 'I had just been given a signal through the police that it was time to tell them.'

Chadwin: 'How did that come about?'

Sutcliffe: 'I was asked if I remembered going to the wall where I had parked the car in Sheffield and I realised that this was the time to tell them, because they were saying, in other words, that they had found the weapons I had hidden.'

Chadwin: 'I want you to explain to the jury; you have said you had been given the signal through the police that now was the time to tell them. You said through the police – from whom?'

Sutcliffe: 'From God.'

Chadwin: 'At that stage, could you understand in your own mind why God was giving you a signal to tell the police?'

Sutcliffe: 'No, I just realised that it was time to tell them everything I had done.' [He also admitted that he told the police he was glad it was all over] 'because I had been through terrible suffering all the time.'

Chadwin: 'In what way did you suffer?'

Sutcliffe: 'Through having to go through with the mission against my will.'

Mr Chadwin then addressed the issue of the voices from God that Sutcliffe claimed to be following and why this had not been disclosed to the police during his confessions. He also wanted to know why there had been no mention of Bingley cemetery, or the fact he had worked there. Sutcliffe told the court that he feared it would lead the police to discover the mission and he was not convinced the mission had come to an end and certainly did not want anyone finding out his true purpose.

Sutcliffe: 'I thought they would ask me all kinds of questions about why I worked there, I just thought it best to steer clear of the place altogether.'

[He was asked how God would be able to get him to continue the mission.]

Sutcliffe: 'I had no definite thoughts in that direction. I did not know how, but God was in control of the situation and anything was possible, so I said nothing about the cemetery.'

Author's note: Stories surrounding Sutcliffe's time at Bingley cemetery emerged shortly after the trial and although his employer, Mr Douglas McTavish, was adamant that bad timekeeping was the only reason he was sacked from the job, other stories surfaced about desecration and grave-robbing. Ex-work colleagues, such as Eric Robinson and Laurie Ashton, spoke of Sutcliffe's fascination with dead bodies and how he would steal rings and gold trinkets off the corpses. Other stories had him prising open the mouths of fresh corpses and yanking teeth with gold fillings out with pliers. He jumped into freshly dug graves and pulled out bones and skulls from other graves that he had disturbed in the process. He would use the bones to frighten passing schoolgirls by the cemetery wall, all the while laughing hysterically at the shock he caused.

Another unsavoury aspect of his character was his habit of discussing necrophilia (having sex with dead bodies). Although we don't know for sure if Sutcliffe sexually interfered with the dead bodies, he had plenty of opportunity to do so. Eric Robinson recalled a time when Sutcliffe mentioned that he had the keys to the mortuary and said he could 'come and see a couple of ripe ones.'

These stories were never presented in court so its uncertain whether they were factual accounts or embellished tales by those wanting to get their story in the newspaper. But with this in mind it is perhaps understandable why Sutcliffe was reluctant to disclose this key piece of employment history with the police. Their investigation would have uncovered the stories told by Eric Robinson and Laurie Ashton and they would almost certainly have been called as prosecution witnesses.

Mr Chadwin now wanted to tackle one of the more controversial witness testimonies which had been heard earlier in the trial; that of prison officer Anthony Fitzpatrick, who claimed Sutcliffe told him that he would not be going to prison but rather an asylum as all the doctors had agreed he was mentally ill.

Sutcliffe: 'I simply told the truth of what I believed and what I had been informed, and that was that the prosecution had agreed to accept the plea of diminished responsibility.'

[He was then asked why he had told his wife that he would only do ten years in a 'loony bin' if he could convince people he was insane.]

Sutcliffe: 'She was very upset, and I thought I could try and make her forget me and start a new life. I suggested that to her, but I don't think she was prepared to do so. She was alarmed by it. I tried, against what I wanted to do, to persuade her and I said I would be serving thirty years or more and it was pointless her wasting her life, waiting for me. I could see the effect what I was saying was having on her and I couldn't go through with it, pretending I didn't care and turning her away.'

Chadwin: [Did you say] anything to Sonia about only serving ten years in custody if he could make people believe he was insane?

Sutcliffe: 'I said something like that, yes.'

Chadwin: 'Could you elaborate further?'

Sutcliffe: 'I had seen what effect my words had on her and how distraught she was and it was my means of cheering her up that I said something to the effect of: "Not to worry, they will probably think I was a loony or I was mad, and I would spend maybe ten years in a loony bin." After telling her this it had succeeded in cheering her up. She was crying and I had wiped the tears from her face and licked them. Combining that with what I had said cheered her up.'

Chadwin: 'Had you by this time any idea of the defences to the charge of murder which might be available to you?'

Sutcliffe: No.

Chadwin: 'Do you think you are mad?'

Sutcliffe: 'No.'

Chadwin: 'Do you think there is anything wrong with you mentally?'

Sutcliffe: 'Nothing serious at all, no.'

Mr Chadwin: 'Do you think you will spend less time in custody if people think there is something wrong with you mentally?'

Sutcliffe: 'No. There would be something wrong with me mentally if I thought that.'

Mr Chadwin told the court he had no more questions at this time and there was a frantic rush from the press benches as journalists dashed to contact their newspapers and pass all the latest information over to the camera reporters still outside in the street.

In their eyes this was pure media gold and every newsman's dream. The most notorious serial killer of modern times had given his own version of events from the witness box and they were quite clear: God had instructed him to rid the streets of prostitutes. A killer with a divine mission. It was the kind of headline-grabbing material that made every newspaper front cover and guaranteed a serious moral debate was to follow. Soon the television networks were broadcasting footage of Bingley cemetery and live reports from around the grave of Bronislaw Zapolski filled every home across the country, which in turn brought new anguish to the life of Mrs Leonora Zapolski, widow of Bronislaw. After the images of her husband's grave had been broadcast around the world, she was made to feel like a prisoner in her own home as press and camera crews camped outside her house in Percy Street, Bingley. She refused to speak to them, but her neighbour, Mrs Florence Shuttleworth, who was comforting her at the time, told reporters that 'the pictures of the grave all over the TV has broken her heart.'

The stage was now set for a dramatic 'Part 2', with the prosecution all too eager to put Sutcliffe's story to the test.

Challenging the mission

Sir Michael Haver's cross-examination of Peter Sutcliffe would focus on dismantling the divine mission defence and lay bare the prosecution case that the murders were sexually motivated, driven by power and revenge. It would argue that Sutcliffe sought sexual gratification in each of the murders. It was in stark contrast to the previous four-hour legal argument put forward by Sir Michael at the start of the trial, when he argued that Sutcliffe was suffering from diminished responsibility.

Shuffling and rearranging the numerous piles of paper work in front of him, Sir Michael rose to his feet to face Sutcliffe in the dock. He started with the same order with which the defence had presented their case – by going through the night of his arrest and subsequent confession to being the Ripper.

Sir Michael: 'On the night of your arrest you picked up Miss Reivers, intending to kill her?'

Sutcliffe: 'Yes'

Sir Michael: 'Because God expected it?'

Sutcliffe: 'Yes'

Sir Michael: 'When did God last speak to you that night?'

Sutcliffe: 'When I arrived and when I picked Miss Reivers up – and on the journey with the girl in the car.'

Sir Michael: 'And then no more?'

Sutcliffe: 'No.'

Following further questions from Sir Michael, Sutcliffe agreed that once the police arrived on the scene, he had initially asked Olivia Reivers to make a run for it and that he had hidden the weapons by the side of the house, plus that he had hidden another knife in the toilets of Hammerton Road police station. Sir Michael then put it to him that all these actions would suggest a desire to escape detection. Sutcliffe agreed, but stated it was more to protect his divine mission than himself.

Sir Michael then emphasised how Sutcliffe, even after his arrest, had continued to try his best to wriggle out of the situation he had found himself in: 'Then for a considerable time after this, you lied, and lied, and lied again.'

To emphasis this Sir Michael read from the police interviews, in particular the part where Sergeant O'Boyle had asked Sutcliffe: 'Why did you go to Sheffield that night?'

Sutcliffe had replied: 'I gave three people a lift to Rotherham and Sheffield from Bradford.

They stopped me on the M606 and offered me £10 to take them home, so I did.'

Sir Michael: 'You had a ridiculous explanation about picking up people on the motorway.'

Sutcliffe: 'Ridiculous, yes.'

Sir Michael: 'All to protect yourself?'

Sutcliffe: 'The mission.'

Sir Michael: 'All to protect Peter Sutcliffe?'

Mr Sutcliffe: 'Yes.'

Sir Michael then turned to the point where Sutcliffe finally confessed to being the Yorkshire

Ripper: He highlighted the key moment:

Sergeant O'Boyle: 'Do you recall that before you were put in a police car at Sheffield you left your car and went to the side of a house?'

Sutcliffe: 'Yes, I went to urinate against the wall.'

O'Boyle: 'I think you went for another purpose .·. Do you understand what I am saying? I think you are in trouble, serious trouble.'

Sutcliffe: 'I think you have been leading up to it.'

O'Boyle: 'Leading up to what?'

Sutcliffe: 'The Yorkshire Ripper.'

O'Boyle: 'What about the Yorkshire Ripper?'

Sutcliffe: 'Well, it's me.'

Once Sir Michael had read out this section of the police interviews, he paused to let it sink into the jury before continuing:

Sir Michael: 'Do you understand the phrase "bang to rights"?'

Sutcliffe: I don't know the phrase.

Sir Michael: 'Do you understand when I say "I have got you? I have all the evidence well and truly. The game is up"?'

[Sutcliffe was silent for a moment but then replied that it was at that moment in the interview that God had told him it was time to confess and that's why he admitted to being the Ripper.]

Sir Michael: 'And God told you to tell, or was it just that you realised the game was up.

Did you say you were the Ripper because you knew the game was up?'

Sutcliffe: 'I knew it was the time to tell them.'

Sir Michael: 'When found out, you decided to tell the truth, like any other criminal?'

Sutcliffe: 'Like any criminal – not any other.'

[Sutcliffe went on to explain that it wasn't a voice telling him to confess but he took the finding of his weapons as a message from God to come clean and confess. He said once he had gotten the divine message he fully cooperated and told the police everything they wanted to know. Sir Michael jumped on this opportunity to pull Sutcliffe on the fact he hadn't told the police about previous victims before Wilma McCann, the attack on Dr Bandara or the murder of Marguerite Walls.]

Sir Michael: 'So, with God's message ringing in your ears, telling you to tell them everything, the first sentence you tell them is a lie?'

[Sutcliffe told the court that he had gone through a great ordeal in giving full and detailed confessions to the police but that he had probably forgotten some of the other victims. Only later when he had thought about it had he come clean about these attacks and murders.]

Sir Michael: 'If God's message was so clearly instructing you to tell the truth why on earth did it take you so long?'

Sutcliffe: 'On the contrary, I wanted to tell them as quickly as possible.'

Sir Michael picked up the piece of rope and inquired whether it was the same piece of rope he had used on both Dr Bandara and Marguerite Walls. Sutcliffe confirmed that it was. He also said that it was the same piece of rope he had in his pocket when he was arrested in Sheffield with Olivia Reivers. Sir Michael added that along with the hammer and the knife, Sutcliffe was 'keeping [his] options open.'

Then it was time to address the issue of the divine mission itself and the voices Sutcliffe claimed to have heard in Bingley cemetery. Sir Michael started by asking him about his friends and family in the early days of first hearing the voice. Sutcliffe spoke of his mother, Kathleen, and described her as loyal and devoted. He said he had a friend called Eric Robinson and described the first time he met Sonia, who he loved and trusted very much. He also spoke of his Catholic upbringing and time spent going to church. Once he had described in detail the close bonds he had with the main people in his life, Sir Michael took the opportunity to ask Sutcliffe directly about how he felt when he heard the voice of God.

[Sutcliffe repeated what he had told the defence counsel and the doctors, that it was an incredible experience and how he felt he had been chosen. The most important event in his life.]

Sir Michael: 'This was the most stunning thing in your life and you did not tell Sonia?'

Sutcliffe: 'No.'

Sir Michael: 'You didn't tell your devoted mother?'

Sutcliffe: 'No.'

Sir Michael: 'In fact, you didn't tell anyone until years and years had gone by and then you told them on your eighth interview in Armley gaol, two months following your arrest.'

[Sutcliffe confirmed he hadn't told anyone and agreed with Sir Michael that it would appear odd that he hadn't. Sir Michael pressed him further about why he hadn't told anyone about the voices, and were the voices telling him right away to kill and did he know why he had been chosen to hear the voice?]

Sir Michael: 'What was so secret about this marvellous message?'

Sutcliffe: 'The first two years were the best. There were no signs of purpose or why I had been chosen to be here. None whatsoever.'

Sir Michael: 'Then there was nothing to be ashamed of in telling Sonia, your mother, your priest or anyone.'

[Sutcliffe said he couldn't tell a priest because he wasn't part of the church anymore. He was then asked what the exact words were when he first understood what the voice was saying to him.]

Sutcliffe: 'That I should have faith and that I should believe and that there was no need to be so depressed.'

Sir Michael: 'Should that not have encouraged you to go back to the Catholic faith?'

Sutcliffe: 'No because I had been chosen when I was out of faith.'

Sir Michael: 'So for all these years, this great miracle – to you it must have been a miracle – was kept entirely to yourself?'

Sutcliffe: 'Yes'

[Going back to Sutcliffe's eventual confession to being the Yorkshire Ripper, Sir Michael wanted to know why he had not mentioned a word about this divine mission during his long and exhaustive confessions to the police.]

Sutcliffe: 'Because I was waiting for a direct message saying that it was over, to fully convince me that the mission was terminated.'

[Sir Michael pointed out that Sutcliffe had already stated he had received a message from God to confess to being the Ripper when his weapons were found, so why did he not confess to the mission aspect of the murders? Sutcliffe stated that although he was told to confess to the murders he wasn't sure if his mission had ended.]

Sir Michael: 'What you are saying is that you had to have a 'mission finished' or 'mission terminated' signal? Did you ever get that?'

Sutcliffe: No.

Mr Justice Boreham: 'Do you mean never? You still haven't, had it?'

Sutcliffe: 'No.'

Sir Michael: 'To this day you believe you are still an agent for God in a mission only partly fulfilled?'

Sutcliffe: 'Yes.'

[Sutcliffe was then asked if, as God's agent, he ever felt he was being asked to carry out an impossible task for one man. Sutcliffe said he didn't know if he was the only one or there might have been others chosen to do similar. He was then asked did it not occur to him that the God he had been brought up with all his life was meant to be merciful and there he was killing people in a painful way.]

Sutcliffe: 'I am quite sure that the ways I killed them meant they never knew anything.'

Sir Michael: 'You mean to say they felt anything as they lay there moaning, groaning, gurgling, a screwdriver in the eye, stabbed and one disembowelled?'

Sutcliffe: They were gurgling, but would not know anything about it.

[He was then asked whether he had favourite cat or dog and Sutcliffe replied that he had and admitted he would never have killed them in any of the ways he had killed his victims.]

Sir Michael: 'When did it first pass your mind that the God you were in touch with was very evil, quite contrary to the sort of miracles you had been told about as a Catholic boy?'

Sutcliffe: 'It seemed similar to the contradiction between the Old Testament and the New.'

Sir Michael: 'It must have been a great experience, this miracle – and you were transfixed – suddenly turns out to be instructing you to become a murderer?'

Sutcliffe: 'Yes.'

Sir Michael: 'And yet you tell nobody?'

Sutcliffe: 'No'

It was then time to focus on the incident where Sutcliffe had been conned out of money by a prostitute. Sir Michael briefly went through Sutcliffe's account of how he had the argument with Sonia then decided seek sex with a prostitute on Manningham Lane, Bradford, which had ended badly with Sutcliffe being out of pocket. But what Sir Michael wanted to focus on was the incident in the Old Crown pub shortly afterwards when Sutcliffe had run into the same woman and she had mocked him in front of the entire pub, humiliating him.

Sir Michael: 'You have stated that after you had been taunted by a prostitute, the first one you had met, you developed a hatred for her and her kind, that is a fact.'

Sutcliffe: Yes.

[Sir Michael then asked whether he realised that his divine purpose in life had now come about after he had been short-changed by a prostitute. The divine mission happened only 'after you began to hate prostitutes.']

Sutcliffe: 'No, I do not hate prostitutes.'

Sir Michael: 'But you were pretty cross, especially after she taunted you – you came out frustrated and tormented?'

Sutcliffe: 'Yes.'

Sir Michael: 'Humiliated, outraged and embarrassed?'

Sutcliffe: [Clearly rattled] 'That is what I said.'

Sir Michael: 'God had not spoken to you then.'

Sutcliffe: 'No.'

Sir Michael: 'So God very conveniently jumped on the bandwagon after that and said: "You have a divine mission, young Peter, to stalk the red-light districts and avenge me by killing prostitutes"?'

Sutcliffe: 'It is a very colourful speech, sir, but it does not apply.'

Sir Michael: 'When forced to accept that you hate prostitutes, God comes to the rescue as far as this case is concerned?'

Sutcliffe: 'That is after the incident when I got into a very depressed condition.'

[When asked whether he had seen a doctor about his condition, Sutcliffe said that he had not. Sir Michael then pointed out that Sutcliffe had claimed to have had a motorcycle accident which led to blackouts and depressions, and surely he would have went to a doctor at some point had this been true.]

Sutcliffe: 'I thought to go to the doctor's would probably result in a brain operation or something like that which I did not want.'

He was reminded that he had given two different versions of the motorcycle accident to the doctors at Armley. In one version he was unconscious for fifteen to twenty-five minutes, and in later version he said he was unconscious for hours. Sir Michael put it to him that he was simply exaggerating the story to create the illusion of a serious mental condition and to 'make the doctors think he was loony'. Sutcliffe denied this. Sir Michael then asked Sutcliffe if he had ever heard or read about the case of a spree killer called Mark Rowntree. Sutcliffe said he hadn't. Sir Michael thought this strange as Mark Rowntree had killed four people at random in Sutcliffe's home town of Bingley, West Yorkshire, during late 1975 and early 1976. It was story that had appeared throughout all the local papers.

Sir Michael explained to the court that on 31 December 1975, 19-year-old Rowntree had stabbed a widow, Grace Adamson, to death, then celebrated with a beer at a local pub. On 3 January 1976 he killed 16-year-old Stephen Wilson at a bus stop. The victim later died in hospital, although he was first able to give a description of his attacker to the police. On 7 January 1976, Rowntree visited part-time model Barbara Booth at her home and stabbed her to death, along with her 3-year-old son Alan. By the time he returned home, the police were waiting for him, armed with the description given by the second victim. Rowntree gave a full confession to his crimes and complained that he had not managed to reach five victims. Mr Justice Boreham interrupted and asked for the relevance of this information. Sir Michael went on to explain that Mark Rowntree was later diagnosed as suffering from schizophrenia and pleaded guilty to four counts of manslaughter on the ground of diminished responsibility at Leeds Crown Court in June 1976. He was ordered to be committed to Rampton secure hospital for an indefinite period.

Sir Michael: When you were being held in Armley gaol, did you ask an officer if you were like Mark Rowntree?

Sutcliffe: No.

Sir Michael: 'I suppose you read newspapers?'

Sutcliffe: 'I get a daily yes – the Daily Mail.'

Sir Michael: 'They covered the Ripper murders pretty heavily?'

Sutcliffe: 'They had items, yes.'

[He was then asked how the newspapers were describing the killer and the sort of man the Ripper was supposed to be.]

Sutcliffe: 'They made me out to be a monster. Oh, a terrible thing.

Sir Michael: 'Did you read articles which seemed almost unanimous that the Ripper had a loathing of prostitutes?'

Sutcliffe: 'Yes.'

[Sir Michael pointed out that there already existed in the public consciousness, an idea that the Ripper was an obvious mad man who hated prostitutes. Someone who was mentally ill and someone who should be locked away in asylum. He then asked Sutcliffe when he first realised there could be a special defence involving his state of mind.]

Sutcliffe: 'I can't be sure exactly.'

Sir Michael: 'You were telling your wife on January 8th that you were expecting to get thirty years in prison, but if you could convince people, you were mad then it would be ten years in a 'loony bin.'

Sutcliffe: 'I said that quite openly.'

[He was then asked how, if he hadn't been planning an insanity defence, he would know he might only get ten years if committed to a 'loony bin'.]

Sutcliffe: 'I couldn't possibly know I would get ten years in a "loony bin". The sole reason was to cheer her [Sonia] up and bring her out of a depression. I tried to comfort her, to tell her things weren't that bad. I didn't like to see her crying.'

Sir Michael: 'You are over 30 years of age, you read newspapers, you have a higher-than-average intelligence, and you have been murdering and attempting to murder people for years. There has been endless talk in pieces in the newspapers. Are you going now to turn round and tell members of the jury that on January 8th you had no idea what you were talking about?'

Sutcliffe: [turning his head to look at the jury] 'Yes, I had no idea it would be less if I got sent to the loony bin.'

[He was then pressed about his gloating attitude to his prison guards on 5 April when he was described as cocky and arrogant at the idea of being declared insane and being sent to an asylum.]

Sutcliffe: 'I can see why he thought I was arrogant.' [He went on the say that his solicitor had told him that the plea of diminished responsibility had been accepted.]

Sir Michael: 'You can take it from me that there was no agreement of any kind.'

Sutcliffe: 'I was told that the doctors were agreed. My solicitor said that the doctors for the prosecution had agreed.'

Sutcliffe was then asked to describe the symptoms his wife, Sonia, had suffered from when she had a mental breakdown and was diagnosed with schizophrenia. Sutcliffe told how she had hallucinations, paranoia and religious mania, including the feeling that 'all the machinery was stopping and the world was coming to an end'. He confirmed that she could not work for three years and that he took care of her. Sir Michael pointed out that Sutcliffe would have learnt a lot about the illness during this time and how remarkable it was that he displayed the same symptoms to the doctors who examined him at Armley Prison. He was then asked to describe in detail how his supposed 'divine mission' would manifest itself.

As with his testimony for the defence, Sutcliffe spoke again of the urges that would build up inside him; of how, when God had told him to go on his mission, he would try to fight it but the urges would become so severe that he couldn't control himself. He had to kill.

Sir Michael pointed out that rather than being out of control and 'forced' to commit murders against his will, Sutcliffe could control himself quite well; his choice of quiet sites to commit the murders, his quick-thinking and play-acting during the events of the attacks, all suggested that he had a great capacity for personal control. He chose his victims carefully, making sure he was alone with them in a quiet spot so as not to be seen.

[Sutcliffe then claimed that urge became so great that he would kill as soon as possible, the fact he killed his victims in the quietest of places was simply by chance.]

Sir Michael: 'Are you saying that if the urge came over you in the middle of Piccadilly Square, London you would have done it?'

Sutcliffe: 'Yes that's what I said.'

Sir Michael: 'Was it your intention to kill your victims as soon as possible?'

Sutcliffe: 'Yes'

Sir Michael: 'Why did you never kill in the car?'

Sutcliffe: 'It was impossible there was no way at all. I always used a hammer.'

[He was asked again]

Sutcliffe: 'Well maybe because they would make a lot of noise and the evidence would be all over the car.'

Sir Michael: 'Well done Mr Sutcliffe you finally got there, you have the capacity for control and you knew you would leave blood there. You always checked your clothes and if there was any blood, you washed it off. There would be blood all over your car. It would make your detection more likely. A messy job to get rid of it. That's what I am getting at: your capacity for control. Do you see?'

Pressing home Sutcliffe's ability to control himself, Sir Michael referred to the murder of Josephine Whitaker. He pointed out how Sutcliffe had remained cool and clam when approaching the 19-year-old clerk. Walking with her and striking up a conversation. During the encounter Sutcliffe had told the girl, 'you do not know who you can trust these days'.

Sir Michael: 'Can you think of anything more sinful and horrible to say to someone you were about to murder?'

Sutcliffe: 'No'

Sir Michael: 'You were trying to convince her she was safe with you?'

Sutcliffe: 'Yes, in a sense.'

Sir Michael: 'Did God tell you to do that?'

Sutcliffe: 'No.'

Sir Michael then pointed that rather than being controlled by a divine force, Sutcliffe was thinking and plotting his murder thoroughly, putting his victim off guard and waiting for the moment to strike.

Sir Michael: 'It was a bit of private enterprise on your part, was it?'
[Sutcliffe then agreed that what he told police about the attack was a confession of a cold blooded calculated sadistic murder he also agreed that he had pretended to have poor eyesight and asked her to look at the time on the Clock to get her to stop.]

Sir Michael: 'Is that a sort of macabre play acting while you got her jockeyed into the right position?'

Sutcliffe: 'Yes'

Sir Michael: 'Did God help you or not? Did he tell you what to do?'

Sutcliffe: 'Yes I had instructions most of the time.'

Sir Michael: 'Did God tell you to tell that poor girl to look at the Church Clock?'

Sutcliffe: 'Yes'

Sir Michael: 'Are you just standing there telling us deliberate lies?'

Sutcliffe: 'No.'

Turning to other murders and attacks Sir Michael pointed out times when Sutcliffe was clearly not being guided by divine instructions but rather thinking on his own.

Sir Michael: 'Did he tell you to hide behind the garden wall when you were escaping after attacking Theresa Sykes?'

Sutcliffe: 'Yes.'

Mr Justice Boreham: 'Are you saying you needed God to tell you that unless you did hide you might be caught?'

Sutcliffe: 'Maybe, maybe not. I am not sure.'

Sir Michael then used the murder of Yvonne Pearson as an example of more individual thinking. In this attack Sutcliffe was disturbed in the act and resorted to stuffing horsehair from the discarded couch down the victim's throat to keep her quiet.

Sir Michael: 'Did God instruct you as far as Yvonne Pearson and the horsehair was concerned?'

Sutcliffe: 'Yes'

Sir Michael: 'When Yvonne Pearson was lying there gurgling and moaning and there was someone in a car nearby, with your high-average intelligence you must have known you were in danger of being caught. You don't need God to tell you to ram it down her throat?'

Sutcliffe: 'No.'

Sir Michael: 'Did God tell you?'

Sutcliffe: 'No.'

The murder of Jean Jordan in Manchester had presented the prosecution with the opportunity to show that Sutcliffe had been thoughtful enough to return to the body to retrieve the £5 note from Jordan's handbag. Here, God wasn't protecting him but leaving it up to him to avoid detection. Sir Michael suggested the attempt to cut Jordan's head off was an attempt to disguise the murder as that committed by someone else. Sutcliffe denied this. Mr Justice

Boreham then asked Sutcliffe why he had tried to remove the head with a hacksaw.

Sutcliffe: 'Because she was in league with the Devil and between them, they had hidden the £5 note and I was going to do the same thing with her head.'

Mr Justice Boreham: [After the £5 note had been found] 'I don't want to get into a theological argument, but are you saying that she and her colleague the Devil had beaten you and your God?'

Sutcliffe: 'Yes. It seemed very much so.'

On the exhibits table, among the grim collection of knives and hammers, lay a bent yellow-handled screwdriver. Sir Michael picked it up and explained to the jury that this was the very screwdriver that Sutcliffe had thrust into the eye of Jackie Hill as she lay dead or dying on the ground in Leeds 1980. He then held it up waving it at Sutcliffe and asked why he had stabbed it into Jackie Hill's open eye.

Sutcliffe: [Her eyes had been] 'Staring at me accusingly.'

Sir Michael: 'You are not going to tell the jury she was not entitled to look accusingly at you?'

Sutcliffe: 'I don't know. I think she was already dead but her eyes were open.'

Sir Michael: 'Did it matter whether she was giving you an accusing look? You had God on your side. She was a mere mortal who you were about to take off the face of the earth.'

[Sutcliffe was then reminded that his answer also meant God had not told him to thrust the screwdriver into Miss Hill's eye that was an independent action of his own.]

Sir Michael: 'Have you got any regret about what you did to her eye?'

Sutcliffe: [silent].

Sir Michael: 'It's difficult for you, isn't it?'

Sutcliffe: 'Yes.'

Sir Michael: 'Maybe it's because you are unsure of the right answer to give the jury'

Sutcliffe: 'You are much quicker than I am. [Another pause] Despite being told what to do, still partly inside I feel guilty.'

Sir Michael: 'So you felt sorry about what you were doing? I'm sure you don't want to say that you enjoyed it.'

Now it was time to address the motivation behind the murders. Sir Michael told the court that Sutcliffe had repeatedly claimed he was on a divine mission and that there was never any sexual gratification gained from them. Sir Michael then went through each of the murders, explaining in detail how the underwear had been removed or displaced above the breasts and below the genitals in most of the murders.

He referred to the specific targeted attacks on the breasts and genitals in cases such as Wilma McCann, Patricia Atkinson, Josephine Whitaker and Marguerite Walls. Sutcliffe admitted that he removed some of his victim's clothes once they were unconscious, but it was only so that they 'would not hinder' him while he stabbed his victim. Sir Michael pointed out that this may explain the bra being removed but not the lower underwear. Sutcliffe explained that he wanted to expose them, 'to show them for what they were'. He denied that there was anything sexual in his actions. Sir Michael dismissed this by reading out Sutcliffe's statements to the police where he admitted he had removed clothing to perform a sexual revenge on both Wilma McCann and Emily Jackson.

Turning to some of the more curious wounds inflicted on the bodies, Sir Michael explained how Sutcliffe had inserted the knife into the same wound repeatedly. In one case, that of Josephine Whitaker, Sutcliffe had done this by stabbing her vagina with a sharpened screwdriver, then repeatedly thrusting it in and out of the same wound, mimicking penile
penetration. Sir Michael showed that a clear and conscious effort was made not to cause injury to any other part of her vagina. This multiple entry wound was no frenzy, but a purposeful act which bore all the hallmarks of a sexually motivated attack.

Sir Michael: 'Do you realise how difficult it must have been to do that?'

[Sutcliffe said he couldn't recall doing it and suggested it was just random stabbing. Sir Michael paused for a moment then began reading from the pathologist's report which clearly described the multiple wounds through the same entry. Careful and precise. Sutcliffe then interrupted him and stated that he might have moved a knife about inside a wound.]

Sir Michael: 'It [the pathologists report] hasn't been challenged, Mr Sutcliffe, by your very experienced leading counsel.'

Sutcliffe: 'I put it in and moved it around to kill her, that is all. I do not mean to contradict you, but I'm trying to express what happened.'

Sir Michael: 'How did you use this rusted old screwdriver that has been sharpened to a hideous point, to stab Miss Whitaker through the same wound multiple times. How can you get that into the same place?'

Sutcliffe: 'By moving it about.'

Regarding the murder of Emily Jackson, Sutcliffe had left her legs spread apart and had pushed a piece of wood up against her vagina. Was this an attempt to insert the wood into her body?

Sutcliffe: 'I was just pushing her out of sight with it. I pushed her with it because I could not bear to touch her again.' [He went on to explain how he didn't want to be contaminated with her blood and left her in that position to show her as disgusting as she was.]

Sir Michael saw an opportunity to put the pressure on Sutcliffe regarding his disgust of prostitutes. He now turned the murder of Helen Rytka in Huddersfield.

Sir Michael: 'You say you feel contaminated by the blood of a victim. You talk about your mission, and then surprise, surprise, here's pretty little Helen Rytka and you have sex with her. Why?'

Sutcliffe: 'I didn't have sex. I entered her, but there was no action. It was to persuade her that everything would be all right.'

[Sir Michael rubbished this account, pointing out that Sutcliffe had already hit her over the head with a hammer and the last thing she would be interested in was sex.]

Sutcliffe: 'I had no choice, I had to keep her quiet due to the nearby taxi drivers.'

Sir Michael: 'Of course you had a choice. God didn't tell you to put your penis in that girl's vagina.'

Going back over Sutcliffe's confessions to the police, Sir Michael asked him to explain in detail why his story changed from killing Wilma McCann because she had mocked him causing him to lose his temper, to later telling the doctors he had left home with the sole purpose of killing a prostitute and that he always intended to kill her? Sutcliffe said that he had misheard (or misunderstood) the police the first time and when he had time to think about it, he then told them exactly how it happened. Sir Michael quickly attacked this by saying the mission relied on ridding the world of prostitutes, this was the story he had told the doctors. This was the foundation of his defence.

Sir Michael: 'Here you are first claiming the murder occurred as an assault that had gone wrong, then on January 22nd you claim you had had gone out with the purpose of killing a prostitute. They are quite different stories, aren't they? Was it because you realised that what you had said about McCann would not be of much help to you if you wanted to pull the wool over the doctor's eyes?'

Sutcliffe: 'No that's not the reason.'

Sir Michael: 'It wasn't going to stand up as an assault that had gone wrong. That wouldn't wash with God's instructions and your mission.'

Sutcliffe maintained that all his victims were thought to be prostitutes. This was his mission. Sir Michael countered this by stating that Sutcliffe's defence relied heavily on all his victims being prostitutes, but there were five or six victims who clearly had no connection to prostitution. He put it to the jury that Sutcliffe knew fine that they were respectable women. When he murdered prostitutes he would drive his car up alongside them and they would get in on the promise of being paid, but it is much harder to entice a respectable woman into your car. This is why each of the non-prostitute attacks occurred by Sutcliffe following his victims on foot. It was clearly no coincidence.

Sir Michael: [To the jury] 'Sutcliffe, having decided to persuade the doctors he was mentally ill and that the series of attacks and murders was part of a divine mission to rid the world of prostitutes, he knew that the mission story would collapse if he admitted to the doctors that he knew five or six of the women he attacked were not prostitutes. [To Sutcliffe] Is that why you had to maintain through thick and thin in the face of the clearest evidence that these six women were prostitutes?'

Sutcliffe: 'No, I knew when I did it that each one was.'

Sir Michael: 'Your story would have gone straight down the drain if you had to say to the doctors that six of them were not prostitutes?'

Sutcliffe: 'It is not a story, sir.'

Sir Michael: 'But the mission requires them to be prostitutes.'

Sutcliffe: 'It didn't require them to be, they were.'

Turning to the confession to the police, Sir Michael read out what Sutcliffe had told them regarding the murder of Josephine Whitaker, 'I had been driving around aimlessly, the mood was in me, and no woman was safe. I realised she was not a prostitute, but at that time I wasn't bothered, I just wanted to kill a woman.' He then read another statement regarding the Vera Millward murder, 'I now realised I had the urge to kill any woman.'

Sir Michael: 'Had you got to the stage where your lust for killing meant that everybody that you saw, if in a quiet spot, could meet their death at your hands?'

Sutcliffe: 'No.'

Sutcliffe explained that he had only told the police this because he couldn't divulge the real story behind his mission; he believed Josephine Whitaker wasn't a prostitute, but the voice had told him that she was and not to believe anything she was saying. Sir Michael put it to him that what he was telling the jury was a pack of lies and desperate attempt to convince the court that he was insane.

Sir Michael: 'Had you realised by about mid-February that you were not getting on too well in persuading these learned gentlemen that you were fit for the loony bin?'

Sutcliffe: 'No.'

Sir Michael referred to the motorcycle accident, Sutcliffe's exaggeration of the events, the suggestion that he may have something wrong with his head, all mentioned before he told the doctors about the voice of God. Was this the early attempt to weave in the insanity plea?

Sir Michael: 'And then did you say, "Right. We'd better pull some more aces out of the pack". The mission was the floater and the bait on the hook was God's message, and they [the doctors] fell for it hook, line and sinker. Is that what happened?'

Sutcliffe: 'No.'

Sir Michael had no more questions, and Mr James Chadwin was given the opportunity to re-examine Sutcliffe further. Chadwin accepted and asked Sutcliffe if he had told the doctors he would kill again if he was released. Sutcliffe confirmed that he had.

Chadwin: 'What is your view about that now, Mr Sutcliffe?'

Sutcliffe: 'I still feel the same.'

Chadwin: 'Under what circumstances might you kill again?'

Sutcliffe: 'If I am allowed out.'

Chadwin: 'Yes, but who would you kill if you were allowed out?'

Sutcliffe: 'Prostitutes.'

Chadwin: 'Why?'

Sutcliffe: 'Because I still do not believe the mission is finished.'

This concluded the testimony and cross-examination of Peter Sutcliffe. Before the court was adjourned the jury spokesman requested the judge to explain the definition of Sutcliffe's defence to them once again.

Mr Justice Boreham: 'What has to be established is, first, that at the material times – that is the times he killed – the defendant was suffering from abnormality of the mind. Secondly, that the abnormality was caused or induced by inherent causes or disease, mental disorder or illness, and, thirdly, that the abnormality was of such proportions as substantially diminished his mental responsibility for what he did – the killings.'

The day's testimony and cross-examination of Peter Sutcliffe highlighted how correct Mr Justice Boreham had been to insist on a jury hearing all the evidence. It was clear to everyone that there was a massive disparity between what they had been told at the start of the trial, when an insanity plea was being accepted up by both the defence and the prosecution, and what they had now learnt from the medical evidence, witness statements and Sutcliffe himself.

There now remained one final chapter in the trial of the Yorkshire Ripper. The doctors who had diagnosed Sutcliffe as a schizophrenic would take the stand to argue their case, show their findings and, in a way, prove their professional abilities to the world. Had they got it right? Or had Sutcliffe fooled them all?

It was now clear to most that Psychiatry as a whole, would soon be on trial.

Chapter 8

Psychiatry on Trial

Dr Kay: 'I understand he was doing it so she would not raise the alarm, she had been expecting sex.'

Ognall: 'You mean after being hit over the head several times with a hammer?'

A full three days of the Yorkshire Ripper trial would be taken up with the examination and cross-examination of forensic psychiatrists, Dr Hugo Mine of Bradford, Dr Malcolm McCullough of Liverpool and Dr Terence Kay of Leeds. These were the three key men who had interviewed Peter Sutcliffe as he awaited trial in Armley Prison. Sir Michael Havers would take a back seat in the prosecution's cross-examination of the medical evidence, instead handing over the job to his colleague Harry Ognall.

All three doctors were all pretty much singing from the same hymn sheet: Sutcliffe was mentally unbalanced, not in full control of his actions and suffered from diminished responsibility. In all the murders and attacks there had been no sexual motivation, and in conclusion of their reports into Sutcliffe's state of mind, they were all unanimous that he was suffering from schizophrenia.

Dr McCulloch had been a consultant psychiatrist for fourteen years and was medical director of the Park Dean special hospital (asylum) in Liverpool (the place Sutcliffe had claimed he would be going when found to be insane). He stated that he had made notes on Sutcliffe's mannerisms during the trial, and nothing he had seen or heard had changed his mind. He said Sutcliffe had appeared unusually passive while evidence of the brutal killings was given to the jury. He also noted a complete lack of 'normal' emotion when he was quizzed about the weapons and injuries he inflicted. He also noticed how Sutcliffe stared into space on thirty-eight occasions, at a point in the glass dome above the judge's head, and had repeatedly moved his mouth, though under cross-examination by Mr Ognall he admitted he may have been mistaken and Sutcliffe might have been chewing a peppermint. However, he was adamant that his diagnosis was sound.

I was expecting to meet a man suffering from an abnormal personality, including sexual deviation of some sort. The possibility of schizophrenia was also on my mind but I considered it a much lower level of probability.

As the interview went on I took the view that he was suffering from mental illness.

However when pressed he admitted he had not seen any external signs of mental illness in the three interviews he had conducted with Sutcliffe, basing most of his conclusions on what Sutcliffe was telling him, but added there were some cases where there were no external signs at all.

Dr McCullough went onto to explain that in his mind Sutcliffe had delusional perception, with this he took a piece of paper and crumpled it up and placed it on the ledge of the witness box. He explained that someone with a schizophrenic experience would see this screwed up piece of paper as a reflection of themselves, that they were all crumpled up and that it had a meaning special to them. Anyone, with no interferences from other sources like drugs, hallucinating to hear a voice lasting for as long as a sentence, should be assumed to be suffering from schizophrenia.

But in a further embarrassment for the doctor it was revealed under cross-examination that he had concluded after only half an hour of meeting Sutcliffe that he was suffering from paranoid schizophrenia. He later admitted he had no access to any of the papers or police reports when he first interviewed Sutcliffe, and although the doctor told the court there was nothing in Sutcliffe's history to suggest the kind of personality disorder often linked to sadistic killers, he admitted he had not seen the prosecution's case or the pathologist reports on the appalling injuries until a day before the trial started. Yet despite this the doctor remained adamant that at the time of the killings Sutcliffe was a paranoid schizophrenic, and although he had made that diagnosis in such a short time, he had continued to check it and still had the same opinion.

Ognall: 'I put it to you that no matter what I say, it will not make you change your opinion doctor.'

Dr McCullough: 'Nothing I have read or seen so far has changed my opinion.'

The next doctor to testify was Dr Terence Kay, a consultant forensic psychiatrist. He had interviewed Sutcliffe eight times. Dr Kay repeated much of what Dr McCullough had stated and referred to Dr Milne's report for guidance on Sutcliffe's state of mind. He did reveal that Sutcliffe had admitted plans to kill himself during one of his severe bouts of depression. On one occasion he claimed Sutcliffe had driven to a place called 'Druid's Altar' in Bingley. This area was allegedly the scene of human sacrifice in ancient times, although there is no evidence for this. Its grandeur and location probably gave rise to its fanciful title, with its wonderful view of Bingley and the Aire Valley. The plan was to take his car up to the top and then drive off the rock, killing himself in the process. He was eventually stopped by the voice of God who told him he had a purpose unfulfilled. He went onto explain that he had a purpose to drive prostitutes off the streets.

He spoke of how he was able to clean his clothes undetected by his wife. She would never allow him to wash his and her clothes together so he did all his own washing separately. When asked if his wife was worried about excessive cleanliness regarding sex, he was told the Sonia did not insist on being clean before sex, but used towels on the bed if she had recently put on clean sheets.

Dr Kay said that when he asked what had brought on his depressions, Sutcliffe told him, 'Quarrels with wife, worries, problem losing licence. Two or three occasions packed my cases. Wife has had nervous breakdown. Hell to pay if I entered the house with boots on.'

Dr Kay said that he felt sure that Mr Sutcliffe was suffering from paranoid schizophrenia:

> I felt safe in the diagnosis, but was uneasy because of other factors. I work in the prisons more than any of my colleagues and have a very good relationship with the prison officers. They told me quite frankly that we were all being fooled. I wasn't troubled with the diagnosis, but as the officers quite rightly said they spent far more time with Sutcliffe than I did. They were with him twenty-four hours a day and he had made that remark about going to a loony bin.

However, the conversation had not given him any cause for concern about his diagnosis.

Dr Kay said Sutcliffe's manner at times did not match the seriousness of what he was talking about:

> At times he smiled almost giggled when we were discussing very serious things. Sometimes he treated almost as a joke and laughed. In the early parts of the interviews, I particularly asked him to describe the first attack he made on a young woman and he described the attack he made 1969 on the woman with a sock he told me he thought it was another prostitute he had met earlier who had embarrassed him and swindled him out of money.

On other occasions Sutcliffe spoke of an inner voice which protected him and made him feel special.

Under cross-examination Dr Kay said he would have expected someone suffering from schizophrenia for fifteen years to be in a far more advanced state of deterioration, but was still satisfied that he was mentally ill. He also admitted that if the common feature in the crimes involved a sexual element, then it would cast considerable doubt on Sutcliffe's 'mission from God' story.

Ognall asked about Sutcliffe having sex with Helen Rytka as she lay dying, and that surely this proved a sexual motive, or at least showed arousal at what he was doing.

Dr Kay: 'I understand he was doing it so she would not raise the alarm, she had been expecting sex.'

Ognall: 'you mean after being hit over the head several times with a hammer?'

Dr Kay: 'No.'

Later he confirmed that the re-insertion of the weapon through the same hole a number of times had a possible sexual meaning.

Ognall: 'Much more like a sadistic killer than someone on a mission?'

Dr Kay: 'Multiple stabbings are a common way of killing, but stabbing through the same hole as a deliberate thing would be extremely rare. I have to balance – was this for sexual excitement or pleasure, or whether it is a man whose feelings of human beings are blunted by schizophrenia.'

[He went on to say that he did know what went through it schizophrenics mind all the time.]

Ognall: 'It is impossible to exclude sexual components in a number of these cases'

Dr Kay: 'That's true.'

In regard to the last six victims, Dr Kay agreed with the prosecution that if Sutcliffe knew they were not prostitutes, then the divine mission failed and so did the diagnosis.

The main medical expert for the defence took to the witness stand next. Dr Hugo Milne, a consultant psychiatrist of twenty years, claimed he had dealt with 200 homicide cases, personally examining them for both the Crown and the defence. He confirmed that he had first interviewed Peter Sutcliffe while he was being held in Armley Prison, Leeds, on 14 January 1981. He would go on to interview Sutcliffe eleven times during the build up to the trial. During their talks together, Dr Milne explored Sutcliffe's early life, his family background and the circumstances leading up to and during the Yorkshire Ripper murders. It was his report and guidance which Dr Kaye and Dr McCullough had followed in their assessment of Sutcliffe's mental state.

Dr Milne mentioned there was no psychiatric history involving any of Mr Sutcliffe's five brothers and sisters. The report said: 'The mother became involved with a policeman and as a result the happy marriage was destroyed and the father became unfaithful with the woman with whom he is now living.'

He said the death of his mother, on 8 November 1978, had greatly distressed Mr Sutcliffe and it was apparent that he was very much fonder of his mother than his father; since his arrest the accused had difficulty with family relationships on the basis that his wife had objected to the Sutcliffe's family visiting him because they have been in contact with the press on frequent occasions.

Dr Milne had also interviewed Sonia Sutcliffe on three separate occasions and stated that she was extremely critical of her in-laws, and he had found it difficult whether or not to accede to her request not to see Sutcliffe's family. Dr Milne went onto to talk about Sonia's mental health and how in 1972 she had to give up a teacher training position because she had a psychiatric episode, but had made a good recovery by May 1976. She had no signs of reoccurrence of the illness.

However, the doctor was highly critical of Sonia as a person, claiming she was temperamental and difficult. In his report he claimed she had admitted on several occasions that she often teased and provoked her husband. He said Sonia was overexcited, highly strung, unstable and obsessed with cleanliness. Often she shouted at Peter to such an extent that it was embarrassing because he thought the neighbours might hear it. Other times, if Sutcliffe was reading a newspaper for example, she would shout at him, swipe at him and as a result he would hold her, but never hit her. She was obsessed by cleanliness and made her husband remove his shoes before entering their home and spent about three hours a day cleaning specks of dust from the carpet with a dustpan and brush. If Sutcliffe was watching television she would pull out the plug and he was never allowed to delve into the fridge for food.

Piece by piece the bizarre life behind the trim lace curtains of 6 Garden Lane was revealed to the whole world. In a way, Sonia Sutcliffe was now in the dock. Her enigmatic façade was stripped away, revealing her as a domineering woman who nagged and henpecked her husband.

She too heard voices. She too was schizophrenic. Where her husband claimed that God ordered him to kill, she was convinced she was the second Christ. Her affair drove him to prostitutes and he also contemplated suicide. Dr Milne told the court that Sutcliffe's version of his wife's behaviour 'accounts for his aggressive behaviour towards many women'. So all of a sudden, to the court, it felt that Dr Milne was suggesting Sonia, not God, was to blame.

The couple had no children, according to Sutcliffe they preferred material possessions. As regards to their sex life, Sutcliffe had claimed it was extremely satisfactory and admitted sexual involvements prior to marriage, but his wife had denied any form of sexual experience other than with her husband. The relationship was described as intense and loving on the one hand, but at the other extreme they became very angry with each other. The report stated that neither Sutcliffe nor his wife were sexually deviant.

Dr Milne said of Mr Sutcliffe:

> He completely denies that he was using the assaults to help in the sexual situation. There is no suggestion that he is a sadistic, sexual deviant. I am convinced that the killings were not sexual in any way and the stabbings which were a feature of the assaults had no sexual component. I have had the opportunity of spending many hours with the accused and there is little doubt that he is friendly and open in his manner and at no time did he withhold information.

Dr Milne had put forward a 10-point analysis on Sutcliffe which led him to believe he was suffering from paranoid schizophrenia. He explained that he reached his conclusions 'by taking into consideration not only one symptom but a series of symptoms together which eventually, like a jigsaw, complete the full picture'.

Below, for the first time in print, is the list of symptoms he claims were displayed by Peter Sutcliffe. (Some of the below points include notes that were added during trial as Dr Milne observed Sutcliffe giving evidence in the dock.)

1. PARANOIA: this concerned prostitutes and formed part of his observation that Sutcliffe was preoccupied with them to the extent of delusion. 'I am referring to his phrases that have come out in court here about prostitutes being "scum of the earth" and "being responsible for all sorts of problems", to the extent that he could not see beyond that idea.'
2. GRANDEUR WITH SPECIAL POWERS 'by that I mean an individual who believes himself, or herself, to have powers greater than those endowed within a normal individual.' He was referring to Sutcliffe's claims to know what his victims were thinking and the thoughts of those around him.
3. HALLUCINOSIS: a description of experiences an individual may have where he or she hears, sees, smells or feels, when there is no identifiable external stimulus to account for it.
4. DEPRESSION AND IDEAS OF REFERENCE: this is a misrepresentation of that which is either written, spoken or demonstrated by some form of behaviour, which misinterpretation implies a different meaning to that which a normal person might apply.

5. MISIDENTIFICATION: 'I use this in particular, relating to what has been given in evidence, this relates to his confusion at times to identify who were, and who were not, his victims – in this case, prostitutes.'

6. OVER-CONTROLLED BEHAVIOUR – 'Sutcliffe's particular ability to remain completely calm in the most stressful situations, such as giving evidence.'

7. PSYCHOTIC DETACHMENT – 'Mr Sutcliffe's case was his ability to detach himself from the enormity of what he had done. Schizophrenics could be both in touch and out of touch with reality, and schizophrenia was a psychosis, and a sign of which would include psychotic detachment.'

8. LACK OF INSIGHT: where an individual begins to lose touch with what he is doing and distances himself from it, no longer realising he is ill.

9. THOUGHT ARGUMENT: this was where an individual may tell you, and it may take him a long time before he does that, he is having an internal argument between his mind and his voice ... or a voice. He may feel torn between the two, not knowing which way to go.

10. PRIMARY SCHIZOPHRENIC EXPERIENCE: 'in this particular case there exists a primary schizophrenic experience. The evidence is in his statements regarding the experience in the Cemetery. That is a classical description of a primary schizophrenic experience. The magical quality and the feeling something miraculous had happened.'

During this breakdown of the key symptoms, the door of the court opened up and for the first time, since the official start of the trial, Sonia Sutcliffe came into the court accompanied by Ian McGill, a journalist and brother of Sutcliffe's solicitor, Kerry McGill. According to the *Yorkshire Post*, she was wearing a blue shirt and grey cardigan, she made her way to the side of the dock, before she took her seat she looked around nervously, once towards the judge and then towards her husband as he sat in the dock flanked by five prison officers. Due to the fact that she may have been a potential witness in the trial, Sonia was unable to sit in and witness first-hand the grim catalogue of atrocities committed by her husband. However, now it was clear her testimony would not be required she was allowed to take her place to listen to the doctors trying to explain her husband's state of mind. To this day it's unclear if she ever knew the full circumstances behind each of the murders.

Defence counsel, James Chadwin, asked Dr Milne if Sutcliffe could be misleading the medical experts and pretending his symptoms. Dr Milne replied, 'I cannot accept that.' He also denied he had suggested to Sutcliffe that if he was found to be mentally abnormal, he would be kept in custody for ten years to satisfy the public. He also dismissed the idea that Sutcliffe might have tried to copy the symptoms of schizophrenic illness from his wife Sonia, after witnessing it for years during her mental breakdown.

Dr Milne: 'On the balance of probability it is unlikely he could have modelled himself on his wife. I have always been very much on my guard [against the possibility of Sutcliffe pretending his symptoms].'

Chadwin: 'What conclusion did you eventually come to at the end of all your examinations?'

Dr Milne: 'I do not believe that the accused is, in fact, simulating mental illness. He is suffering from schizophrenia of a paranoid type.'

Mr Justice Boreham: 'When you talk of simulating mental illness, do you mean simulating the symptoms and manifestations of the illness?'

Dr Milne: 'Yes, I think it is what lay people may think what madness may be.'

According to his report, Dr Milne felt Sutcliffe had been a paranoid schizophrenic since the date of the primary experience in Bingley cemetery, when he was aged 19 or 20. This incident in the graveyard when Sutcliffe first heard voices speaking to him was, in his view, the most crucial symptom in the diagnosis of schizophrenia. It was this that had swayed most of the doctors into reaching their conclusions.

Dr Milne: 'With that initially and after the other aspects relating to his delusional content and his hallucinations, and disappearance of perception – one would confirm a diagnosis of schizophrenia. ... Sutcliffe's account of the graveyard voices and how he described them were particularly significant during my interviews and to a certain extent in court his whole demeanour in recounting his graveyard experience changed, he suddenly livened up as if he was describing something which at the time was mystical and magical, which he had never experienced before.'

Milne pointed out this was a classic symptom of the illness and that this played on Sutcliffe's religious and moral background when he was surrounded by angels, crucifixes and cherubs in the cemetery.

Dr Milne: 'It was a wonderful place for someone like Sutcliffe to have the primary schizophrenic episode. Much more different than had he been working on a factory floor at the time.'

From here the doctors felt that Sutcliffe believed he was being guided and that he had got to a stage where he might have gone into town while people were shopping and, now quoting from Sutcliffe's interviews, 'attacked any woman,

I knew I could do nothing to stop myself carrying on killing I did not want to kill anyone at all I just had to get rid of all the prostitutes.'

Chadwin: 'Do you regard him as dangerous?'

Dr Milne: 'Not dangerous, extremely dangerous.'
Chadwin: [That some of Sutcliffe's victims were not prostitutes] 'is that fact in your opinion inconsistent with the diagnosis you have made the fact the last six were not prostitutes?'

Dr Milne: 'The answer to that question is no, it is not inconsistent.'

He explained that the reasons for thinking they were prostitutes was either they were walking slowly looking at cars or had a slit in their skirt.

Dr Milne: 'In very practical terms his control was going, he was unable to identify whether one woman was or was not a prostitute, his internal argument with himself was becoming more and more obvious and he was, in a very practical term – the lay term – becoming madder.'

Milne said that Mr Sutcliffe's account of his early relationship with his wife, Sonia, also had some significance due to his reaction to being told that she was interested in another man. Sutcliffe seemed to have also over-exaggerated what might have been taking place.

Dr Milne: 'He became, if one accepts his testimony, distressed by it, distressed to the extent he walked out of a job. He seemed to see things in Sonia's behaviour in a way we know could never be borne out in fact. For example, he wondered whether she might be a prostitute.'

[When asked if there was any significance in the case were Sutcliffe had been mocked in a public bar by a prostitute.]

Dr Milne: 'Many men are mocked, no doubt, by prostitutes and somewhat cheated. We do not know whether he was mocked. He thought he was mocked. … Perhaps this was the beginning of Mr Sutcliffe's "ideas of reference", where he misinterpreted what prostitutes, or women who might not be prostitutes, were saying. It appeared that at a later stage Mr Sutcliffe would, based on very flimsy evidence, assume that a woman was a prostitute.'

Chadwin: 'Would an example of that be saying a woman was a prostitute because she was wearing a split skirt?'

Dr Milne: 'That is correct.'

[When asked why nobody in Sutcliffe's inner family and friends circle had noticed this supposed madness, Dr Milne explained that this was not unusual and there was nothing inconsistent with his diagnosis of paranoid schizophrenia that he appeared as an ordinary man going about his ordinary business.]

Chadwin: Were there any other symptoms, apart from what the patient told you?

Dr Milne: 'The way he might behave as if he was suspicious of other people's behaviour. The way he may misinterpret people's behaviour and the way he may react to what he believes. The great difficulty is that what the individual says is the symptom, is in fact very often the sign of underlying schizophrenic disorder. If a man says that he is the king of Siam when it is patently obvious he is an ordinary office clerk, the symptom he presents is "I am the king of Siam", but the [truth] would be that he has grandiosity.'

Mr Justice Boreham: 'It sounds as if you are saying that you are very much dependent upon what you are told and, in these courts, you have to test its accuracy.'

Mr Chadwin turned to what he called 'perhaps the most striking part of the evidence', that Sutcliffe had deliberately taken weapons with him when he went out to kill.

Chadwin: 'It is suggested for the purpose of killing he created that horrible, sharpened screwdriver, you have all seen a deal of deliberation and people might say premeditation of what he was going to do. Is that inconsistent with someone suffering from paranoid schizophrenia?'

Dr Milne: 'No not at all'. [He then explained to the jury that Sutcliffe had to kill prostitutes because he believed they were evil and scum. There was a disorder in him on the basis of his delusion, they had to be removed at the direction of God.]

During his first interview Dr Milne said he entertained the possibility that Sutcliffe could have been considered a normal, sane person. But by the second interview, he was slightly more suspicious that Sutcliffe was not as mentally well as he made out to be. In the 27 January interview, Sutcliffe continued to have paranoiac ideas in relation to prostitutes. Uncontrollable impulses, in relation to the 'stone in sock' attack in Bradford and to the attack on Olive Smelt in Halifax, were other symptoms observed. When asked about the third interview Dr Milne said, 'if I could have detached myself from the reason why I was seeing him I would have thought he was a paranoid schizophrenic.'

Milne said that a further interview on 5 February was of particular importance, as it was then that Mr Sutcliffe first mentioned having a mission. 'I didn't respond to this in the clinical sense because I wanted to avoid getting drawn into what might have been an attempt to persuade me that he was mentally ill.'

Dr Milne: [Sutcliffe told me] 'I know it is wrong to kill, but if you've got a good reason, it's justified and alright.' [I asked if he felt justified in killing, he replied] 'yes I have no doubt whatsoever, I was not as rational then as now but if there were women around now it would not take me too long to get those thoughts again, the prostitutes are still there, even more on the streets now they say the mission is only partly fulfilled.'

Dr Milne finished his testimony by saying nothing had happened from the time of the interviews and through the entire trial to affect his opinion that Sutcliffe had been a long-time paranoid schizophrenic.

Harry Ognall for the prosecution commenced his cross-examination. He reminded the doctor that Sutcliffe had never said what the voices had told him when he first heard them in the cemetery, only that they were described as 'being a benign and joyous experience, he was transfixed by it'. Ognall suggested that a man getting evil signals which perhaps tempted him to commit criminal misconduct might want to keep them a secret, but these weren't evil signals at the time and still Sutcliffe told nobody; in fact he displayed none of the symptoms to anyone close to him.

Dr Milne: 'Yes, I agree that my inquiries have shown that Sutcliffe never displayed to family, friends or workmates any external indications of mental disturbance.'

Ognall: 'But if it is joyous and a benign experience, why should it not be shared?'

Dr Milne: 'Because that message was for him and him alone, I do not know whether there was an indication that it should be shared and he might feel people might make fun of him and laugh at him.'

Ognall: 'What? Even his own mother?'

Dr Milne: 'It is possible.'

Ognall: 'It is possible that he was very much on the alert as to what you and other doctors wanted to hear?'

Dr Milne: 'If he knew the symptoms and signs of schizophrenia and he was as cool and calculated as he might have been, then it is possible.'

Ognall: 'Sonia Sutcliffe suffered from schizophrenia in 1972. She heard voices talking to her, she is described as having grandiose ideas. That is what this man has set out to display to you. This man has spoken of being in communication with the Almighty and Jesus, hasn't he?'

Dr Milne: 'Yes.'

Ognall: 'And Sonia Sutcliffe had the delusion she was Christ, didn't she?'

Dr Milne: 'Yes.'

Ognall: [Turning to Sutcliffe's confessions to the police, highlighting some key phrases used during the interviews.] '"Morbid depression." That's a very learned phrase for a lorry-driver? And "pathological hatred". That's a rum phrase for a lorry-driver to use? He is an intelligent lorry-driver.'

Dr Milne: 'Yes he is.'

When pressed by Ognall, Milne admitted he had conducted an IQ test on Sutcliffe which showed he had an IQ of between 108 and 110. The average was between 90 and 100. Milne accepted that 'while not a genius, Mr Sutcliffe was of above average intelligence'. He also admitted that Sutcliffe was 'articulate' and 'astute'.

When asked what external evidence was used to determine Sutcliffe's illness, Dr Milne said that he had photographs of Bingley cemetery, where Mr Sutcliffe claimed to have first heard God's voice, and pointed out the gravestone in question and Sutcliffe's own evidence. Other than this, there wasn't any physical evidence other than Sutcliffe himself.

Mr Ognall then stated how he found it extremely strange that when Sutcliffe was asked by the psychiatrists whether he had any special confirmation or special protection from an outside source he never spoke of his mission. Here was the ideal opportunity to finally explain his motivations to real medical experts yet he says nothing. Ognall then went on to suggest that in reality the doctor's questions had directly planted a seed in Sutcliffe's mind which he pondered over, considered his story then came up with what they wanted to hear at a later date. Dr Milne denied this was the case.

Ognall: 'Prison officers have told us that Sutcliffe has claimed "I'm going to do a long time in prison thirty years or more, unless I can convince people here that I'm mad. Then I'll do ten years in the loony bin." What do you make of that Dr Milne, in the context of your evidence?'

Dr Milne: 'I think it is a very straightforward decision to make. Is this man pretending to be mad, and has duped me and my colleagues, or am I, from my clinical examination, right in saying that he is a paranoid schizophrenic? As far as I can see in this particular case, either he is a competent actor, or I am an inefficient psychiatrist.'

[The judge then reminded Dr Milne that it was up to the jury to weigh up the evidence presented and decide accordingly. Mr Ognall went on to describe the dates and timings on which Sutcliffe committed his murders and attacks.]

Ognall: 'Exactly half of the twenty attacks had taken place on a Friday or Saturday night when Mr Sutcliffe's wife was working. This is a man who is prompted by God, the hapless and hopeless victim of God's will. This is a man who believed he was God's instrument. Why did God direct him only on Friday and Saturday night?'

Dr Milne: 'Some paranoid schizophrenics are extraordinarily cunning, extremely involved in premeditation and determined not to be found.'
Ognall: 'A very great proportion of normal criminals are also cunning, clever and anxious not to be found. That isn't the hallmark of a schizophrenic. It is the hallmark of the normal criminal. I suggest that this pattern is a badge of a premeditated killer.'

Dr Milne: 'I don't accept that.'

[The doctor went on to explain to the court that Sutcliffe had been open and honest, explaining all the crimes in a calm manor and that he truly believed he was an instrument of God, doing nothing wrong but God's will.]

Ognall: 'In reaching this conclusion were you satisfied you had all the necessary information at your disposal?'

Dr Milne: 'Yes.'

Ognall: 'Did Sutcliffe ever relate to you the incident in 1969 when he had been caught armed with a hammer in a garden off Manningham Lane, Bradford. A time when he was subsequently charged with going equipped for theft but the true intent was to attack a prostitute.'

Dr Milne: 'No.'

Ognall: 'So how can you possibly say that he has not withheld information from you and has satisfied you that he has told the whole truth? ... [To the court: Sutcliffe is] a selective liar to suit his own purposes. He has deliberately told lies to both the police and to the doctors. He has said that his first attack was on Wilma McCann when, in fact, he had attacked three times before then.'

[Ognall pointed out that the central weakness to Dr Milne's diagnosis was that it was based almost exclusively on what Sutcliffe had told him.]

Dr Milne: 'I agree that as he lied to the police, he could have also lied to me. [But I still feel that Sutcliffe has not] wilfully misled [me].'

Mr Ognall then turning to the lack of criminal activity during the period in which Sutcliffe had moved to London to be near Sonia.

Ognall: 'This appears to be a very local God, speaking to him in Yorkshire but not in London.'

Dr Milne: '[It is possible that] Sutcliffe's schizophrenia might have been in a period of remission.'

Ognall: 'You take the view so far as this man is concerned that there is no underlying sexual component to his homicidal attacks?'

Dr Milne: 'Yes that is correct, in simple terms, although his victims were female and it might be thought he might be a sexual killer, I am not of the opinion that he is primarily a sexual killer.'

[It was then put to the doctor that if Sutcliffe could be shown to have mutilated or shown an unhealthy interest in the victims' sexual parts it would go against the idea of a divine mission theory which was at the heart of Milne's diagnosis. The doctor agreed. Mr Ognall then pointed out key points of Sutcliffe's confessions that he pulled up the clothing of one victim in order to satisfy some sort of sexual revenge. Dr Milne continued to disagree that the murders were sexually motivated.

[Mr Ognall turned to Dr Milne's own report that suggested that injuries caused to Josephine Whitaker's vagina might have been accidental rather than deliberate. While reading out the report Ognall held up the seven-inch sharpened screwdriver, used by Sutcliffe to inflict the ghastly wounds.]

Ognall: 'How on earth are we to reconcile the pathologist's evidence of three stab wounds deep into the vagina with what you said? There is no doubt that this wicked agent was introduced with almost no injury to the external parts of the vagina. I suggest that indicates the most fiendish cruelty, deliberately done for sexual satisfaction, do you agree?'

Dr Milne: 'It may be a most vicious and foul thing to do, but not necessarily for sexual satisfaction. Mutilation of the genitalia for sadistic satisfaction would have to be repetitive, and there is no evidence, as far as I know, that this man has attacked any of the other victims in this way. There is no other evidence that he has in any way despoiled them or carried out any unnatural acts with them during the killings.'

Mr Ognall said that the screwdriver attack on Josephine Whitaker was certainly not the only example, although by far the most horrendous, of a sexual component. He reminded the jury of how Sutcliffe's attacks had included both the upper and lower underwear being displaced. There was the stabbing of Jackie Hill's breasts, the fingertip scratches on the genitals of Marguerite Walls and the injuries inflicted on both the breasts and genitals of Patricia Atkinson.

Ognall: 'He had told the police that he did it because it's just something that comes over him, but unless I'm very naive, that betrays a specific, clear sexual element in his killing.'

[He then asked Dr Milne if Sutcliffe had ever told him that the injury had been accidental, Dr Milne replied that he had not.]

Ognall: 'Did Peter Sutcliffe tell you there was no sexual element in the attacks?'

Dr Milne: 'Yes.'

Ognall: 'Well, that doesn't seem to be right, does it?'

Dr Milne: [Flicked through the pathologist report, before replying] 'No.'

Mr Ognall: 'He deceived you. Why did he do that?'

Dr Milne: 'Perhaps he might have been very reluctant to talk about this because of what people might think of him.'

Mr Ognall: 'He had admitted thirteen killings and seven attempted killings. But he thought he might be worse thought of, because he stabbed one of them in the vagina? Is that a considered reply?'

Dr Milne: 'It is a considered reply. He has said he never ever wanted to be seen as a sexual killer.'

Mr Ognall: 'I expect he has never wanted to be seen as a sexual killer because if he puts himself forward as a sexual killer the divine mission goes out of the window. That's why, isn't it?'

Dr Milne: 'It could be.'

Mr Ognall: 'If you were to find a number of instances of sexual molestation, the more instances you find, the more it would erode the validity of the diagnosis?'

Dr Milne: 'It would lead to erosion, yes. If you interpret it in that way, it does suggest that there may be a possible sexual component.

Mr Ognall: 'What else could it have been? I will have an answer.'

Dr Milne: 'I do not think it could have been anything else other than sexual.'

Mr Justice Boreham: 'If the prosecution was correct, would the observations made in your report still stand?'

Dr Milne: 'On reflection my report may not be as accurate as I first thought.'

Dr Mile agreed to withdraw the observation that it was accidental, but added that he still did not believe that Sutcliffe was a sexual sadist. Ognall now saw his opportunity to really hammer home more examples of sexual motivation by discussing the evidence of how Sutcliffe had attacked Olive Smelt in Halifax and then scratched her buttocks with a hacksaw blade. When asked what he made of that, Dr Milne replied: 'I don't make very much of it, apart from the fact he thought she was a prostitute and I don't see any particular sexual significance, certainly not as a sexual sadist.'

Turning to the murder of Emily Jackson, where Mr Sutcliffe had pushed a 2–3-ft piece of wood against her vagina, Ognall reminded the doctor that Sutcliffe had already told police that he pulled her clothes up: 'In order to satisfy some kind of sexual revenge as, on reflection, I had done with Wilma McCann.'

Dr Milne: 'If in fact you believe what he said, then it obviously could imply a sexual component.'

Ognall: 'And what about Helen Rytka – he had sexual intercourse with her.'

[Dr Milne said that although there may appear to be a sexual component to the murder, it was not an abnormal act. Mr Ognall reminded Dr Milne of Sutcliffe's description of the murder of Helen Rytka, by hitting her with a hammer, having sex with her, stabbing her, and taking her clothes off. When he had sex with her after hitting her with the hammer, he complained: 'She just lay there limp and didn't put much into it.']

Ognall: 'Normal?'

Dr Milne: 'Not normal, no.'

Ognall: 'Can you think of anything more obscenely abnormal than his behaviour with that unfortunate girl?'

Dr Milne: 'I agree with you, but I still think that this was a use of sexual behaviour for entirely the wrong reason – to avoid detection, quieten her and get away.'

Ognall: 'Why did he have to have intercourse with her to keep her quiet? I don't suppose he could have just put his hand over her mouth?'

Dr Milne: 'As he himself said, this was what the girl expected.'

Mr Justice Boreham: 'At that stage, did she really expect it, doctor?' [Dr Milne conceded that he didn't know whether she did or not.]

Ognall: 'This isn't a missionary of God; it is a man who gets a sexual pleasure out of killing these women.'

Dr Milne: 'I don't accept that.'

Ognall: 'It is not God telling the tortured soul, "You must kill." It is a man who craves for it like an addict for the next shot of heroin. What he is saying is: "I am hooked on it."'

Mr Justice Boreham: Could any of this come to pass without the primary schizophrenic experience [the voices Sutcliffe heard in the cemetery].

Dr Milne: 'No'.

Ognall: 'Without the incident at the grave, this man is a murderer?'

Dr Milne: 'Yes.'

Ognall now finished his cross-examination by returning to one of the most crucial aspects of the case. The divine mission.

In Dr Milne's report he had identified the time when Sutcliffe believed he was now being instructed on a divine mission to rid the world of prostitutes. It was during the Irene Richardson murder. However, no such mission was involved in the earlier murders of Emily Jackson or Wilma McCann, or indeed any of the several prior non-fatal attacks. He was asked to explain what excuse Sutcliffe was using to explain this. Dr Milne conceded that during the early murders Sutcliffe was harbouring a grudge against prostitutes and that in itself would sensibly account for the killings, but that it was all based around Sutcliffe being a schizophrenic to begin with at the time. He admitted he could not find any evidence that Sutcliffe was possessed with a divine mission during this time.

Dr Milne: 'I think he was suffering from diminished responsibility at the time ... under a delusion about prostitutes that they were people that caused him harm, which McCann had done. He would develop a pathological hatred and wish to kill them because they had done him harm.'

Ognall: 'A divine mission at the time he killed was central and cardinal to the diagnosis of paranoid schizophrenic.'

[Without the divine mission driving Sutcliffe to commit the murders then the diagnosis fails. Ognall went on to state that there was a logical fallacy in Dr Milne's opinion, if Sutcliffe was cheated by a prostitute as he said he was and if he felt humiliated and developed a hatred of prostitutes that is not schizophrenia.]

Dr Milne: 'It was not on its own schizophrenia, but it was when the whole picture is taken into account.'

Ognall: '[Are you] saying that a grudge or hatred of prostitutes was not a perfectly sensible and rational explanation for the killings?'

Dr Milne: 'It can be yes.'

Mr Justice Boreham: 'Assuming a man had been so humiliated by a prostitute it made him angry enough to want to kill, would there be any delusion involved?'

Dr Milne: 'There doesn't need to be any delusions to feel this way.'

Mr Justice Boreham: 'If the grudge or hatred continued, then how he could offer up delusion as the motivation for murder?'

Dr Milne: 'The hatred developed into the divine mission.'

Ognall: 'If he was swindled by a prostitute and if he hated prostitutes and killed them because of his hatred, then until he believes in a divine mission any killings do not stem from an abnormality of the mind do they?'

Dr Milne: 'On that logical thinking no.'

Ognall: 'Therefore if it is right that you can only confidently identify the sense of a divine mission at the time of the killing of Irene Richardson, then the earlier killings of McCann and Jackson were murder.'

Dr Milne: 'Yes.'

After three long days of expert testimony and cross-examination, the court proceedings finally came to an end. All that would be left now was for the closing arguments to take place, before the jury could retire to consider its verdict.

What happened in court was, in a way, an indictment of the inexact and subjective science of psychiatry. For the prosecution sliced incisively and sceptically through the medical jargon to make two simple points.
These were:

> That Sutcliffe already had a ready-made model for his feigning of insanity ... the mental illness that Sonia had suffered after her nervous breakdown brought on by her study for college exams.
>
> And that psychiatric opinion was suspect, anyway, because it was based solely on what Sutcliffe had told the doctors ... statements they had accepted from a known, accomplished and cunning liar.

Meanwhile in Bradford, Sonia's mother was making her feelings about the court revelations about her daughter's private life well known to the press. In a loud and angry interview she proclaimed:

> At least all the women he killed are at peace, I wish with all my heart that our beloved Sonia was with them. Instead she has to live through the hell that faces her now. ... the defence have crucified my daughter to try and save that man. The wrong person is being pilloried for Peter Sutcliffe's crimes. The solicitors said all the doctors seem to be laying the blame for what he did at my daughter's feet. The defence seemed more concerned with dragging our Sonia through the muck than telling the truth about Peter. ... But she's the most innocent person of all in this, I think so low of them. They have ruined my daughter's life forever.

She rubbished the claims made Dr Milne that suggested her daughter had refused Peter food and had bitter rows about housekeeping.

> I was at their home nearly every day I know what went on there. It was said that Sonia wouldn't even let Peter go near the refrigerator that is ridiculous, my daughter made him good meals there was always one on the table for him when he came home, what they didn't tell was all the time Sonia made meals for him and never came home.

She then turned her attention to the talks about Sonia's mental condition.

> My daughter had a mental breakdown she was in hospital for just three weeks, in that time she didn't eat and her weight dropped to under six stone. When we saw what the hospital was doing to her we signed a form and brought her home. We threw away all the medicines. We nursed her

back to health with love. She was ill but the schizophrenia they talk of is something different from the illness she suffered. It was all in the past. They dragged up things that happened years ago and rolled my Sonia in the mud. They said nothing about Peter … about the downright rotten family he's from. They should have looked at his background for a motive instead of my daughter.

I'm not just speaking as a mother, there couldn't be a kinder, nicer person than my Sonia. She is a very intelligent girl. She'll help anyone. Even when we get into an argument, she was always the one to smooth it over. I left my daughter alone in London after the first few days of the trial because I couldn't bear it anymore. Now I wish with all my heart I'd stayed. Just to be with her.

I've no respect for any of the people who have done this terrible thing to my daughter in the name of justice. Making everything so public and so dirty. Filth for all the world to read and hear.

Chapter 9

Summing Up and Verdict

'I do not mean to be flippant but this is very much like claiming to have swum the channel and your friends doubting it and then taking them and showing them the channel, as proof.'

Mr Justice Boreham

On 19 May 1981, both defence and prosecution presented their closing arguments on arguably the most important trial in criminal history. Two weeks of witness testimony, cross-examinations and medical evidence had ended. It would soon be up to the jury to weigh up all they had heard.

In his final ninety-minute address, Sir Michael Havers took to the floor:

if all the facts presented in the case were true then Sutcliffe is a sadistic, calculated and cold blooded murderer who loved his job. The crimes are horrific and sadistic beyond our comprehension. Does it mean he must be mad? Or just plain evil?

He told the jury that of the three doctors who had given evidence in the courtroom it was possible to put their reports to music.

They could be compared to a symphony. There had been a very quiet opening with little of great interest happening, a pianist passage where things needed to be stirred up and then Sutcliffe's primary schizophrenic experience in the Bingley cemetery.

He told the jury that Sutcliffe's graveyard experience when he heard the voice of God must have been something worth treasuring, but that it raised its own problems with his account.

This was a moving experience and he wasn't going to tell anyone? Another explanation is that he simply hadn't thought of it before. It must have been the most joyous occasion of his life. Yet he never told his devoted mother or his fiancée. If he had said to someone at the time he heard it then there would be no question of him just making it up.

He reminded the jury that the doctors had decided to base their views on just one man. 'That man was Peter William Sutcliffe.'

Sir Michael asked the jury to base their verdict on all the evidence presented, and to look at the whole broad spectrum, to examine all the plusses and minuses.

If they decided they didn't know where the truth lay, or if they were evenly balanced in respect of any one of the thirteen counts and were not satisfied on the balance of probabilities in respect of each count, then the verdict has to be murder. But if they can say on the balance of probabilities that this is a case of diminished responsibility because the defendant has discharged that burden to justify returning that verdict, then the verdict will be one of manslaughter.

He emphasised that the medical evidence was going to be a crucial matter for the jury to decide. They had to test the medical evidence against the facts of the case which were not in dispute and that evidence also has to be tested against what Sutcliffe had said in evidence.

Sir Michael went through all the crucial details of the murders, showing where a clear sexual element was present. He described the bite marks on Josephine Whitaker's breast and the penetration of her vagina. The numerous victims whose bra and underwear was displaced to expose their bodies. Sutcliffe's confessions where he claimed to have been carrying out a sexual revenge on both Wilma McCann and Emily Jackson, the latter having a piece of wood thrust up against her groin. There were fingertip scratch marks of Marguerite Walls' genitals and stab wounds to Jaqueline Hill's breasts. All these points and more mounted up to an undeniable conclusion that Sutcliffe was clearly seeking sexual gratification in all his attacks and murders.

You must not flinch or feel afraid. It may be the most notorious or infamous multiple murder case of the decade but it is no different from any other ordinary case. The gruesome details should not cause you more anxiety than if it was a man charged with one murder. You are going to have to ask yourself how much you believe of what he said. It is the doctor's belief in what he said about Bingley, the voices of god and the mission to kill prostitutes which leads them to their diagnosis. If you do not believe that he is telling the truth, then the doctor's diagnosis collapses. If you are not satisfied that he did hear voices of god or he did have a mission that is the end of it.

Sir Michael did point out that one thing they might agree on was when Sutcliffe said 'I am not stupid', he was telling the truth; Sir Michael stated that Sutcliffe was in fact of high-average intelligence and with a good command of the English language, and from the time of the arrest, there was at first outright lying coupled with some skill as Sutcliffe sought to maintain his innocence. In his first interviews with the police he began with outright lies coupled with some degree of skill – even after admitting he was the Ripper he began his voluntary statement with a lie by wrongly saying Wilma McCann was the first woman he had attacked when she was really the third; he had not mentioned several other attacks because, as he said, he wanted to save time – or was it just another example of his well-developed instinct for self-preservation? He denied everything until he had been cornered on his hidden weapons find. Only when he saw there was no alternative, he admitted he was the Ripper. The truth then came out inch by inch.

He stressed the importance of when the mission from God first appeared, after Sutcliffe had been left humiliated and enraged by a prostitute in a pub. The hatred had already been born. 'Then and only then does God finally jump on the bandwagon. How convenient after that for the mission to have appeared.'

Referring to the incident where Sutcliffe had attacked a prostitute with a stone in a sock following being cheated out of £10 and being laughed at by another prostitute:

Was not this a classic example of provocation? God hadn't told him to hit prostitutes or kill them, it was a reaction which you may think was not altogether surprising, the reaction of a man who had been fleeced and humiliated; it was a sort of loss of control which you don't have to be mad for a moment to suffer.

…

Would it be unfair to describe this man as a calculated and skilful man who is quick to protect himself? He was quick to inflict pain, especially on the last girl who he stabbed in the eye with a screwdriver. He was willing to enjoy what he was doing, willing to prolong death, willing to deceive others and offer false protection to them. He was willing to take the unexpected opportunity, and willing to kill any woman. Is that an unfair catalogue of this man's vices?

The jury was asked if they truly believed there had been any message from God, or any voices at all, that directed Sutcliffe to commit the murders. Sir Michael then highlighted, to his mind, a more likely scenario:

that it is just a pack of lies. He never heard any voices in Bingley graveyard and never had any voice telling him to kill. He is a cold-blooded, calculated murderer who has made this up because he knew he was going to go to a 'loony bin' for ten years instead of thirty years in prison

Sir Michael stated that it was clear that all the doctors believed Sutcliffe when he said he heard the voice of God. The jury should pay particular attention to this point, and he ended by saying, 'Softly, softly, catchee monkey, so they say. The monkeys were the doctors perhaps?'

Sir Michael now recalled the evidence given by Dr Milne. He told the court that the doctor had never doubted a word of what Sutcliffe had told him, and yet he had admitted that there were occasions when Sutcliffe had lied and he could have been deceived. As for Dr McCulloch, he had made his diagnosis after only half an hour and without reading the police interviews. 'What sort of an expert is that, who forms his opinion without knowing all the facts or without knowing very many facts at all? All he knew was what Sutcliffe told him.'

Sir Michael then hammered home the final part of his closing argument by telling the jury that there was no shame or disgrace for the doctors if the jury decided to take another view or disagree with them.

> it is your job and not theirs to decide this case. Of course you must pay attention, particularly when they, the doctors, are all agreed. But do not be frightened to form your own views. That is why you are here. If you found this man was guilty of murder, or some of the murders, thus perhaps in the public eye rejecting the doctor's evidence, it is no disgrace to them. They are only, in the end, giving you an option. They are not lying or being dishonest. They certainly are not. They are only doing their best and have formed an opinion ... But you will have to give a common sense view to these sickening and nauseous events.

Sir Michael took his seat and gave way to Mr James Chadwin to present the closing argument for the defence. Chadwin set about highlighting Sutcliffe's loathing of prostitutes and stating that his mission to rid the world of them was at the very heart of the case. He told the jury that he:

> was in an unusual position to be representing a man who had admitted killing thirteen women and attacking seven others. With the intention to kill them. But it was even more unusual for the defence to prove the defence's case and not for the prosecution to prove anything.
>
> Normally it was up for the defence to attack the prosecution's case and convince a jury there was reasonable doubt in the case.
> ...
> Because Peter Sutcliffe has admitted these killings and said they were done with the intention of killing, it follows that they are murders unless I can persuade you that because of the evidence it is probable that Peter William Sutcliffe at the time of these killings had a sick mind, a diseased mind, a diseased mind which had the effect that it substantially impaired his responsibility for what he did.

The jury was told that the defence, unlike the prosecution, was not going to go into each little intimate detail of the murders, not in an attempt to distract them from or diminish the enormity of Sutcliffe's gruesome murders, but more to the point, 'if this man is to face justice, not vengeance, we mustn't be overawed by the enormity of these acts'.

Mr Chadwin explained that the doctors had expressed their belief that the series of events arose because of schizophrenic illness, and the prosecution claimed Sutcliffe must be a man who enjoys killing. The prosecution had claimed that the murders all started because of Sutcliffe's hatred for one particular prostitute: 'Now you may think that any young man cheated by a prostitute would be angry and have a resentment against any one prostitute, but to react against any prostitute that crossed his path you may think would be extreme.'

Mr Chadwin then went on to explain a remarkable feature of the case. Sonia's cheating and Sutcliffe's encounter with the prostitute happened in 1969, yet the murders did not happen until 1975. 'A grudge makes a poor explanation in all senses. What had happened to Sutcliffe's seething hatred of prostitutes between 1969 and 1975? If it lay dormant for so long, why did it take so long to reawaken in 1975?'

He explained to the jury that Sutcliffe had already accounted for this by saying he was in turmoil and wondered if the urge to kill could be right.

A man with a healthy mind as opposed to one which was diseased would have been most unlikely to start killing and attacking prostitutes in 1975 because of an incident in 1969. But a man who had become convinced through sickness of mind that it was God's will that he should attack prostitutes might well have taken time to become so convinced to start the attacks.

Turning to the suggestion that Sutcliffe's actions had a sexual element or motive, Mr Chadwin dismissed the idea put forward by the prosecution, stating, 'This man was obsessed with prostitutes, paranoid about prostitutes and would see special significance about a part of a prostitutes body. But is there anything to suggest he enjoyed anything sexually?'

He drew the jury's attention to Sutcliffe's own explanation of why he positioned some of his victims in the way they were found, 'to show them for what they are, to show them as a disgrace.'

Looking at the pattern of the murders, Mr Chadwin told the jury that Sutcliffe used the same method each time, giving stunning blows to the back of the head followed by a knife.

is this a man who enjoys watching his victims suffer and manifests that enjoyment by knocking them out before he stabs them? Knocking them out from the rear is not the mark of a sadist who likes to watch the fear in his victim's eyes. It may point quite the other way when you bear in mind the fact that this man who has repeatedly said he did not enjoy killing at all. If you are persuaded by the evidence that it is more probable than not that, at the time of killing, Sutcliffe was suffering from a disease of the mind that subsequently impaired his responsibility then that is enough. Then the defence succeeds and the verdict should be one of guilty of manslaughter and not guilty of murder. I suggest it is a man with a diseased mind who is under the influence of what he is convinced is god, and he has a mission to kill.

He said there were two essential alternatives in this case. Either Sutcliffe attacked all his women victims from 1975 because he enjoyed killing, or there was some other explanation that he had to kill. That reason was based on his illness and the delusion that causes him to believe that prostitutes were responsible for all the troubles in the world, and that he was the instrument from god to carry out these killings.

Mr Chadwin pointed out that Sutcliffe had used extreme violence on his victims, in one case fifty-two stab wounds, and that the violence against Josephine Whitaker and Jackie Hill may at first appear sexual but that the jury should bear in mind that it correlated with everything Sutcliffe had said about his attitude to prostitutes. 'That he loathed them, they were responsible for all the troubles in the world and that they were scum of the earth.' This explained his actions and the injuries caused to each of the women. Mr Chadwin also emphasised that during all this the pattern was always the same, Sutcliffe attacked from behind quickly and with no desire to prolong suffering. He told the jury that the prosecution had 'desperately' drawn attention to only six cases with some small hint of sexual gratification, yet had ignored the fourteen other cases where the injuries did not point to any sexual enjoyment.

Although the wounds were sometimes directed in the victim's private parts, Mr Chadwin asked whether, 'it was necessarily a pointer of someone who enjoyed suffering, or was it consistent with the feelings of a man who deluded himself into thinking he was destroying what he regarded as the scum of the earth'.

Tackling the issue of those victims who were not prostitutes, Mr Chadwin pointed out that it has been suggested there was some significance in the fact that in most cases where Sutcliffe's victim was a prostitute, the victim was usually brought into a car and attacked. All the other victims had been attacked as they walked, suggesting Sutcliffe knew they were not prostitutes.

It has been suggested in Sutcliffe's voluntary statements that he had reached the state where he wanted to attack all women. I accept that if this is right then there can be no basis for the argument of his delusion. But is there really a clear pattern or is it chance pattern? Meaning he simply saw a woman whom he thought was a prostitute and went to attack them. On foot the risk factor was also higher but this showed that Sutcliffe was convinced God was protecting him. He had been interviewed time and again, his car had been seen and he was questioned about it, he was questioned about the £5 note, then there were the letters, the tapes and the attack on Teresa Sykes, he was chased and escaped and that's why you may think he was convinced God was protecting him.

...

what we are looking for here is to see if this man is telling the truth, or the truth as to how he sees it. We are looking to see if he deliberately manufactured material in a cold, calculating clever way to fool all the forensic psychiatrists.

Mr Chadwin said that the prosecution was presenting Sutcliffe as a clever, cunning and devious individual, but asked the jury to look at the first interview Sutcliffe had after his arrest with Sergeant O'Boyle. He asked whether Sutcliffe really came across as a clever, calculating, self-serving liar, or was it at that point a ham-fisted attempt to mislead the officer.

he was totally incompetent, see what the officer said at the time; he had no chance to mislead me with a story like that, he had never heard such a load of rubbish in his life', so, is this a cool, calculating liar, so good at telling a tale he could fool those [the doctors] who were on their guard against it?

As for not confessing to the attacks Anna Rogulskyj and Olive Smelt, as well as the murder of Marguerite Walls, in his statement to the police, Chadwin dismissed the claims from the prosecution that it was 'self-serving'. He asked the jury:

does anyone seriously suggest that the man who had just admitted he was the Yorkshire Ripper was serving some purpose that benefited him by restricting his admissions to twelve killings? I hope I do not sound in any way frivolous, but can you see in what way a man is worse off if he admits thirteen killings rather than twelve, or if he adds four more attempts to the two attempts he is admitting? I suggest you have to look elsewhere for the reasons why that statement was incomplete.

Mr Chadwin also warned the jury not to get bogged down with use of the single word 'mission'. He added that the prosecution had made much of their claim that Sutcliffe's references to his mission did not come about until his later statements – but earlier he had used other terms to indicate that he might be under some form of control. Chadwin was referring to the murder of Emily Jackson in Leeds, not long after the first alleged murder of Wilma McCann. Sutcliffe had claimed to have had 'an inner compulsion' to kill a prostitute. That word he had used again and again in his statement to the police. Later following the murder of Manchester sex worker Vera Millward, he claimed that the compulsion inside him had lain dormant but then came 'welling up'.

Mr Chadwin said that, 'curiously enough, in suggesting the elements of Sutcliffe's mental illness were manufactured at a later date, the word compulsion had appeared very early on in for instance the case of Maureen Long who was attacked in Bradford in 1977.' He suggested that other phrases such as 'urge to kill', and 'being taken over completely by this urge', could be a strong indication of his mental deterioration and might not have been recognised or followed up thoroughly by the police. 'The police may not have followed up those claims, but a psychiatrist hearing the words might have said "What is this urge? What is he talking about? Let's explore it further."'

The prosecution had heavily relied on Sutcliffe's statements that in his last attacks he knew that his victims were not prostitutes and that he was now killing women in a random and indiscriminate way. Mr Chadwin explained to the jury that Sutcliffe was not being totally honest and was hiding the fact he believed God had told him they were prostitutes.

What I am contending is that was a lie. A lie that he subsequently retracted, because he explained afterwards that the slightest thing would make him think of a woman as a prostitute and that, in the medical evidence, is exactly what would happen if you had paranoid schizophrenia: the misinterpretation, the delusional perception. He said all those who said she wasn't a prostitute must be wrong because God cannot be wrong. He convinced himself that all his victims were prostitutes. The police knew, and he knew that there were reports in the press and everywhere else that she was not a prostitute. But how could he explain it? How could he say it was God that told him?

It fits in with what the doctors said – that it is not unusual in persons with this illness to be reluctant to indicate the original source of the illness, the primary schizophrenic experience.

Mr Chadwin spoke of how Sutcliffe had not wanted a solicitor present when he finally confessed to being the Ripper. He asked the jury to stand back from this case for a moment and ask themselves this simple question:

a man is arrested as the suspect in a long catalogue of murders, not unnaturally described as the most notorious in the last decade – and it may be a far longer time than that. What would you expect a normal man with a healthy mind to do? Would you expect him to have a solicitor there? But he did not want one, he turned down the offer. He sat alone for fifteen hours making this extensive admission, and before being taken to the Magistrate Court he was again asked did he want a solicitor and he said no. Who needed one more? Why did he not want one? Sutcliffe's explanation was God was protecting him, can you see any other way this makes sense?

As for Sutcliffe trying to fake mental illness so he would 'only do ten years in a loony bin', Mr Chadwin explained that it would have been hugely emotional moment for any woman when their husband told them to go away and make a new life without him. He added that Sonia had the unfortunate task of being the wife of the Yorkshire Ripper, yet had decided to stand by him regardless.

> In these circumstance a man would clutch at anything to console his wife about the length of time he might be detained. If this is a key piece of evidence and that all the doctors have been quite deliberately mislead because he told everyone he was going to do it, does that really make sense?

Mr Chadwin said that prison officers were listening to all the conversations, 'so is it likely this clever, calculating man can bamboozle and make monkeys out of skilled doctors, that he is so clever he gives the whole thing away not once but more than once? His explanation that he was calming her down makes, in human terms, in ordinary terms, far more sense.'

He then stressed to the jury that each of the doctors had independently diagnosed the disease in a situation in which they had borne in mind the very real possibility that Sutcliffe might be trying to con them. He quoted Dr Milne's dramatic description of his evaluation of Sutcliffe 'that either he is a very good actor or I'm an inefficient psychiatrist'. He also said it would be absurd to think that these three experienced men had not applied their own skill and wisdom to the danger that Sutcliffe was trying to dupe them.

Mr Chadwin closed his argument by telling the jury that although there was a human need to seek revenge on Sutcliffe for his crimes, that they should put aside those feelings and focus on the evidence before them. They should disregard any ideas that their verdict would somehow change the sentence, that it was not up to them to decide what sentence Sutcliffe might get. He thanked them and took his seat next to Sir Michael Havers.

Before a jury can be allowed to retire to consider its verdict, the judge must give his summing up of the case as he sees it. Mr Justice Boreham had continually made detailed notes throughout the whole trial as well as getting involved, posing his questions to all the witnesses who appeared. He was now ready to begin his closing remarks.

Mr Justice Boreham began summing up with a call to the jury for a 'quiet, calm and objective look at the evidence'. Was Sutcliffe's mind abnormal at the time of each killing, and if it was, then was the abnormality strong enough to affect his mental responsibility? 'If the answers to these questions is no, there one verdict. Guilty of murder.'

He also warned the six man, six woman jury to consider carefully the evidence of three top psychiatrists. The doctors' evidence is important, but not conclusive by any means:

> It was no disgrace to a judge if a jury took a different view of the facts from his own ... or a disgrace on a doctor if you were to put a different view on

the evidence to which they hold. This is not a trial of doctors, if you think that it will distort your judgement concerning the defendant. It is his trial, and no one else's.

Drawing the jury's attention to the fact that after admitting he was the Yorkshire Ripper, Sutcliffe went on to say how he dumped the knife and hammer at the corner of the house in Melbourne avenue, were he was first arrested. Mr Justice Boreham advised that he did not know if it was relevant to the medical evidence regarding the mission from God, but that Sutcliffe claimed he panicked and hoped he would get bail to come back and retrieve his weapons at a later time. He also asked the jury to decide whether, during his long statement in which Sutcliffe said he wanted to unburden himself about the killings, he had in fact done this. 'He certainly made no mention of God or divine intervention in his statement.'

Turning to the medical evidence and to the crucial question of what made him do it, the judge said that when the jury came to consider this central point they might get some help – or draw some inference from Sutcliffe's wife Sonia and her mental breakdown 1971–72. Mr Justice Boreham emphasised that forensic physiatrist Dr Milne had seen her, indeed she had actually been his patient, and he had taken account of the possibility that Sutcliffe could have learned sufficiently of this illness to make her the model, the starting point, for his assertions that God had intervened in his life. The judge referred to Sonia's belief that she was the second Christ, and that it was curious that none of Sutcliffe's friends or family had detected any signs of the same illness in Sutcliffe.

Now it is said that this man, whom nobody thought was abnormal in any way, was in fact a schizophrenic for years before she was, and has now been schizophrenic for some fifteen years. What the jury is to make of that, is entirely up to them.

He drew the jury's attention to the evidence put forward by Sutcliffe's friends, Trevor Birdsall and Ronald and David Barker, and their trips around the red-light district. They described Sutcliffe as a rather quiet man who had certainly shown no indication that he was in any way mentally abnormal. That, however, would fit in with the diagnosis if the jury accepted that Sutcliffe's illness was a very rare type of disorder. The judge pointed out that schizophrenia itself is not particularly rare, paranoid schizophrenia is rather more rare.

But the judge said that the encapsulated form of the illness, one that is kept hidden for so long, is very rare and the doctors have said the rest of his personality was left untouched.

The judge then moved onto some of the individual killings in light of the medical evidence. He pointed out that the case of Wilma McCann – the first murder – there was no hint of divine intervention – Sutcliffe admitted he was merely provoked into killing her.

In the case of Emily Jackson, the killing was carried out as a hatred of prostitutes built up after the first murder. The judge reminded the jury of Sutcliffe's references to the inner compulsion and that the first alleged murder unhinged him completely. He drew the jury to Sutcliffe's description of how he had pulled up Emily Jackson's clothes to satisfy some sort of sexual revenge on her as he had done on McCann – 'revenge', the judge emphasised, 'not sex'.

There was also a long series of statements that Sutcliffe had made in his evidence which he felt had shed light on his motives. The judge mentioned that Sutcliffe believed he was being taken over completely by his urge to kill and he could not fight it. When describing the murder of Yvonne Pearson, Sutcliffe had stated the urge inside him was practically uncontrollable. And again just before he went to Manchester on one occasion, Sutcliffe had said 'the urge inside me still dominated my actions'.

Mr Justice Boreham said:

I refer to these things. I suggest you mark them because they are relied upon as being matters of considerable relevance. Certainly here is the first revelation, if a true revelation, of what the defendant's feelings were and his motivations. One of the questions to ask is have we witnessed a man who was really wanting to unburden himself truthfully, or is it more likely this was a man who just had a secret of a divine mission and was still keeping it a secret ?

The judge asked the jury to carefully look at what these urges to kill were. He asked them to weigh up the opinions of the Crown verses the doctors.

He then turned to Sutcliffe's conversation with Sonia during a visit to him in Armley prison Leeds. This was the time when Sutcliffe said he would try and convince the doctors he was mad, thus he would serve ten years in the 'loony bin' rather than thirty years in prison.

The judge said it was entirely up to the jury to decide if Sutcliffe had made up his mind to be deliberately deceitful and try and prove he was mad, then it would be very significant.

But if you think it was something said at the spur of the moment in order to comfort his distressed wife, then I suspect it would be something to invoke your admiration, being a kindly thing to do. It is significant only if there is not a question of calming his wife.

The judge pointed out Sutcliffe's time in the graveyard and heard an echoing voice and words on a gravestone which he took to be a direct message from Jesus. He pointed out there was nothing on the gravestone that resembled that phrase, although an inscription could be taken to suggest something of that sort. He emphasised that it was right to challenge the doctors' diagnosis as it was mainly based on what was being told to them by Sutcliffe. He referred to Dr Milne's evidence and reminded the jury that the doctor had cited the fact that Sutcliffe had once worked in Bingley Cemetery as some confirmation of his claim to have heard the voice of God. 'I do not mean to be flippant but this is very much like claiming to have swum the channel and your friends doubting it and then taking them and showing them the channel as proof, well it doesn't prove very much does it', he commented.

Moving onto the Sutcliffe's private life, he reminded the jury of his argument with Sonia over her fling with Antonio, an ice cream salesman. Sutcliffe had hoped she would stop seeing this man, but as the months went on he decided to begin his encounters with prostitutes

He mentioned the evidence of the prison officer who told the jury that Sutcliffe appeared bright and cheerful at the prospect of having his trial at the old Bailey. 'I don't think he fancied the idea of a trial in Yorkshire', and you will not blame him for that.

As for the encounter with the prostitute who 'ripped him off' and mocked him, the jury would need to take note of 'how humiliated and embarrassed she had made him. She made a fool of him. If you think they are true revelations and complete revelations which resulted in his attacking women then they are very different to what he would say later.'

Finally the judge reminded the jury that when interviewed by police Sutcliffe had lied, but would later claim he was waiting on instructions from God. He claimed that the signal from God to confess only came when he learnt the police had found his weapons hidden behind the oil tank in Sheffield. 'The Crown argue that this is not the case and it was not the voice of God but a simple fact of life that he had been caught and decided to confess.'

Mr Justice Boreman told the jury: 'It would be humbug to pretend I have not got my own views. I have been sitting here as long as you, and of course I have my own views.'

He went on to say that the jury should reject his views if they did not agree with them. Pointing out the most important witness was the defendant himself, only he could tell what was in his mind. 'Has he told you the truth as to what moved him to kill and kill again? That in the end is going to be the fundamental question.'

Of Sutcliffe the judge said:

it is said this is a very articulate young man, it is said he is of average intelligence and given the broad span of average he comes in the top part of that bracket. If you take a hard, calm, quiet look at the evidence and abide by the facts you decide are true, you will come to a just verdict.

He ended with a warning to the jury that he wanted a complete and unanimous verdict, before ordering them to retire and deliberate on the evidence.

As the court adjourned Sutcliffe scanned the public benches and seemed relieved to see Sonia there. Their eyes met, they nodded a greeting – and then he was led down to the cells.

Soon after lunch the jury returned to inform the judge that they could not reach a majority verdict. Visibly disappointed, Mr Justice Boreham conceded and said 'I am prepared to accept verdicts upon which at least ten of you have agreed', the jury once again retired to chambers were they spent the next four hours trying to get a majority agreement.

By 4.18 pm on Friday, 22 May 1981, the jury declared they had reached a verdict. In total it had taken five hours, fifty-eight minutes, from when had first sat down to weigh up the evidence.

The crowds filed back into court number one. Among them, David and Beryl Leach whose daughter Barbara had been murdered by Sutcliffe in Bradford. There was Doreen Hill, mother of final victim Jackie Hill, she was accompanied by Jackie's fiancé, Ian. For the first time since the trial began, Irene Macdonald, mother of the murdered Jayne Macdonald, had made an appearance. She couldn't afford to stay in London throughout the trial but friends and neighbours had rallied up funds for her travel from Leeds to come and hear the verdict.

At 4.30 pm Peter Sutcliffe once again climbed the steps from the cells below the courtroom and took his place for the final time in the dock. He was still in the same grey suit, with open neck blue shirt, that he had worn since the trial began. He gave a quick glance around the room, but if he was hoping to see Sonia, he was disappointed. She had decided not to be there. Sutcliffe now stood alone in the oak-panelled dock surrounded by five guards – he stared straight ahead. A deathly hush fell over the court.

The clerk of the court, Michael McKenzie, addressed the jury. 'In the case of the Crown versus Peter William Sutcliffe, have you reached a verdict?' The foreman of the jury, a middle-aged man with a red beard, declared that the six men and six women of the jury had reached a verdict.

McKenzie: 'To the charge of murder of that of Wilma McCann on 30 October 1975, how do you find the defendant Peter William Sutcliffe, guilty or not guilty on the grounds of diminished responsibility?'

Jury Foreman: 'We find the defendant guilty of murder.'

A jubilant sigh rushed across the public gallery as the first verdict was read out, followed by loud whispers and mutterings. The judge called for order and threatened to clear the court. Once the crowd had fallen silent the clerk continued and asked if this was a unanimous verdict or majority verdict. The jury foreman replied that it was a majority verdict of ten to two.

For the next nine minutes the jury foreman announced that Sutcliffe was guilty to each of the remaining twelve counts of murder, ending with the killing of Jacqueline Hill.

As the name of her daughter was read out, Mrs Doreen Hill bowed her head slightly and stared forward; had she lived, Jacqueline would have been celebrating her 21st birthday the day before and also announcing her engagement to her boyfriend Ian. Mrs Beryl Leach, mother of murdered student Barbara, tried to remain composed but began shaking; as the verdicts were announced she took off her glasses and sobbed, tilting her head forward as the name of her daughter was heard in the court. Meanwhile, outside the Old Bailey a crowd of about 250 people cheered loudly when news of the verdicts reached them.

Back inside court number one all eyes were fixed firmly on Peter Sutcliffe for any glimmer of emotion, but he showed no emotion as he heard the guilty verdicts read out one by one, and only looked at the jury twice in the nine minutes it took to go through all thirteen charges.

As the final guilty verdict was announced and Mr McKenzie and the foreman of the jury had taken their seats, the sound of relief and mutterings faded away in the court. Sir Michael Havers immediately stood up and said, 'this man, in the view of the doctors, should be locked up for the rest of his life'.

Dr Terence Kay, one of the psychiatrists who had earlier given evidence on Sutcliffe's state of mind, was then called to the witness box by Sir Michael and told the judge that with the present knowledge of the illness of schizophrenia, Sutcliffe should remain in custody for the rest of his natural life Mr Justice Boreham told Havers that he was entitled to make a recommendation to the Home Secretary on how long Sutcliffe should serve.

Turning to Sutcliffe the judge said, 'Peter William Sutcliffe, the jury have found you guilty of thirteen charges of murder. In each case by a majority of ten to two.' (Sutcliffe had already pleaded guilty to seven cases of attempted murder.)

They were murders of a very cowardly quality, for each was a murder of a woman and it was a murder by getting behind her and belting her on the head with a hammer from behind. It is difficult to find words that are adequate to describe the brutality and gravity of these offences I'm not going to pause to find those words and will let the catalogue of the crimes speak for itself. I am left in no doubt that women from a wide area lived in the deepest fear and I have no doubt to that fear spilled over to their menfolk.

There are two things I must consider and they are these. The first is the extent in geographical terms and the depth in human terms of the terror you introduced into a wide area of West Yorkshire. The second thing I have to assess is the danger you would still represent, and, perhaps more accurately, would represent in the foreseeable future if you were at large. I have no doubt you are a very dangerous man indeed. The sentence for murder is laid down by the law and is immutable. It is a sentence that you be imprisoned for life ... but so far, on the counts for which you are convicted of murder are concerned, I shall recommend to the Home Secretary that the minimum period which should elapse before he orders your release shall be thirty years. This is a long period, an unusually long period; in my judgement you, I believe, are an unusually dangerous man. I express hope that, when I have said life imprisonment, it will mean precisely that.

Sutcliffe remained as impassive and unmoved as ever, staring straight ahead at the judge. One of the prison officers then opened the door to the dock and beckoned to him to come with him. As he stepped out of the dock he was flanked by four other prison officers and for the final time was led down the stone steps to the cells below. He barely glanced around as he descended out of view.

Once Sutcliffe had disappeared, Mr Justice Boreham thanked the jury and officially excused them from jury service for ten years. He then took time to praise the officers of the West Yorkshire Police.

I would like to convey to the members of the Ripper Squad, as I think they are called, my commendation for the tenacity with which they kept at their task and I would like to mention in particular Sergeant Desmond O'Boyle, Sergeant Peter Smith, and Detective Inspector John Boyle. It is unfortunate but true that there are often allegations of impropriety against policemen. Sometimes, they are, unhappily, well-founded, often they are ill-founded. In this case these three officers behaved quite immaculately. They never put a foot wrong, and that can be said of few of us. I hope the commendation which I give – and give these very rarely – may be conveyed to their chief officer of the police.

As for Sergeant Robert Ring and PC Robert Hydes of the South Yorkshire police, the two officers who had arrested Sutcliffe in Sheffield, he said:

They were engaged in what I suspect from what I heard, sitting in this court, is often a very humdrum, routine duty. They must be very grateful, and the public in general and Miss Reivers in particular must be very relieved, that these basic police tasks which they perform were carried out assiduously and with such attention to duty. I do not mean to introduce levity but I cannot help but recall the remarks of the officer that he had not fallen off a Christmas tree. We are very grateful that he had not.

Finally Mr Justice Boreham said of the West Yorkshire Police:

I am sure every sensible member of the public feels the greatest sympathy for them for this reason, if no other, that the scent was falsified by a cynical, almost inhuman hoaxer – I refer to the tape and letters. I express the hope that one day he may be exposed.

The court session was then was officially ended.

Outside in the hallways, and on the steps of the Old Bailey, the pressmen were clambering over each other hoping to get a story out of anyone who was willing to talk to them. Out in the street, angry shouts could be heard from the crowd as the green prison van, carrying Sutcliffe behind darkened windows, was driven from the Old Bailey and on to HMP Wormwood Scrubs.

Despite his grief, Mr David Leach, father of Barbara Leach, announced that he did not wish to see the death penalty reintroduced because of the case.

At the time of my daughter's death if I had met this man it would have been him or me, but I would not like to see the death penalty reintroduced. I think if anything this is strengthened my belief in not having a death penalty ... I do not think you should take anyone's life just like that, I think this man should be locked away for the rest of his life but the danger is that in twenty or thirty years' time someone may want to get him released. I hope that now the trial is over things will start to quieten down we're just ordinary people who've been thrown into a series of events.

Beryl Leach was still crying when she left the court but managed to tell the press, 'I'm glad it's all over and that it was a murder verdict. He will be 64 before he could ever come out so I do not think we have to worry too much about that, it was a verdict we very much wanted.'

Doreen Hill had made her way to the phone booth to telephone her husband, who had been in ill health and couldn't attend. Once she told him the news of the verdict, she gave a few words to the press. 'It was the right verdict I am relieved, I wanted him in a normal prison so other prisoners could get to him. I would like him to be hanged, I would have preferred the death penalty to have been in force.'

Mrs Irene McDonald, mother of Jayne said:

hanging would be the best solution in a case like this, it was like he was stepping on beetles not killing humans. I have no sympathy for his wife and this has had a terrible effect on all my family. Fortunately I have two daughters and a son and we all pulled together if one of us had cracked we would have all gone.

Olive Smelt, who survived one Sutcliffe's vicious attacks, was also in court to hear the verdict and gave her opinion, 'it was the right one [the verdict], I don't care what happens to him now, lock him away for a very long time. I am still living with the memory of my attack.'

Although not present for the verdict, Sonia Sutcliffe had commented on the case to the *Daily Star* newspaper:

> I could not believe it was him, he had behaved so normally at home, he would tell me to be careful if I ever went out alone and once even escorted me because of the Ripper. I shall go on seeing him wherever he is but I won't be able to live in Bradford again. I could be rich if I decide to sell my story but it would be blood money if I did sell it.

Mr David Friendly, editor of *Sheffield Star* later confirmed that neither Sonia nor her relatives had been paid a penny for the interview.

Peter Sutcliffe's father would later issue a statement saying:

> we share the anguish of the families of the Ripper victims, their sorrow will also be our sorrow and sadness forever. It is an impossible task to put into words what we all feel for them as no words can bring these girls back into the world. The greatest shadow hanging over us is a terrible suffering and the unspeakable anguish caused to the families and friends of the victims. Can anyone possibly imagine how the world collapsed when he was arrested and charged with these horrible murders, it is still almost incomprehensible to me.
>
> He was a loving son and brother that we all loved dearly and who loved us equally. To me he was a lad who would never let me down. His love for his mother was such that he literally learned to walk holding her dress. Having weighed just 5 pounds at birth he took a long time to develop, right through his school days he never had the physical attributes to enjoy the rough and tumble of childhood games so he was content to stay indoors and read or draw pictures, even on a lovely summer's evening, yet he was a happy little fellow in his own way, always obedient and rarely having been chastised at school. He was not brilliant but adequate all around.
>
> I do not wish to appear to condone any of the endless things that he is done when in the throes of the terrible mania which from time to time engulfed him.

Epilogue

There were two reports made following the arrest and conviction of Peter Sutcliffe in 1981: a Home Office-appointed public document, the Byford Report, and an internal West Yorkshire Police inquiry, the Sampson Report.

The main part of the Byford Report was released to the public in 2006 following a Freedom of Information Act request. On 30 June 1983, the Sampson Report, led by former Assistant Chief Constable Colin Sampson, since promoted to Chief Constable, was released amid press and TV news coverage. As expected, the report was highly critical of those in charge of the inquiry. Heads would roll and the four main players would all leave their jobs before long. First in the firing line was Chief Constable Ronald Gregory. The police inquiry concluded that the bungled Ripper investigation may have cost the lives of Sutcliffe's last six victims. However, Gregory responded by saying Sutcliffe had been 'extremely lucky and very clever. The truth is that we never had sufficient evidence to charge Sutcliffe.' Gregory added: 'He was interviewed several times at home. His wife gave him alibis and nothing was found in his garage or car.'

In January 1982, Home Secretary William Whitelaw told Parliament that Gregory would not be sacked for the 'major errors of judgement' uncovered by the various reviews. Nevertheless, over dinner at the Garrick Club a month later, when the Conservative MP Alan Clark asked Whitelaw why he had not fired Gregory for making 'such a balls-up of the Ripper case', Whitelaw hinted that Gregory's departure was imminent. In the event, he remained in the post for a further year, retiring in June 1983. In his final annual report in 1983, Gregory wrote: 'The Ripper is a thorn in my career. I wish we could have caught him earlier. But I know the men on the case could not have worked any harder.' After his retirement, Gregory moved to Cyprus where he came under fire once more for selling his story to the *Mail On Sunday* for £40,000. Relatives of some of the Ripper's victims accused him of taking 'blood money'; the then Home Secretary Leon Brittan called him 'deplorable' and – particularly hurtful to Gregory – a police review branded him 'disloyal' and a 'hypocrite'.

Ronald Gregory died on 9 April 2010, aged 88.

Assistant Chief Constable George Oldfield, at one time the most famous detective in the UK, stayed in his position for two years following the Ripper trial. Dogged by ill-health, he announced his retirement in July 1983. He was heavily criticised by press and public alike for getting too personally involved in the case and for the next two years refused to acknowledge any fault behind his decisions. On 5 July 1985, he passed away from chronic heart disease at Pinderfields Hospital in Wakefield. He was 66 years old.

PC Andrew Laptew is regarded by many as the man who originally nailed the Ripper, even though his report was ignored by his superiors at the time. He continued to serve with West Yorkshire Police until his retirement in 2001. He later returned as a civilian investigator compiling financial profiles of drug dealers and money launderers. He finally became a volunteer at Bradford Police Museum and was a regular face on documentaries regarding the Yorkshire Ripper investigation. Andrew Laptew passed away in September 2019 at the age of 68.

Judge Justice Leslie Boreham, continued on the bench until his retirement in 1992. During this time he chaired the Lord Chancellor's advisory committee on the training of new magistrates and became vice chairman of the parole board, eventually succeeding to president of the central council of probation committees. He died May 2 2004 , aged 85

Sir Michael Havers, the Attorney General who lead the prosecution remained in his position until 1987, and served as member of the House of Commons, representing Wimbledon. During the Falklands war he was part of Margaret Thatcher's war cabinet, advising the Prime Minister on international law and rules of engagement. He ended his career as an appointed Baron to the House of Lords. He Died 1 April 1992 aged 69

Harry Ognall continued serving as a barrister until 1986 when he was appointed to the high court as a judge. In 1994 he presided over the infamous Rachel Nickell murder on Wimbledon common. He ruled that the police had gone to inexcusable lengths to incriminate the defendant Colin Stagg, calling it a 'deceptive conduct of the grossest kind'. Stagg was acquitted of the crime and the real killer, Robert Napper, was convicted by DNA sixteen years later. After retiring from the bench Harry Ognall released his memoirs in a book entitled, *A life of crime: the memoirs of a high court judge.*

He died on 13 April 2021, aged 87

Defence council James Chadwin, went on to represent other notable murderers, including Anthony Arkwright, who committed four murders and mutilated his victims over a space of fifty-six hours in August 1988. In later years, Chadwin was bestowed the title of master of the bench and leader of the northern circuit. He Died 16 January 2006, aged 75

As well as having to live the rest of her life being known as the wife of the Yorkshire Ripper, Sonia Sutcliffe faced the very real prospect of being homeless. Following the trial and conviction of her husband, solicitors for murder victim Jayne MacDonald applied to Bradford County Court for damages. Several of Sutcliffe's surviving victims, including Maureen Long, Marilyn Moore and Theresa Sykes, also won substantial damages against him.

A court ordered that the couple's house in Garden Lane be sold and her husband's share be given in compensation to the victim's families. The house was put up for sale but at the last minute an anonymous buyer stepped in to cover Peter's share which meant Sonia could keep the house and has remained at the property ever since.

In May 1989, Sonia was awarded a record £600,000 damages from *Private Eye* for libellous claims that she had been aware that her husband was the Ripper. This was later reduced to £160,000. A further bid to sue the *News of the World* failed as she lied about her financial resources. She was ordered to pay huge costs which nearly bankrupted her, but further successful lawsuits brought her in another £200,000.

In 1994 she was finally divorced from Peter and she went on to marry hairdresser Michael Woodward in a low-key ceremony in 1997 but so far, Michael has refused to move into Garden Lane, perhaps due to its history. He lives alone in a flat in a converted mill in Saltaire, a fifteen-minute drive away.

As for Peter Sutcliffe, he was rarely out of the press. Within a short period of arriving at Parkhurst Prison, he convinced some doctors that he was suffering from schizophrenia. On 13 December 1982, Home Secretary William Whitelaw ruled that Sutcliffe should stay in Parkhurst Prison despite reports recommending he be transferred to a psychiatric hospital. Both the prison psychiatrist, Dr David Cooper, and Professor John Gunn, a psychiatrist called in by the Home Office, have certified that Sutcliffe was mentally ill in accordance with the Mental Health Act.

On 10 January 1983, while in Parkhurst, he was seriously assaulted by James Costello, a 35-year-old career criminal with several convictions for violence. Costello had followed Sutcliffe into the recess area of the hospital wing and twice plunged a broken coffee jar into the left side of his face, creating four wounds requiring thirty stitches.

On 27 March 1984, at the direction of the Home Secretary Leon Brittan, Sutcliffe was sent to Broadmoor Hospital for the criminally insane.

In November 1992, Sutcliffe finally admitted responsibility for the 1975 attack on Tracy Browne to Keith Hellawell who was then Chief Constable of Cleveland. He has never been charged with her attack. In December 1994, it was reported that Sutcliffe would be notified by Home Secretary Michael Howard within six weeks that he would never be released. He had been sentenced in 1981 to a minimum sentence of thirty years.

On 23 February 1996, Sutcliffe was attacked in his room in Broadmoor Hospital's Henley Ward. Paul Wilson, a convicted robber, asked to borrow a videotape before attempting to strangle him with the cable from a pair of stereo headphones. Two other convicted murderers, Kenneth Erskine and Jamie Devitt, intervened after hearing screams.

In 1996, Keith Hellawell revealed that he had examined seventy-eight unsolved murders and attacks that could possibly have been Ripper attacks. Eventually, he reduced this number to twenty, which he believed may have been the responsibility of Sutcliffe. These offences were linked by a number of factors including similar descriptions of the offender, the use of a hammer as a weapon, and similar head injuries.

In 1997 Sutcliffe was attacked in Broadmoor again, this time by fellow inmate Ian Kay who stabbed him in both eyes. Sutcliffe lost the vision in his left eye, and his right eye was severely damaged. Kay admitted trying to kill Sutcliffe and was ordered to be detained in a secure psychiatric facility.

In November 2002, the law lords prevented Home Secretary David Blunkett from being able to increase the minimum life sentencing tariff recommended by the judiciary. A few months later in 2003, fearing that Sutcliffe might be released, the retired detective who had handed the murderer's trousers to police contacted *The Yorkshire Evening Post* and informed them of the existence of Sutcliffe's leggings. He said he could not understand why no mention was made of the leggings at Sutcliffe's trial. Other newspapers took up the story but to this date it is unknown if any tests have been carried out on Sutcliffe's 'killing kit'. However, the revelations about the leggings reopened public debate about whether Sutcliffe was mentally ill or a cold and calculated sexual serial killer.

On 24 March 2003, David Peace wrote a long article for the *New Statesman* which asked: 'Should the Yorkshire Ripper really be in Broadmoor?' Sutcliffe's father, John, died in 2004 and was cremated. On 17 January 2005 Sutcliffe was allowed to visit Grange-over-Sands where his ashes had been scattered. The decision to allow the temporary release was initiated by Blunkett and ratified by Charles Clarke when he succeeded him as Home Secretary. Sutcliffe was accompanied by four members of hospital staff. Despite the passage of twenty-five years since the Ripper murders, his visit was the focus of tabloid headlines.

On 22 December 2007, Sutcliffe was attacked by fellow inmate Patrick Sureda, who lunged at him with a metal cutlery knife while shouting, 'You fucking raping, murdering bastard, I'll blind your fucking other one.' Sutcliffe flung himself backwards and the blade missed his right eye, stabbing him in the cheek.

In early 2010 Sutcliffe, by now calling himself by his mother's maiden name Coonan, made an application to have a minimum term set to give him a chance of parole. It was a frightening prospect for the families of his victims and naturally they fought against it. Their prayers were answered in July 2010 when the High Court ruled that he would never be freed. Sutcliffe appealed against this decision but on 9 March 2011 his appeal was rejected.

Mr Justice Mitting said:

This was a campaign of murder which terrorised the population of a large part of Yorkshire for several years. The only explanation for it, on the jury's verdict, was anger, hatred and obsession. Apart from a terrorist outrage, it is difficult to conceive of circumstances in which one man could account for so many victims.

On 29 June 2015, *Yorkshire Ripper: The Secret Murders* was published by Chris Clark and Tim Tate. It identified a further twenty-three murders in the UK, which they believe were committed by Sutcliffe. Despite the strong evidence put forward for each case, Sutcliffe was never charged with any more crimes.

In August 2016, it was ruled that Sutcliffe was mentally fit to be returned to prison, and that month was transferred to HM Prison Frankland in Durham. Doctors had confirmed Sutcliffe was no danger to anyone as long as he continued to take his medication. By coincidence, at the same time it was reported that he would finally be leaving the comfortable life of Broadmoor, it was also reported that he was claiming to hear voices again, telling him to kill. All the symptoms he had displayed with the doctors at his trial had suddenly come back again.

Thankfully, his claims fell on deaf ears this time and he was back behind the bars of a proper prison, where the jury decided he should be in 1981. There he would stay for the next four years.

On 27 October 2020, he told a prison nurse he felt 'unwell and very dizzy'. His health had already been in rapid decline and he had several long-term physical health conditions including Type 2 diabetes, impaired vision and heart disease. In April 2020, when the COVID-19 virus was running rampant across the UK, he was asked by prison staff if he wanted to shield on a different wing due to his health issues but Sutcliffe declined.

Sutcliffe was sent to University Hospital of North Durham to have a pacemaker fitted the following day, while there he was tested twice for Covid. On his return to prison on 4 November he was found to be positive. It therefore appears that Sutcliffe had contracted COVID-19 in hospital.

From here his condition continued to decline, with prison staff noting he was coughing continuously, vomiting and suffering from severe diarrhoea. He was also unable to get out of bed. On 10 November the prison GP spoke with the hospital consultant about Sutcliffe's low oxygen saturation rate and it was agreed he should return to the University Hospital of North Durham.

The prison service has a duty to protect the public while escorting prisoners outside prison so, regardless of his condition, Sutcliffe had to restrained and handcuffed to the stretcher while being transported to then hospital and remained restrained for the next two days.

By 12 November it was very clear that Sutcliffe was dying and thus doctors asked for his restraints to be removed as they administered end of life care.

He continued to deteriorate and he died at 01:45 GMT on Friday 13 November 2020 aged 74.

Within the hour all news channels in the country were reporting on the death of the Yorkshire Ripper.

Sonia was named as his next of kin and took over the funeral arrangements. As everyone had anticipated, there would be no burial. This was due to the controversy this would cause in trying to find a graveyard willing to take the body, but also to avoid any chance of the grave becoming a pilgrimage for morbid true-crime ghouls. It was decided to have the body cremated. Such a process was used in other notable serial killer cases such as Fred West and child killer Ian Brady.

On Friday 27 November 2020, Sutcliffe was cremated in a secret funeral service attended only by Sonia and the funeral director. None of the killer's family, including his two brothers and two sisters, were invited.

His remains were eventually given to his brother Mick to disperse accordingly.

Peter Sutcliffe's desire was for some of his remains to be buried in an unmarked location in Bingley, close to where the Sutcliffe family grew up and the rest given to a female friend who had stayed in constant contact with him throughout his incarceration. She took his ashes to Lanzarote and scattered the ashes by a rocky cove near the Playa de Los Pocillos beach.

What happened the rest of the ashes remain a mystery; however, a location which is in Bingley – a stone's throw from the family home on Manor Road Cottingley, and would have been of significant interest to Peter Sutcliffe – was the garden of remembrance in Nab Wood cemetery on Bingley Road, Shipley, Bradford. It was here that Peter's mother Kathleen had her ashes buried in 1978, three years before her son was arrested for the Yorkshire Ripper murders. By all the accounts of how close he was to his mother, it's not unreasonable to assume this was the location in which Sutcliffe wanted his own ashes buried.

So is this the end of the Yorkshire Ripper story? Sadly not. There are still many unanswered questions regarding just how many people he may have killed or attacked. There is evidence to suggest he may have committed many more murders than he was convicted for, others disagree and thus we will never be 100 per cent sure, and with his death it feels that these victims, if they do exist, will be forever robbed of justice. Research continues through authors and experts on the case, promising new information, if it exists, will be found and made public.

There is no doubt the story of the Yorkshire Ripper will continue to linger like a dark shadow over the North of England, in among the streets and alleyways he made his killing ground. Like a real life bogeyman character, it's almost fitting he died on Friday 13th.

I hope his death will bring closure to the families of his known victims and to his own family, who found themselves thrust into the media spotlight through his crimes. Hopefully now he has left this world, those who carry the physical and emotional scars to this day will finally be able to lay the ghosts of the past to rest.

Time will tell.